MY BRAIN ON FIRE

MY BRAIN ON FIRE

PARIS AND OTHER OBSESSIONS

LEONARD PITT

SOFT SKULL PRESS
AN IMPRINT OF COUNTERPOINT

Library of Congress Cataloging-in-Publication Data Is Available

Cover design by Kelly Winton
Interior design by Tabitha Lahr

ISBN 978-1-59376-634-4

Soft Skull Press
An Imprint of Counterpoint
2560 Ninth Street, Suite 318
Berkeley, CA 94710
www.softskull.com

Printed in the United States of America
Distributed by Publishers Group West

10 9 8 7 6 5 4 3 2 1

For my nieces and nephews, Erin, Jeffrey, Jesse, and Joanna; my grandnieces and grandnephews, Asher, Isaac, Ariella, Julius, Annalise, Jemma, Elia, and Micah; my grandson Miles; and my son Stephen.

CONTENTS

INTRODUCTION

MANY YEARS AGO WHEN MY BROTHERS began having children, I thought, *My nieces and nephews will grow up and never know anything about the interesting life I've had.* So with them in mind, I began writing.

Those nieces and nephews have grown up, married, and now have children of their own. Life's unexpected turns have made me a father and a grandfather. My younger brother has passed away. And undeniably, I have entered my later years. I'd better finish this tale soon.

The subjects here range far and wide. Life is big, and I'm easily distracted. Because I never went to college or followed any formal academic education after high school, I never learned about boundaries or the discipline that keeps one "on track."

That's why I've never been a fan of the five-year plan. Too limiting. There's something to be said for those who become fixated by an idea or a passion and doggedly follow it throughout their life. But that's not me. Instead of the straight line, I'm the zigzag. I believe in the Great Meander. Every experience no matter how small has the potential to be a door into an interesting world.

While my zigs and zags appear to have no connection, to the contrary, there is a through line. Hopefully this will reveal itself here as I navigate through fields as diverse as the history of dance, the pre-Socratic philosophers, the European witch hunts, the birth of modern science, the origins of modern architecture, the birth of rock and roll, and much more. It all relates.

Anyone who reads this book from beginning to end deserves a medal. I expect most readers to skip over parts, and that's fine. Each of the fields I've studied and write about here has seized me and carried me away as I've tried to understand human nature and the body: how we think, feel, and conceive of our bodies, and how we understand this within the totality of who we are. This varies from person to person and culture to culture and changes through time. All of this comes together to make the world we have created and is part of the vast drama of humans trying to live on this earth in a commodious fashion. On the whole, we have not done well.

Unschooled as I am, this study has not been easy. Working in my favor is a curiosity that won't give up. I'm a highly motivated autodidact. In a classroom, I always fell asleep. On my own, I don't stop. This is my brain on fire. I get to work by 7 AM and don't stop till near midnight. The word *vacation* is not in my vocabulary. Getting away? Where? To do what? Call me the joyful workaholic. My motto: find your inner maniac. All the fun goes to the obsessed.

*   *   *   *

The principal people I write about here are all people I knew. In some instances, I've changed names or put words in their mouths to make a point, but everything they say is true to character. No one is misrepresented. There is, however, a dose of fiction in these pages. I allow myself a fantasy with my Paris landlady Madame Ragout. Sex! Years after I left Paris, it dawned on me one day that "Damn, she was coming on to me!" She was young—only a few years older than me—attractive, and lonely. I too was young, studying with a master, and wasn't bad looking. In my naiveté, though, I missed the situation completely. How slow can I be? Pretty slow. It would have been perfect. Or rather, it would have been a disaster not unlike the fantasy played out in these pages.

*   *   *   *

If I've learned anything it is that we must work to create a condition where the marvelous can happen, for the marvelous can happen in the most unexpected ways. Doing little, or nothing, guarantees little or nothing. Partake in the world, and much is possible.

NOTE: The number of photos accompanying this book is too great to include. The reader is, therefore, invited to www.leonardpitt.com where they can be viewed in chapter order, each with an explanation related to the text.

CHAPTER 1

EARLY MISERY, LATER SALVATION

When I was a little boy I thought that my shoes were alive. Every night before going to bed, I would bend them back and forth to make them feel better after a hard day's work.

When I was a little boy I thought that God had given everyone only so many words to speak in a lifetime, and that if I wasn't careful and spoke too much, I would use up all of my words too soon and die young.

IT WAS A WEEKEND NIGHT IN 1946, in my hometown, Detroit. I was five. We were driving along in the family car. My father was behind the wheel with my mother at his side. I was in the backseat with my brother Murray on my left. He was seven. I sat on the edge of the seat holding onto the rope handle that cars had on the backs of the front seats in those days. We were dressed up. I wore a cap. I remember this in such detail because of what happened next.

"Well, boys," my father said, "your mother's going to have a baby." I was stunned. *A baby! Who needs a baby? We're fine the way we are. A baby will only bust things up!* Bust things up. That was my very thought.

My father was hoping for a girl. When he learned that it was another boy, he exclaimed, "Oh, shit!" But I saw it differently. Now I had a little brother! This put everything in a new light. I loved Barry. We played at fighting all the time. We called it tussling. Standing at the top of the stairs, we'd play at hitting and pounding each other—Bang! Pow! Ooh!—and then tumble down to the bottom, groaning all the way.

We shared a bedroom, but because he was younger, he went to bed earlier than me. Every night before I went to sleep, I would kneel at his bedside and whisper into his ear, "Barry, I love you."

*   *   *   *

I received my formal sex education at age six or seven. By "formal" I mean an adult telling me something concrete about sex. It was brief. I was walking in a park with my mother and aunt. I asked how babies were made. "They put a pill in your cup of coffee," my aunt said, with a nervous laugh.

A couple years later (I was about seven or eight years old), I sat on the porch swing under the awning on a warm summer day. I hiked up the leg of my shorts and pulled out my penis. It was like a little mushroom. All I knew about sex was that certain things had something vaguely to do with other things. I knew that a penis was important. I knew that a bigger one was supposed to be better, but I didn't know why. I did know something about where babies came from. I knew that a man did something to a woman, that something from his body got into hers, but I wasn't sure how. Maybe it was from the penis. I hoped not. I knew my middle finger had to do with sex too, but I wasn't sure how. Maybe it was my middle finger that got a woman pregnant. Maybe there was a tiny hole that I didn't know about. I examined the tip of my finger but couldn't find anything.

* * * *

My first encounter with the real world took place when I was nine years old. Lucky me. Many children learn this lesson much earlier. It was at Roosevelt Elementary School. My third-grade teacher, Miss Stone (note the name), was bone thin with jet-black hair pulled back tight into a bun, and bright red lipstick that accentuated her lizardy lips. I sat in the front row.

One day, she walked up and stood ramrod straight in front of me. Her taciturn face bore down on me with ball bearing eyes. "Leonard Pitt, stand up!" I rose from my chair. "Leonard, what is three times three?" I froze. "Well?" she said, impatiently. "I, I don't know," I said, barely audibly. Thwack! She slapped me across the face. The sound of the metallic bracelets she wore on her skinny arm jangled in my ears for days.

The next morning I sat motionless in class, still smarting from my rude awakening of the day before. Midway through class Miss Stone looked at me and said, "Leonard, I want to talk to you after class, alone. Don't leave." I shrank inside. *What's she going to do now? Bend my fingernails back? Rip off my eyelids?* At the end of class everyone filed out. I sat in my chair, petrified. Miss Stone looked at me and gestured to the chair in front of her. I went slinking over.

"Leonard," she said, "your mother called me this morning and told me that you told her that you didn't like me. Now why did you say that?" I was stunned. I never said a word about my slap in the face to anyone, not my parents, my brothers. I was too terrified. She was making it up. My mother never called her. "I didn't say that, Miss Stone." I could barely speak.

"Yes you did, Leonard," she said, pointing her bony finger at me. "You told your mother you didn't like me. Now why did you say that?" Dumbstruck by the impossibility of what was happening, I shook my head no, repeating barely above a whisper, "But I didn't say anything." She went on harping.

From that day on, anything to do with numbers made me sick. I had so many attacks of diarrhea in school that I was given a special hall pass to leave at any time to go to the bathroom. My parents took me to see doctors, but they couldn't find anything wrong. They thought it might be the chocolate milk I liked so much.

I found refuge in my art class with Mrs. Hammer. What can crayons, construction paper, and paint mean to a child? Plenty. And there was music too. I liked singing. The highlight of the class was when we all lined up at the door, waiting for the bell to ring at the end of class. I made sure I was first in line, for there at perfect eye level for a nine-year-old were the enormous breasts of our teacher, Miss Belkin. I was struck by the strangeness of her face and arms gesticulating vigorously as if detached from her body that stood stock-still just a few inches before me as she directed us.

My parents recognized my interest in things artistic and sent me to Saturday-morning art classes at the Detroit Institute of Arts. This was early salvation for a little boy like me.

*   *   *   *

Maybe it was that slap in the face. Maybe it was my feeling so out of place, but I began to stutter. I had it bad. Stuttering is like having a knife stuck in your throat. Worst of all are the nice people who try to finish your sentences for you. They think they're helping, but they're not. They make it worse. Any stutterer becomes like an agile football player dodging all the troublesome words before they take you down. Sometimes it was words that start with a *T*. Other times it was an *S*. I hated talking.

My parents put me into a speech therapy class in school. Standing in front of the blackboard, Mrs. Ogelsby made large gestures in the air with her small, delicate hands as she gave a shape to each word she spoke. "Now, children, you must speak sloooowly. And above all, think before you speak! All together now, let's repeat, 'How now, brown cow'!"

* * * *

Somewhere in those early years, I developed a twitch in my left eye. This went along great with my stuttering. Then it started in my right eye too. Uncontrollably my eyes would twitch, one after the other, or in unison. Some people thought it was cute, as if I did it on purpose.

To complete this picture, I developed a twitch in the fingers of my right hand, my thumb, and sometimes my index finger. Suddenly it would start jiggling. My parents took me to the family doctor. His pronouncement was clear: "It's not organic, it's functional," he said. That cleared things up. I was a mess.

* * * *

Another visit with a doctor was of a different nature. I was about twelve. During the appointment he asked me to take off my pants and bend over for an anal exam. I knew there was something wrong, really wrong, but I didn't know what. Why would a doctor give a fourteen-year-old an anal exam? I knew that a man did something to a woman in that part of her body, and if the doctor did that to me, it could only mean one thing. I walked home crying, profoundly disturbed, repeating, "I'm not a man, I must be a woman, I must be a woman."

* * * *

I woke up with a start. This was it, the big day. My Bar Mitzvah! The year was 1954. I sat in bed with my stomach in knots. For more than a year I studied my *mafter* with Rabbi Loewy. The *mafter* is the portion of the Torah that I was to sing at the synagogue in front of all the invited guests.

Every Saturday my father drove me to Rabbi Loewy's house. He was orthodox, and the one thing you didn't do on the Sabbath if you were orthodox was drive a car. We were reformed Jews and didn't follow the same strict rules. Out of respect, my father drove me to within a block of the rabbi's house and dropped me off.

Rabbi Loewy was a tall, slender man with a resonant voice and a long, black beard with matching sideburns. Everything he wore was black—his hat, jacket, pants, horn-rimmed glasses, shoes. Everything except his shirts. They were white and immaculately clean. Sitting hunched over our desk week after week, I couldn't take my eyes off his long, silky white fingers that turned the pages of our book with the sensitivity of a snail's antennae.

My mother called out from the kitchen, "Lenny, it's time to get dressed!" I glanced at the suit draped over the chair. *Oh, God!* My brother Murray had already been through this ordeal and came out alive, so I knew I would survive too. From my bed I could hear my little brother Barry running around the house, playing blithely with no idea of the enormity of the day that lay ahead of me.

Aunt Doris stopped by to pick up the name cards for the lunch after the service. She sat at the kitchen table and munched on rye crisp crackers as she went through the stack. Aunt Doris was the movie star of the family for the simple reason that her lips never touched her food while she ate. She was afraid of smearing her lipstick. I thought only movie stars did that.

My mother looked at her watch. "Lenny, get your jacket, it's time to go." The plan was for me to walk to Rabbi Loewy's house. No ride today. I was a man and had to walk all the way. From there we would walk to the synagogue together.

I left the house and headed down Calvert in my new suit and tie and, best of all, blue suede shoes with tassels. Approaching the corner of Linwood, I gazed across the street to Neeley's Drugstore, a young boy's temple of candy, comics, and cherry Cokes. *Better not stop. I might be late.*

As I waited for the light, something on the ground caught my eye. I leaned down and picked up what looked like pages torn from a book. My heart stopped. Dirty pictures! Whoa! Pen-and-ink drawings of men and women in erotic poses with all the right body parts exaggerated. I ogled them all the way to the rabbi's house, going over the pages again and again. "Wait till Murray sees these, and Raymond too!" Standing in front of the rabbi's door, I stuffed the pictures into my back pocket and knocked.

"Good morning, Lenny. Please, come in. I'll be with you in a minute." I walked into the living room and sat down as the rabbi gathered his things. "OK, we can go now," he said. I got up and moved towards the door. "But before we leave, there's one thing," he said, looking down at me. "Today is the most important day of your life, and in accordance with the holy tradition of the Jewish Sabbath, we mustn't carry anything in our pockets. Would you please empty your pockets on the table." I froze. I knew you couldn't drive a car or use the telephone or even turn on the lights. But no one ever told me about this, the pockets! Slowly I took out my wallet and my handkerchief and handed them over. I emptied my pocket of a few coins and put them on the table.

Rabbi Loewy looked down at me. "Is that all you have in your pockets, Lenny?" Terror stricken, I nodded yes. Then, of all things, he frisked me! My body snapped taut as I sucked in my breath and felt his hands running over me.

"OK," he said, patting me on the shoulder. "That's fine, we can go now."

Dazed, I muttered, "Huh, what? Oh, yeah, we can go. Sure." He didn't find them. He didn't find them! This had to be God's Bar Mitzvah present to me! *Thank you, God! Oh, thank you!* We walked out the door into the crisp October air, and I breathed in the most beautiful day of my life. I was alive!

*   *   *   *

When I was around fourteen, I tried to run away from home. I left the house after dark not sure where I would go. My parents caught on quick. I was walking down Seven Mile Road when a police car pulled up. "Are you Lenny Pitt?" asked one of the police officers. "Uh-huh," I said. "Turn around and go home." Funny how they didn't put me in their car and drive me. I walked home.

*   *   *   *

In 1956, my parents opened a toy store just outside Detroit in the small community of Redford Township. Pogo sticks were a big item then. I stepped onto one and fell over. I couldn't keep my balance. A few minutes later, a boy came in, stepped onto the same pogo stick, and began bouncing away. As I watched him I could feel in my body everything that was going on in his body as if I were on the stick myself. I could feel him balancing, shifting his weight from side to side; I could feel what it felt like to shoot up and down. He stepped off, put the stick back, and left. I picked up the pogo stick, stepped on, and began bouncing like a pro. I was surprised at the sudden ease of bouncing up and down and enjoyed it greatly. This was my first experience of learning directly through the body.

*   *   *   *

Junior high was a variation on the nightmare of elementary school. By then I had an aversion to anything resembling academia. My new defense was to fall asleep. Not that I wanted to, but I just couldn't keep my eyes open. To stay awake I taught myself how to write backwards. When that got too easy I taught myself how to talk backwards. I sat through Miss Fennel's English literature class holding my book up to hide my mouth. Everything she said I repeated backwards under my breath. The word *room* is *moor*. *Man* is *nam*. I started with short words and learned to add prefixes and suffixes. *Walking* was *klaw* with *gni* at the front, *gniklaw*! My favorite word was *probably, ylbaborp*. Another was *elbow*, pronounced *wobly*. I made up arbitrary rules. *y*'s backwards could be pronounced as *e*'s, and so on. I can still talk backwards. Sometimes when people are talking, I automatically repeat in my mind what they're saying backwards.

*   *   *   *

Even with two brothers, friends, and a loving family with lots of aunts, uncles, and cousins, I felt lonely. I was an artist and didn't know it, and felt out of place. In my boredom I kept wishing I could skip over life and just get to old age. Surely there could be nothing interesting in between. TV was my salvation. Situated away from the world in our basement converted into the rec room ("rec" for "recreation"), I did my homework in front of the TV, ate my meals there, and practically lived in front of the thing. My parents knew what time it was by when I came upstairs during commercials to grab something to eat. Their pleading could not unglue me from the box. *December Bride, My Little Margie, The Life of Riley, Soupy Sales, Laurel and Hardy, Racket Squad, G-Men, The Lone Ranger, Ozzie and Harriet, Father Knows Best, Red Skelton, Superman*, Milton Berle, Sid Caesar, *Ed Sullivan*—I watched it all. Eventually my parents had a custom lock made for the TV, a small box that fit over the on-and-off switch, and they held the key. My misery increased.

My first year at Mumford High went poorly. All the other guys were jocks in training without knowing it, or academic types headed for careers as doctors, dentists, lawyers, or accountants. I knew I didn't fit in, but I didn't know why.

My parents told me about a school in downtown Detroit that I could transfer to, Cass Technical High School, a thirty-minute bus ride from home. Cass was organized like a college, where each student chose a major in a subject that interested them and took academic classes around that major. There was a remarkable choice of curriculums to choose from—

arts, humanities, dance, journalism, science, biology, automotive engineering, chemistry.

I enrolled in the Commercial Art program. This was a godsend, but it took me a while to realize it. At first I couldn't stand being at Cass and longed to return to Mumford. I did poorly in my classes. My parents sent me to the school counselor, Mrs. Jacobs. "Leonard, do you want to go back to Mumford?" she asked. "Will that make you happy?" I wanted nothing more, but for some reason I lied and told her I wanted to stay at Cass. How lucky. Had I gone back to Mumford, I would be living in retirement today in a posh Detroit suburb looking back on my years as a commercial artist and wondering about the real career in the arts that I might have had.

Everything at Cass changed in the eleventh grade. That's when my brain exploded for the first time. I was an average student until one day, my teacher Mr. Johnson explained a project he was giving us in his advertising design class: "When you're thinking about your design, dramatize!" he said.

My brain lit up. In an instant, I was transformed. What had been vague and uncertain suddenly became clear. Without moving a muscle I sat there in my seat, with no one having any idea of the lightning that had just struck me. If there is anything like satori in the American experience, this was it. From that day on I was an A student in design.

That was the first before-and-after moment of my life—when a sudden realization hits and nothing is the same afterwards. There were others to come.

*   *   *   *

Spontaneous affinities between people are mysterious and inexplicable, but can the same thing happen between people and cities? It was during those teenage years that I began dreaming of Paris. I imagined myself living in a garret drinking wine and eating bread and cheese. In the late 1950s, Michel Legrand's "Under the Bridges of Paris" received equal play in my house along with "Tutti Frutti," "Shake, Rattle and Roll," and "Good Golly, Miss Molly." How does a sixteen-year-old growing up in Detroit come to such dreams?

I think about the scores of American artists who traveled to Paris over the years. What is the connection between France and the United States? I thought about *An American in Paris*. Could it have been an American in London or Rome? An American in Athens?

Paris had all the allure of a famous movie star—a beautiful woman, intelligent, admired throughout the world. A woman I surely could never approach much less meet. But then we did meet. Not only that, but we fell madly in love. We moved in together. I grew from her wisdom and grace, her subtlety of spirit. Then, with time, we both changed. We fought, argued, and grew apart. When we finally split up, we couldn't wait to be out of each other's sight. Years later, we met again, and weary from the long separation, we fell into each other's arms. But wiser, we knew better than to live together. Life has taken us in different directions. So keeping our respective grounds, we see each other periodically and revel in the pleasure of our closeness.

*   *   *   *

I did well in my art classes in Cass, but my academics were each a different shade of misery. On the last day of my eleventh-grade geometry class, I sat with my report card in hand and was thrilled. I got a D. I passed! As we filed out, my teacher, Mr. Leach, called me over. His thick, dull puss looked like the leather sole of a shoe that had been walked on for years. "Pitt," he said, putting his face into mine, "you passed geometry one, but I bet you flunk geometry two." He was right. Once again, my summer vacation was spent going to school to make up for the failure.

Our summer-school geometry teacher, Mr. Henderson, was a study in stillness. Sitting erect at his desk, hands folded before him, he didn't move a muscle. The only thing that proved he was alive was the slight movement of his lips when he spoke. But everyone liked Mr. Henderson. For some inexplicable reason, during our weekly tests, he kept a sheet of paper on his desk with the answers to all the problems. We caught on fast and one by one we'd line up at his desk with our test papers in hand and pretend to be confused about a problem while carefully glancing at the answers. I got an A! God bless Mr. Henderson.

My senior year at Cass was no better. I failed chemistry. Instead of crossing a stage to receive a diploma at graduation, I went to summer school yet again.

I knew college was not an option. Instead I applied to the Art Center School in Los Angeles to pursue a career in advertising design. But I had to pass this summer chemistry course. And things looked bad. I begged my teacher. "Please, Mr. Lance, you've got to pass me. Please!" He passed me. I got a D and went home ecstatic.

*   *   *   *

In 1958, the Broadway show *Once Upon a Mattress* came to Detroit. Based on the Hans Christian Andersen fairy tale *The Princess and the Pea*, this is the story of a king who takes a vow of silence until his daughter, the princess, is married. The mute king was played by the one and only Buster Keaton. The princess was played by popular comedienne of the day Dody Goodman, and the prince by the just-as-popular TV comic, skinny, scrawny Arnold Stang.

Keaton never got much play on TV in the 1950s, and by then his career had been in eclipse for years. He never made the transition to talkies like Laurel and Hardy, Charlie Chaplin, or Harold Lloyd. But nevertheless I had seen enough of his films to know that he was part of my particular brand of soul food. My mother often reminded me how when I was a little boy, I would ask her if there was a school for comedians. Of course there wasn't, but Keaton was part of my rich, informal education.

Keaton did a scene in this show of miming the birds and the bees to his son. This remains vividly etched in my memory. Detroit was the last stop on the tour, and I saw the last performance in the run. Keaton was retiring afterwards. This means I had the uncanny luck of seeing Buster Keaton in the last stage performance of his career.

*   *   *   *

Receiving my acceptance letter from Art Center was a thrill I could not have imagined. The pain of high school had a weird kind of payoff after all. What a testimony to art education at Cass Tech! Most people completed high school first, then did four years of college, and only then applied to Art Center hoping to get in. I was going straight from high school.

I was told Art Center was going to be tough. But I was not prepared for how tough. It was grueling. Each teacher assigned homework as if we students had nothing else to do during the week. There was no time to breathe. Rise at 8 AM. Dress, rush through breakfast. Arrive at school for a 9 AM class. Finish at 3 PM. Rush home. Get right to the drawing board. Grab dinner. Back to the drawing board and stay there until 5 AM. Sleep. Rise at 8 AM, ad infinitum. That's three hours' sleep a night.

Free time was only a vague memory. Driving to school in the morning, I'd see people strolling down the street and try to remember what it was like to do that. In time I got to hate the unrelenting pressure. Every semester one student would crack and had to be sent home. But strangely I thrived. What I learned there has served me throughout my life.

*   *   *   *

One day I walked into a drawing class and found a mime standing on a pedestal striking a pose. Mimes in whiteface carried no stigma in those days and were not the object of ridicule they would become years later. It was a more naive time, and the romantic nature of this stage figure stimulated the public's imagination. During a break I learned that our model taught classes. The following week I signed up.

Eliot had a small studio in a storefront on Fairfax Avenue in the Jewish section of LA. At the end of our first lesson he said that anyone thinking of studying mime seriously should go to Paris to study with the master Étienne Decroux, an eccentric with long hair, he said, who kissed his students good-bye at the end of each class. Long hair, kissed his students? That really was eccentric. Little did I know that I would travel to Paris and spend four years studying with Decroux, become his assistant, and perform in his company.

Decroux's most famous student was Marcel Marceau. Eliot warned me that they had little in common. Marceau appealed to a popular audience and would tickle your funny bone or hit you in your pathos. Decroux's work was serious, technically demanding, and appealed to a smaller audience. If Marceau was like a Broadway musical, Decroux was classical music. Eliot pulled a book off the shelf and opened it to a photo of Decroux. He looked serious and imposing. "He developed all the mime technique," Eliot said, "the walk in place, pushing and pulling, but he never made it his stock in trade like Marceau. He doesn't try to dazzle in that way."

Eliot flicked off the light in the studio as we walked outside. "You can see him tonight at the movies. *The Children of Paradise* is playing in Hollywood." *The Children of Paradise* is a classic of French cinema made in 1944 during the German occupation, a tale of love, intrigue, murder, and jealousy set in nineteenth-century Paris in the heart of the city's entertainment district along the Boulevard du Crime, where today's Place de la République stands. Decroux's first student in the 1930s, Jean-Louis Barrault, stars in the role of the legendary mime Deburau. Decroux played his stern father the theatre director, and as I learned years later, the character was not far from Decroux himself.

*   *   *   *

Before moving to Los Angeles, I read a newspaper article about two heroes of my youth, Laurel and Hardy, and saw that Laurel lived in Santa Monica. The early years of television were filled with hours of their movies, and I watched them all. They were the pabulum that nurtured my very bones. Being too young to know fear, I decided to look Laurel up when I got to LA. I grabbed the phone book and there he was: Stan Laurel, 849 Ocean Avenue, Santa Monica. I called him that day. "Hi, Mr. Laurel. I've been a fan of yours all my life. Can I come over and visit?" "Sure," he said. "How about Saturday morning? Ten o'clock, OK?" Imagine my excitement.

To get in the mood, the night before the visit, I went to the Silent Movie Theatre on Fairfax Avenue to see a couple of early Laurel and Hardy shorts. The next morning, I drove out to Santa Monica full of anticipation.

Mr. Laurel lived in a small apartment with his wife Ida. Because he had recently suffered a mild stroke and walked with some difficulty, he told me that his wife would leave the door ajar. I knocked. "Come in, come in, Lenny!" I peered through the crack and entered slowly. There he was, sitting at his writing desk. He gestured to the chair opposite for me to sit down.

The apartment was small, nothing fancy, and was filled with Laurel and Hardy memorabilia. On the television stood the Oscar he received for their 1932 classic *The Music Box*. Thrilled does not express my feeling.

I sat there looking at Mr. Laurel and searched for the man I knew from the movies. That Laurel was younger, in his twenties and thirties. Here was a man in his late sixties. I felt like I was talking to Stan Laurel's father.

I told him about one of the movies I saw the night before, where he and Hardy played rookie soldiers in World War I and were being drilled by their sergeant, played by the inimitable Jimmy Finlayson. In a funny sequence, Laurel fumbles with his rifle while trying to salute at the same time. I described the scene, but it drew a blank for Laurel. "Gosh, it's been almost fifty years," he said, straining to remember. I sprang from my chair and mimed the action from the movie to jog his memory. Suddenly he burst out laughing. "Oh, that one! Yes, of course!" One thing that doesn't change with age is a person's laugh. He sat there laughing and did the same moves from the movie. No doubt about it, I was with *the* Stan Laurel.

We talked about a million things: his early films, the fun of shooting movies in the early days with no schedule, the last time he saw Charlie Chaplin, Jerry Lewis's movies, etc. He never liked doing his signature gesture of crying and scratching his head, he told me. I asked why, and he shrugged his shoulders. "I only did it because people liked it."

I asked him if a recording existed of the Laurel and Hardy theme music. Only one, he said, a 78-rpm record they made in London in 1939. But the building was bombed during the blitz, and everything was lost, including the master recordings. There were only a few copies left in the world, and he had one, but a child had scratched out one side with a nail. The other side was intact and had their theme music along with some gags. "Would you like me to play it for you?" I nearly gasped. He opened the lid of the phonograph player, placed the record on the platen, set the needle, and turned up the sound. From the scratchy sound came:

"Well Stanley, here's another fine mess you've gotten us into. Here we are in London and you forgot our return tickets back in America. Now we'll have to swim back!"

"It wasn't my fault, I didn't know . . . Uh, how far is it?"

"Only about two thousand miles!"

"Well, that isn't so bad. It's only a thousand miles each!"

"Oh, you be quiet. I'll take care of you later. Ladies and gentlemen, here is a medley of our theme song, 'The Song of the Cuckoo.'" The apartment filled with the strains of Laurel and Hardy's music, and I was delivered away onto cloud number nine.

Laurel then told me a story about the most touching moment of their career. In 1953 the two comics set out on a tour of one-night stands around the world with their first stop in Dublin, Ireland. During their entire film career, Laurel and Hardy rarely ever saw each other off the set. In fact they hardly mixed socially at all during their twenty-six years together. Hardy was always on the golf course and left the filmmaking decisions to Stan, who was the real creative force behind the duo. It was only after their film career was over that they grew close.

Going on tour in the 1950s was a risky venture, they thought. They hadn't made a good movie since the late 1930s and were certain the public had forgotten them. The local newspaper in Ireland, *The Cork Examiner*, ran a short notice mentioning that Laurel and Hardy would be docking in Cobh, a small town on Ireland's southern coast, and then would continue on to Dublin. The children in town heard the news and descended on their schoolteachers, demanding that they be allowed to miss school that day so they could greet the two comics at the dock. Things snowballed, and before long, a town holiday was declared. Everyone wanted to be there for the big reception.

Laurel and Hardy had no idea of what lay in store. As they sailed into the harbor at Cobh, they saw great crowds lining the docks and parties of people in sailboats waving and cheering. They had no idea what was going on. "I thought the bloody Pope was there!" Laurel told me, laughing.

On a hill overlooking Cobh is Saint Colman's Cathedral, with one of the finest set of carillon bells in the world. As Laurel and Hardy were trying to figure out what all the commotion was about, the cathedral bells began ringing out with their theme music. The two comics thought they were in a dream.

On shore a frenzied crowd of adoring fans greeted them along with the Lord Mayor of Cork and other local dignitaries. The two were so touched that they wanted to buy some cream pies at a bakery and do a bit of slapstick for the crowd, but they couldn't—all the bakeries were closed for them.

Mr. Laurel regretted that because of their hurried schedule, they never had a chance to collect any press clippings or photos from that treasured day. A couple of years later, I would have the pleasure of doing him that favor.

CHAPTER 2

BREAKING AWAY

AT THE END OF MY SECOND YEAR at the Art Center, I returned to Detroit and got a job at one of the biggest ad agencies in the country, Campbell Ewald. My plan was to work for a semester, earn some money, and then go back to school for a third year. It didn't turn out that way. I never went back.

Striding across the lobby of the General Motors Building to my office on the fourth floor, I was on top of the world. There I was, twenty years old and on the fast track to a lucrative career in an exciting field. It was 1961, a great time to feel good in America. An unmistakable buoyancy filled the air, and everyone felt good about the future. The Motor City was king— the Silicon Valley of its day—and had plenty of muscle to flex around its industrial power.

In those days Americans had love affairs with cars—their American cars, that is. It's hard to imagine, but back then, new model cars were introduced every September with huge fanfare and suspense in the media. Speculation ran high about what design features the new Ford or Chevy was coming out with: wraparound windshields, bigger tail fins, push-button transmissions. Tantalizing ads on TV and in newspapers teased readers with images of new cars under a huge sheet, giving only a suggestion of their outline. Cars were sex and America was turned on.

I was an apprentice at the ad agency and worked in the bullpen. There were five of us—young ones with promise. Each of us was assigned to an art director and an advertising account. Every three months, we rotated to another account. I began on the Chevy account and went to all the meetings with the big executives.

Marie sat at the desk in front of me. She was a painter, a real artist, and was disillusioned after only a few months on the job. Her plan was to only stay long enough to make some money and then retreat back to her art studio full time. One morning we were at the water cooler. She glanced around and whispered, "You gotta get outta here. This place is bullshit. You wait and see, they'll warp your mind. You think you're going to do anything creative here? Forget it. They'll squash you like a gnat."

I didn't know what she was talking about. I was new and loved it there. I loved going to the office every morning, striding across that marble lobby floor along with the thousands of others. I loved riding up the crowded elevator to the fourth floor, my briefcase in hand, even if it did contain only my lunch. I loved wearing my blue blazer, necktie, and button-down shirt pressed to perfection. Marie sipped her water. "Take my word for it," she said. "People around here wear little mental hats saying, 'No creativity, please.' You keep working on that Chevy shit. You'll see—you'll turn into a male version of Dinah Shore." Her face popped into a loopy grin, and, mimicking Dinah on the popular Chevy commercial of the day, she sang, "See the USA in your mindless way!"

The next day Marie came into the office and threw a book on my desk. "Here, read this," she said. It was Hermann Hesse's *Siddhartha*. I'd never heard of him or the book. "What's it about?" I asked.

"Read it; you'll find out," she snapped.

A few days later, I handed the book back to her. "I don't know," I said. "What's he getting at? Is it supposed to be symbolic or something?"

"You don't get it? What's wrong with you?" she fumed. Marie gave me a psychological drenching that left me speechless. The next morning as I sat at my drawing board, she looked at me over her shoulder. Still smarting, I pretended not to notice her as I busied myself sketching. She spun around in her swivel chair. "C'mon, Lenny, don't be so serious. Nothing's that important. Besides, don't worry, you're still the coolest guy around." She chuckled and spun back around to her drawing board.

*   *   *   *

After leaving Los Angeles, I corresponded with Stan Laurel. I told him of my quandary of whether I should continue in advertising or give it up to pursue a career in mime, theatre, etc. He advised against the latter:

> Note you are undecided on the career you want to follow "Mime" or Art Design. I agree with your family Lenny, show bus. is so unpredictable, heartbreaks & disappointments & once you get involved in this medium of make-believe it's very difficult to get away from. If you would like to make your "Miming talent" a hobby & to make occasional appearances for your own satisfaction that would be a sensible solution to your problem, but I think you would be foolish to take the profession seriously.
>
> Incidentally, I had a nice letter from Marcel Marceau yesterday.
>
> Good luck and God Bless,
> Stan Laurel

I wrote Eliot, my mime teacher in LA, and he gave me some solid advice: "Do what you think is right Lenny. And if you're not sure, then do what your heart tells you." Corny but excellent.

*   *   *   *

The Cup of Socrates was a new coffeehouse in Detroit and announced the arrival of the Beat culture to the Motor City. In the early 1960s, this was radical. People read poetry or performed offbeat plays on a tiny stage under a couple of coffee-can lights used for artistic effect while the audience sipped on that new exotic drink from Italy, espresso coffee. Hippies hadn't been invented yet. That was still a few years off. This was the Beat era. Everyone wore black and was very cool. As an antidote to the slick boredom of the advertising agency, I worked up a couple of mime routines and performed there on the weekends.

Marie came back from a vacation in New York and told me she had heard that Étienne Decroux was living and teaching there. I tracked him down and took my two-week vacation from the office to go to Manhattan to take classes with him. I caught him just in time. He had been in New York for five years, and this was his last two weeks there before returning to Paris for good.

Decroux taught in the living room of his small apartment in midtown Manhattan. *This is where the great master teaches?* Most of his students were members of his touring company and had performed with him at Carnegie Hall. I felt very out of place.

In contrast to the lithe, slender body of the ballet dancer, Decroux had the corpulence of a grizzly bear with his large, flat feet; strong, thick legs; and large hands with fingers as round as sausages. His long gray hair fell back from his high forehead onto his collar, highlighting his broad face with small eyes and wide nostrils. The large amounts of beer he drank during New York's sweltering summers left him with an abundant midsection. His mime clothes—a polo shirt, black swim trunks, and gymnastic slippers—seemed comical against the regal bearing he seemed to work at.

The warning that Decroux's work was nothing like Marceau was truer than I expected. No white face or illusions here. No pulling on ropes or walking up imaginary stairs. His work was stylized and very abstract. It was dancelike in its grace and fluidity but unlike any dance I had ever seen.

About halfway through my first lesson, Decroux announced that today was improvisation day. We sat down on stools, eight or nine of us, and he began talking. In French, of course. After five years in America, he had never learned English. He gazed over our heads into the distance as he spoke as if he were somewhere else. I looked quizzically at the girl next to me. She leaned closer and whispered, "Sometimes he imagines he's an orator speaking to great crowds." Decroux paused and looked through the group. "*Voyons . . . qui va passer en premier?*" "What's he saying?" I asked. "He's looking for someone to go first." Decroux motioned to me and said something. "What's he saying now?" I asked. "He wants you to go first."

My heart stopped. *What, me, go first? This is my first day! I don't know a thing!* I rose from my stool and moved slowly to the front of the room. "What am I supposed to do?" I asked my friend nervously. "Is there a theme or something?" "No, just do whatever you want," she replied. Suddenly I was falling out of an airplane at ten thousand feet without a parachute, and the ground was coming up fast. I needed something to grab onto, anything. A piece of classical music burst into my head. I didn't know what it was; it was just there. I began to move to the music in my head. For a few minutes I went blind. I couldn't see anything or anyone in the room. All I saw was bright, white light, and I heard music. A few minutes later, dripping sweat, I stopped and looked at Decroux. He said a few words. I looked at my friend for a translation. "Mr. Decroux said it was better than he expected."

*   *   *   *

As the office grind set in, I began having doubts about the advertising business. Then one day, riding home on the bus, it hit me. Marie was right! I was working in a factory whose sole purpose was to numb people into a torpor of stupidity. Create superfluous needs and then artfully convince the public that they can't live without them. Capitalize on their fears and insecurities and cleverly manipulate the emptying of their pocketbooks in your direction. Drive them crazy, in fact, until they feel that their lives are utter failures unless they have that second car, that electric can opener. Life itself was reduced to a commodity. I sat on the bus hearing my boss's voice ringing in my ears: "Babies are markets, Pitt! Don't forget that!" I thought about the TV show, *Racket Squad.* Every week at the end of the show, a cop sat at his desk closing one more case and warned viewers to watch out for the con man. "He'll slap you on the back with one hand and pick your pocket with the other," he intoned. Isn't that me? Wasn't I the con man? How can I spend the rest of my days churning out this garbage? That was my aha moment, when I knew that I couldn't return to Art Center. *What'll I do now? Thanks a lot Marie!*

*   *   *   *

While trying to figure out my life, I'd often drive downtown to pick up a couple of Coney Island hot dogs and sit on the riverfront to ponder my future. One day, I saw a young boy, about ten years old, jump onto a moored barge. He raced all over the place, lifting up tarps, trying doors and windows. When he couldn't get back up, I went over and offered a hand.

His name was Homer Banks. He was a shoeshine boy and gave all the money he earned to his mama, he said.

I was interested in photography, and at times I wandered through the Detroit slums taking pictures. Homer was interesting, and I wanted to photograph him but didn't have my camera with me. So I asked if I could visit him at home. "Sure!" he said and gave me an address near the ballpark.

A few days later, I knocked on the door of a rundown Victorian house expecting to find Homer. Naive me. He gave me a wrong address, and no one knew who he was. Stumped, I walked around the neighborhood asking people on the street if anyone knew Homer Banks the shoeshine boy. Someone actually did and gave me directions.

I knocked on the door of another house. Homer's mother answered and was concerned. She thought I was a cop or a welfare worker since no one else ever visited. "Was Homer in trouble?" she asked. "Was he hurt?" I reassured her, he was fine.

She introduced herself as Della Slayton and invited me in to wait for Homer. She had moved to Detroit from Hazard, Kentucky, a few years ago with her six kids after her husband tried to stab her. She picked up odd jobs here and there.

With the TV blaring, two girls sat on the floor eating snacks. A third daughter, Larny, walked through the room hiding her face behind her hand. A few minutes later, Homer walked in and did a double take when he saw me. "Why'd you give me the wrong address?" I asked. "I didn't know you," he shot back. "I wasn't gonna tell you where I lived."

This was 1961. I was twenty and knew nothing about nothing. But I knew what was interesting, and this was interesting. The Slaytons and I became friends, and I went to visit them about once a week. Larny was the oldest, an attractive nineteen-year-old yearning for a man and affection. She had little education and no social skills. Asbel was next, about seventeen. He couldn't read or write and had all the dysfunction of a young man with no clue of how to enter society. He was terribly awkward and afraid of going out in public. Clarence, about sixteen, was more socially adept, a brooding teenager in the Elvis mold with his cool demeanor and hair combed with the perfect wave. Then there was Homer and the two younger girls, Sis and Mary Lou.

Della was never far from her bible and often read to her children. She was kind and gracious within her means. As they had no car and never ventured far from home, on occasion I would take them out for a ride. Asbel only came along with great urging. He cowered in the backseat and never left the car.

Because they were "hillbillies" they were the brunt of neighborhood hostility. One night Clarence was jumped by a couple of local youths who beat him up for simply being there. But as neighbors noticed a shiny car pulling up every week, this hostility abated. This could only mean that they knew someone rich and important. When I began shooting portraits of the family at night, the bright light from my crude setup impressed the neighbors more so.

When I brought them clothes from home, Della thanked me and said she would take them to church for her friends. What she was really saying was that it was demeaning for me to say these clothes were for her. It made her feel even poorer. In the future, anything I brought I offered for her church, knowing she would take the pick of the best, as intended.

I tried to teach Asbel how to read. This was an impossible task. The letters *m* and *n* were particularly difficult for him to decipher. He had trouble distinguishing them. "The *m* has two points on top, and the *n* has one," I'd say, as he stared at the letters with incomprehension.

Friends at the ad agency became interested in my involvement with the family, and in time I took up a collection so Asbel could work with a private tutor to learn how to read and write. For his first tutoring session, I rode on the bus with him so he would know how to get there on his own. He sat huddled in his seat throwing frightful glances left and right.

*   *   *   *

One Monday morning I ran out of the elevator and down the hall to the office. I was late. A lousy weekend trying to figure out what to do with my life left me exhausted and bleary-eyed. Marie was working at her desk and half-smiled when she saw me. "Here, this is for you," she said, handing me a note. I opened it. "When a bird is at last quiet it spreads its wings and flies, then it knows the sky."

I walked around the office at Campbell Ewald saying good-bye. The forlorn looks everyone had told me I was doing the right thing. Most of these guys had rushed from college straight into a wife and kids, a mortgage, maybe a stint in the military along the way. Dick shook my hand with a blank expression on his face. "So you're going to Europe . . . damn."

The following week, I left Detroit. It had been a year since I met the Slaytons, and we had grown close. When I told Della I was going to Europe, she didn't understand. "I'm going to Paris," I said. "Paris!" she exclaimed, "Is that a movie star?"

CHAPTER 3

PARIS AT LAST

I STOOD ON THE DECK OF THE *Queen Elizabeth* as we sailed out of New York harbor and watched the Manhattan skyline disappear on the horizon. It was October 1962. I had just turned twenty-one. This was the week of the Cuban Missile Crisis. Only a few days earlier President Kennedy had gone on television to tell the American people that Soviet missile bases had been discovered in Cuba. A Communist threat only ninety miles off our coast was too close for comfort. The United States, Kennedy announced, was setting up a naval blockade to stop the Soviet supply ships from heading there. His ultimatum to the Russians was clear: dismantle the missile bases, or else. Here was the showdown at the O.K. Corral, but now with nuclear weapons. I was unsure that I would ever see New York again.

Once on the ocean, I went below to my cabin and lay down on my immaculately clean bed. *I must be crazy*, I thought. *The world's going to blow up, and I'm heading to Europe!* I only had a vague idea of where I was going and couldn't speak a word of a foreign language. I was both excited and scared out of my wits. The world was a more dangerous place then.

My plan was to be away for only five or six months, just enough time to clear my mind and figure out what I wanted to do with my life. Then I'd head back home and settle down to the serious business of making a living, whatever that was. I never dreamed I'd be away seven years. As my plans for Europe became real, I decided to go to Ireland for Stan Laurel.

After a five-day crossing of the Atlantic, I arrived in Southampton and caught a train and a ferry for Cork, Ireland. I arrived in town and went directly to the offices of *The Cork Examiner* to get copies of the press photos of Laurel and Hardy from that day as they stood with the Lord Mayor of Cork and other dignitaries. There were no Xerox machines then, so I hand-copied the news article and sent everything along in a small package to Mr. Laurel.

In Cork I struck up a conversation with a shopkeeper who asked what brought me to Ireland. There was little tourism in those days, and a foreigner like me was an event. "I'm doing a favor for Stan Laurel," I said. His eyes lit up. "So, you're bein' a friend of Mr. Laurel's!" he exclaimed. "Well, have you met Mr. so-and-so? He was there that day. And how about so-and-so, he was there too!" He picked up the phone and began calling around, "Indeed, he's a friend of Mr. Laurel's!"

Before I knew it arrangements were made for me to meet the man in Cobh who played the bells that day, Dr. Staf Gebruers. The following Sunday evening I took a train the few miles out there and, as instructed, waited on the cathedral steps as the townsfolk filed out after the evening Mass. A man peeked around the corner and called out, "Are you bein' Mr. Pitt?" He introduced himself as Charlie and led me through a small side door into the cathedral.

Dr. Gebruers greeted me warmly and told me something about Laurel and Hardy's visit that the two comics never knew. The British press created a huge uproar because he played their profane music on the sacred church bells, and above all because Laurel had been married more than once—as many as seven times, I heard. The good doctor almost lost his job.

He thought I was an American journalist who had come back to stir up the controversy all over again and was apprehensive. I assured him there was no danger. He looked pensive for a moment. "OK," he said, "I tell you what. Bein' that you're a friend of Mr. Laurel's, how would you like it if I played the bells for you tonight? My eyes opened wide. "Now I can't be playin' you their theme music, but I'll play you something nice just the same." He motioned towards the door, and we stepped outside. "You go with Charlie onto that hill over there and stand next to that block of apartments. That's where the bells sound the most beautiful. Notice how everyone will be openin' their windows because no one's expectin' the bells tonight and everyone loves them so much."

As Charlie and I reached the top of the hill, it started to drizzle. The bells began to ring, first with "Danny Boy." We walked through the village under our umbrellas and stopped at a terrace overlooking the port. Charlie pointed to the docks below. "Mr. Laurel and Mr. Hardy were standing over there, you see, and the Lord Mayor was there . . ." We walked back to the cathedral, and I thanked Dr. Gebruers. He shook my hand vigorously and asked if Mr. Laurel could send him an autographed picture of Laurel and Hardy so he could put it in the church sacristy. I wrote to Mr. Laurel, and he did send the photo to Dr. Gebruers.

*   *   *   *

From Ireland I went to England, to Stratford-upon-Avon, Shakespeare's birthplace, and stopped by the theatre to see what was playing. By chance *King Lear* was opening that night, directed by Peter Brook with Paul Scofield in the role of Lear. I ended up in the center of the tenth row. The stars were well aligned for this trip.

After a short stop in London, I went to Paris for a few days and caught a train south to the village of Montignac in the Dordogne region to see the prehistoric caves of Lascaux. These had been a highlight of my education at Cass Tech and were not to be missed. I paid a couple of francs for my ticket and walked the short distance to the cave entrance with my guide.

In my broken French, I asked if he was the one who found the caves. He nodded yes. He was out walking in the hills with a friend one day in the 1940s when they lost track of his dog. They heard him barking but couldn't find him. They followed the sound to a hole in the ground that the dog had fallen through. The young man slid through and dropped to the bottom. He lit a match and was stunned to find himself in a large cave surrounded by walls covered with strange paintings. No human had seen these paintings for over ten thousand years. And the world was stunned.

We walked down a flight of stone stairs cut into the earth that lead to large, heavy iron doors. It was November 1962, and I was the only one there. To wander these caves alone amidst the liveliness of this ancient art was overwhelming. The guide stood leaning against the cave entrance smoking a cigarette while I walked around.

Not long after my visit, mold was found growing over the paintings— the effects of human breathing, the experts said. The following January the caves were closed to the public. Given the little tourism in those days and the time of year, this means that I was likely one of the last people—if not the last person—to see the actual caves before they were closed. Some years later an exact replica was built nearby for tourists.

I traveled around Europe for a couple of months visiting Spain, Italy, Greece, and Israel and then headed for Paris! Little did I know that I would stay for seven years. I'm still reeling from the experience, all the beauty and the misery of it. To be young, to be living in Paris, to be poor and not know it, to be studying art with a master, and, oh yes, to be in love—I have known it all.

At the train station I phoned a distant relative, Marcel, a cousin of my mother's. When my family left Russia for America, his family traveled to Paris.

Marcel insisted that I stay with him and his wife Ethyl in their large apartment on Rue de Turenne. I hopped a taxi and was there in a few minutes. Marcel was a short, balding man with a ruddy complexion and a face like a bulldog. He was in the garment business and had a small factory in the République quarter of Paris.

He lived in a constant state of brooding because of the loss of his manufacturing enterprise in Algeria after that country achieved independence in 1961. His large apartment had all the tattered feeling of an empire on the wane. We took our meals at a long table that sat sixteen. Marcel sat at the head of the table, his foot nervously ringing a bell on the floor to call the maid for the next course, to clear the dishes, to bring the coffee. Ethyl served the dishes, kept the patter going, and was clearly the charming, hospitable wife who picks up after her abusive husband.

One night, during the hors d'oeuvres, he asked me what I was doing in Paris.

"I'm going to study mime," I said.

"What's that?" he said, not looking up. He'd never heard of mime. Searching for something, I said, "Uh . . . it's like Marcel Marceau." *He must know who he is.* "Who's that?" he said, looking at me with a blank expression. Searching for something more, anything, I said, "It's like . . . uh . . . Charlie Chaplin." His face burst into stupefaction as his head shot across the table. "What! You're going to do what? You came all the way to Paris to do that?" His voice grew louder. "That's mime? That's it? You came here to do that?"

Ethyl tried to distract him. "Marcel, have some bread, have some salad, it's good, eat, eat." His eyes riveted on me, he kept yelling. "Mime? Impossible! It's *caca! Le mime, c'est du caca!*" His pudgy face turned beet red. I thought he was going to explode. His shrill voice hit me like shards of glass. "You should be working in the store with your father, or become a doctor, a lawyer, an architect even! Then I would help you! I'd give you an apartment, a car. But mime? *Caca!* Out of my house! Out!" The rest of the meal passed in a silence as dense as the innermost part of a glacier. The next morning I stood at the door with my suitcases in hand and said good-bye to Ethyl. She kissed me on both cheeks and with a philosophical shrug wished me well.

I trudged down the stairs and walked to the Métro station. What now? It was January 1963—cold, wet, gray skies. Weather made for the depressed. I took the train to the Left Bank, to Place Saint-Michel, and wandered around looking for a cheap hotel. I passed a bookstore—Shakespeare and Company on Rue de la Bûcherie opposite Notre Dame. Taped to the window was a Help Wanted sign. Inside, a thin man with a goatee sat at a large desk reading a book and smoking a cigarette from a long holder. I walked in and struck up a conversation with George Whitman, the owner, and was offered free lodging in exchange for a couple of hours of work each day. That was good enough for now.

I had no idea that I had wandered into a literary institution. This Shakespeare and Co. had no connection to the famous bookstore of the same name run by Sylvia Beach on Rue de l'Odéon in the 1920s and '30s. Nevertheless, this Shakespeare and Co. had its own niche in the literary landscape of Paris. No American writer would go to Paris and not visit, as thousands have done over the years since it opened in 1951.

Once settled into the bookstore I continued my ritual of walking to the American Express every day to pick up my mail. Can we imagine a time before cell phones and email when people actually wrote letters?

Even telephones were hard to find in Paris. Few people had them at home. The Minister of Communication was famous for his pronouncement that he thought telephones were only a gimmick. Phone booths were nowhere to be found in the city. The only pay phones were in cafés.

Phoning home to America was a complicated affair. You went to the post office and made an appointment for a long-distance phone call. The woman behind the counter gave you a time to return. "Come back at two thirty, Monsieur." You showed up at your appointed time and waited to be called. "Monsieur Pitt, booth number three!" The connection was never good, and you always shouted into the phone.

Approaching the American Express that day, I saw big semi-trucks parked on the street, with thick electric cables running inside the building. *Must be doing some work*, I thought. I walked downstairs to the mail department and was surprised to see bright lights everywhere with crowds of people standing stock-still in total silence. *Hmm . . . odd.* Everyone was neatly dressed in clean, new clothes. *Usually the place is full of commotion and everyone is as scruffy as me.* I walked over to the mail counter and said, "Anything today for Pitt?" The woman, who I had seen every day, gave me one of those looks like, *What the hell are you doing here?* and quickly fingered through the letters in her hand as she nervously glanced left and right. "No, nothing today," she said, forcing a smile.

That's odd, I thought, *why didn't she pull the P's out from the cubbyhole on the wall behind her like she usually did?* Then I heard, "ACTION!" I froze. I glanced to my left. Standing next to me was Cary Grant. There on the floor next to him was a big movie camera. *Oh God!* Slowly I moved off to the side. I turned around, and there was a movie crew of about a hundred people. Next to me, right next to me, was Audrey Hepburn. The film was *Charade*. Somehow I stumbled onto a movie set and walked in on the middle of a scene with such perfect timing that no one realized I was out of place. The doors had been open for a few minutes to bring in some equipment, and I slipped by, totally unnoticed. Now with the doors locked, I couldn't leave. During a break in the shooting, Grant bought me a Coke at the soft drink machine. That was the Coke of a lifetime.

*   *   *   *

Several weeks later, I found a small room on the Avenue de l'Opéra, one of the fanciest streets in the heart of Paris lined with fine shops and cafés. Located between the Garnier opera house and the Louvre Museum, I was at the lower end of the avenue at number 16, on the sixth floor under the eaves, one of the many maid's rooms in Paris lived in by poor students, workers, or struggling artists. The building was organized in the same manner as the old French boulevard theatres, where the top balcony, known as "paradise," was reserved for the rabble known as "the children of paradise," while the wealthier crowd sat below.

On the floors beneath were the French Chamber of Commerce and the Swiss Embassy. The elegant entrance to the building was a deceiving introduction to my meager quarters above. The large glass-and-steel door on the street, a door with heft, opened onto a marble hallway that led into a small lobby with an elevator, the old-world kind with a steel cage you could see out of.

My room was small. You opened the door, walked three steps, and that was it. On the sloping wall of the eave was a window overlooking a courtyard six floors below that I could not see because of the pitch of the roof. Overhead was a small, drafty skylight. I had no telephone, no central heat, no bath or shower—only a toilet at the end of the hall that I shared with two other rooms across the hall. Bathing meant regular trips to the public bath a few blocks away. I shared a small kitchen with the people living in the other rooms. We had no refrigerator. We cooked meals on a small two-burner stove that sat on top of a wooden table. My rent, $40 a month, was just manageable. I lived in these quarters for seven years.

When I was in Detroit dreaming of Paris, I imagined myself living in a large one- or two-bedroom apartment. It never occurred to me that this would be so out of reach. It didn't take long to decompress out of this fantasy and to accept my modest quarters on the Avenue de l'Opéra as how life was in Paris. Nevertheless it took a while for me to acclimate to living within four walls that were so close to each other that if they wanted to talk to one another, all they had to do was whisper.

Once I was settled in, I found that the smallness of my room imposed a discipline. The only things that I could acquire were objects of necessity that allowed me to move forward in my work. This made it easy to focus on the important things. No radio, television, or telephone eliminated those distractions as well. This little room was my cockpit to the universe, and everything in it was a tool to get me somewhere.

*   *   *   *

My landlady, Madame Ragout, was only a few years older than me and had all the good looks of a Leslie Caron: full, pouty lips, big dark eyes accentuated with eyeliner, black hair pulled back into a ponytail. But her good looks were melting on her face. Madame Ragout was lost in alcohol. Her budding career as a dancer had veered so far off course that she spent days alone in her large apartment down the hall with her Pekingese dog Gigi in a losing battle with the bottle. She wasn't much older than me, but I still saw her as a much-older woman. She being the landlady and my calling her "Madame" put years on her.

"Lay-oh-nahr," I said quietly looking out my window. That's French for *Leonard*. I repeated my name again. "Lay-oh-nahr!" I liked the sound, especially the accent over the *e*. Back home I was *Lenny*. That was fine when I was younger. But now I was older and was living in Paris. I never liked *Leonard* very much. The sound was too short; it had no shape to it. But *Lay-oh-nahr*. Ahh! That sounded like a bird unfolding its wings and flying.

*   *   *   *

Decroux was the locus of my life in Paris. He lived in a small gingerbread of a house built in the 1890s by his father, a brick mason, on the outskirts of Paris in the Boulogne district. The house sat at the end of a narrow courtyard and was bordered with colorful flowers. The front door led into a small kitchen with a potbelly stove in the corner. Madame Decroux wore wire-rimmed glasses and, wrapped in a large white apron, explained the rules of the house: Classes were held Monday through Saturday, ten to eleven thirty every morning. Tuition was eighty francs a month, about $16. Take off your shoes and put them around the edge of the potbelly stove. Change clothes upstairs. I put my money on the table and signed up for a month. Through a crack in the door I saw Decroux in his study sitting at his desk writing with a crow quill pen and smoking his long-stemmed clay pipe. Who said the nineteenth century was over?

Classes were held in the basement of the house, a long, narrow converted coal bin with a ceiling so low I could not stretch my arms up overhead. But the place sparkled. The stairs leading down from the kitchen were painted bright pink; the walls and ceiling were baby blue. The concrete floor was covered with speckled blue linoleum.

Word hadn't gotten out yet that Decroux was back in Paris, and he didn't advertise, so there were only six or seven of us students. Even after my classes with him in Manhattan, I had no idea what his work was really about. I kept waiting for the "fun stuff," the illusions, but instead we studied rigorous technical exercises: how to move the eyes without the head, the head without the neck, etc. And there were the "Counter-weights," movements of pushing or pulling: simple movements stripped down to their essential components and amplified through every part of the body. Saturdays were reserved for a variety of walks. Then there were the "Figures," sequences of stylized movements strung together. This wasn't mime. It looked more like some obscure form of artistic Yoga. I wanted to know more about what we were doing, what it all meant, but whenever I asked Decroux about mime specifically, he only gave an evasive smile.

Studying how the body moves instilled within me an appreciation for all movement. Anything that moves is interesting. I began intently watching people. The streets and the cafés became my laboratory with an endless flux of humans in motion to study. I became sensitive to how people walk, sit, gesture. Watching is not only watching; it is also feeling. I developed feelers on my eyes like antennae that reach out and touch bodies. I felt their weight, consistency, tension, knottiness, fluidity. We all experience this to some degree. I developed an acute sense of this way of seeing. It is an animal way of experiencing. Simple, direct, no judgment, just taking in.

One day, a small coleus plant in my room wilted because I forgot to water it. I saturated the soil with water, sat down, and without taking my eyes off it, I watched it for over an hour while it revived almost imperceptibly.

Riding home on the Métro one day after class, my mind was bubbling. Decroux had pointed out the connection between much of his work and cartoons, an odd juxtaposition. "The movement in the cartoons is clean," he said. "There's nothing extra or too much. Just enough. Very expressive." Decroux often drew parallels between things I never thought about, and these became my windows onto a new world. Much that I had discounted as boring or uninteresting became intensely interesting. This forced me to a simple conclusion: I had to rethink every thought I ever had, see everything I had ever seen and reevaluate it all. What might I have missed because I didn't know how to see?

*   *   *   *

Decroux had made no progress with his English since leaving Manhattan. The language was too impossible to learn, he said. The only word he liked in the whole of the English language was *elbow*. Slowly he would pronounce it with all the sweetness of a bird cooing. The word he detested most and found impossible to pronounce was *fire*. It was as if he needed something to tee him off now and then, and this word was it.

As students congregated in the kitchen after a lesson, the conversation would often turn to the subject of the differences between French and English. Inevitably Decroux would ask someone to pronounce the word *feu* in English. "Fire," an innocent soul said one day. And with that the grand debacle began. Decroux stammered as he contorted his mouth. "Fa-yer, Fay-yeer!"

"Very good, Monsieur, that's it."

"No, that's not it," he barked. "Say it again, once more, but this time slowly," he fumed. "Fire," the innocent repeated.

"Fah-yeere, fuh-yire!"

"Very good, Monsieur."

"No, no, once again!"

Like a mechanical engine laboring under too great a load, hissing, jerking, and sputtering, Decroux leaned into the face of his unwilling accomplice, bending his ear towards his mouth so as not to miss an inflection or an errant syllable, and continued mangling one of the simpler words in the English language. In this battle, the word always won. At the end of his wits, Decroux reassumed a state of composure, held himself upright—as if to say, "You see, the damn word didn't get me"—and, forcing a smile, shook hands with the students as they left.

One night, instead of the normal lesson, we all sat on wooden stools while Decroux pulled a table and chair out and sat down with his hands clasped in front of him. "From now on," he said, "Monday nights will be reserved for lectures. What would you like me to talk about tonight?" In response to our questions he came back with what sounded like riddles: "Mime is weight . . . mime is gravity . . . everything in the world weighs . . . don't try to express yourself . . . to the contrary, empty yourself so you can express the soul of God . . . think of yourself like a bull when moving . . . you are not a gazelle, you are a bull. Each step has weight."

It was this principle of weight, he told us, that distinguished his art from the ballet. The ballet tries to free the body from the ground. Decroux encouraged us to plant ourselves on the earth. Another time he talked about stillness: "Mime is immobility . . . the sun radiates but does not move . . . you must know how to move so you can know how to stop . . ." What was he getting at? I enrolled for another month.

*   *   *   *

As I settled into Paris, it hit me one day how difficult it must have been for my parents to raise the three of us boys. How did they do it? My mother was not the stay-at-home mom I know she would have liked to be, but rather she worked as much as she could. I wrote them a letter and thanked them.

*   *   *   *

One day, about a year after being in Paris, I took stock of my life as I crossed the footbridge across the Seine, the Pont des Arts. I was living in Paris studying with a master. I had a circle of friends made up of artists and writers. I lived two blocks from the Louvre, not to speak of the other museums. My mind exploded the day I arrived, and a year later, it was still in a state of explosion. The world was before me, and it was mine for the taking.

I knew I wanted to make art and theatre my life, but how? When I thought about the future, I saw a door before me that I had to pass through in order to attain the life I wanted. It wasn't wide open welcoming me in, but it wasn't closed either. It was open just a crack. That was all I needed.

*   *   *   *

How was I going to support myself in Paris? Getting a real job was impossible. Those were reserved for the French. With classes every day, I couldn't manage a full-time job anyway. Surviving in Paris made me feel like an animal foraging for food in the dead of winter—you had to know the landscape, keep your eyes open, know when to move, when to wait, when to jump.

Someone told me about a job selling *The New York Times* on the street. I went to an office on Rue Lafayette and after a short interview was hired. I had a guarantee of twelve francs a day, about $2.20, plus 4¢ a paper. Three days a week I paced up and down in front of the Garnier opera house, Notre Dame, or on the Champs-Élysées crying out a spiel I made up:

> *New York Times, ten cents!*
> *All today's news, one dime.*
> *Printed this morning right here in Paris.*
> *Hot off the press, the ink is still wet.*
> *Cheapest thing in Paris. Ten cents, one dime, two nickels, ten*
> *pennies, one tenth part of a dollar!*
> *Sports! Baseball, football, basketball, high jumping, Pole-vault-*
> *ing, discus throwing, mumblety-peg.*
> *It's cheap; get homesick for a dime!*

Little did I know that I had become part of a centuries-old tradition of Paris street hawkers crying out their wares. And I was probably one of the last.

On my days off I earned a few extra francs working with Gaston the one-armed photographer and his son Guy. We met at the entrance to the Louvre, set up his box camera on a wooden tripod, and waited for the tour buses to arrive. With the museum as a backdrop, Gaston hunched down under the large black cloth and took group photos of American tourists. Then we'd jump into his old Citroën and rattle on back to his apartment to develop the negatives in a makeshift darkroom and print up forty or fifty copies on postcards that I sold to the same tourists once we caught up with them at the end of their tours at Notre Dame. I made 50 centimes for each postcard sold.

On Sundays I walked over to the foot bridge across the Seine, the Pont des Arts, and sat next to the old organ grinder to sell my pen-and-ink sketches of Paris to the tourists for five or ten francs.

My big coup was landing a job as a technical translator. Me, a technical translator? Massey Ferguson, an American manufacturer of farm machinery with an office in Paris, needed someone to translate the operating manual of a tractor from English into French. At the interview the company manager wanted proof of my expertise in this field. He opened the manual to a drawing of the tractor with lines drawn to each of the thousands of parts showing the names in English. With a pencil he pointed to the hand brake. "How about that?" he said, "How would you translate that into French?" I stared blankly at the page. Here was the easiest part of the whole damned machine, and I had no idea what it was called. I stumbled. "Yeah, sure, I know that, *hand brake*, in French that's the uh . . ." "*Frein a main*," he chimed in. "Ah, yes, *frein a main*! Right, sure, the *frein a main*." I smiled with satisfaction at my knowledge. I guess it was good enough because I got the job.

Back in my room I pored over the manual wondering what I had gotten myself into. This was as arcane as *The Tibetan Book of the Dead*. The technical terms were bad enough in English, but to know them in French? I called my friend Ben, a real technical translator, and told him of my dilemma. He laughed uproariously. "People spend years learning this stuff. They have huge specialized dictionaries for this kind of work. And you didn't know *hand brake*?" Lucky for me he took the job.

CHAPTER 4

LOUIS'S HIGH HEELS

STUDYING WITH DECROUX WAS a seesaw ride between joy and despair. I never thought that learning how to move my body could be so challenging. Every movement has a source somewhere in the body, and I struggled to find those places. Head movements come from the neck. Chest movements from the back. Arm movements from the biceps and triceps. Putting the body under a microscope and focusing on such detail brought out the innate expression of every movement of the body. Intensity of experience sharpens perception. I began to look at body movement as I never had before.

One Friday night I walked to the Latin Quarter for a coffee. It was a warm evening, and the crowds were out enjoying the first days of spring. Cafés are great for people-watching, and I was hooked. I liked the Café Favorite at Place Saint-Michel near a Métro exit that continually disgorged crowds of people out of the ground.

That night I watched people's feet as they walked by, and I saw much I had never seen before. The feet are the critical point between the body and the ground. All of our body weighs down and is concentrated there. A part of us is essentialized in the way our bodies sit on the ground through our feet.

Some feet as they walk are bland; others are vivacious. I've seen them frightened, nervous, cocky, staid, overconfident, and sometimes insecure. Some are afraid to walk on the ground. Some sit naturally; some grapple with it.

When we meet someone for the first time, we look first at the face. Sometimes feet confirm what we see there. Other times they contradict. You might think it's difficult to see feet with all the coverings of pants, cuffs, and heels, but no. There is still movement, and where there is movement, something is being said.

There are not nearly enough words to describe the different feet that I have seen walking. If I tried to put a word to all the feet walking that I have seen, I wouldn't have seen half the feet walking that I have seen. All I can do is look at them like an event of nature without trying to judge or evaluate, but just to witness.

Every aspect of a person is present and is funneled down there. In the rhythm and tempo of the step, in the way the feet make contact with the ground, in the length of the step, in how the foot hits the ground heel first. I watch how the weight of the body moves from the heel to the ball of the foot. I see the qualities, features, and idiosyncrasies of a person.

Some set their weight on the outside of the foot when their heel hits the ground and then, as it moves forward towards their toe, their weight moves to the inside of their foot. With others their weight goes straight up the center of their foot, from heel to toe. Each of these sequences has a different expression.

Some feet land almost flat on the ground in the step. Some people angle their feet into the ground as their heels make contact. Some people walk imperceptibly on the balls of their feet. Infants walk this way, but as they mature, their heels find the ground first.

Everything going on down there speaks of someone. I look at feet and see eyes and faces. I see minds posturing and gesticulating, telling us who they are. I see a million stories down there.

Then there is the leg as it angles into the ground. The bend of the lower leg, its tension and resistance like a pillar or bow. There is the upper leg, the thigh, the pelvis, all supporting the thrust of the body's weight.

I have seen underdeveloped pelvises beneath overdeveloped, thick chests moving through the world like a closed fist. I have seen sunken chests that have given up long ago, surrounded by fortressed shoulders telling the world that the fight is not over yet.

I have seen chins and necks screaming because someone violated them over and over again in an obscure past. I have seen chests breathe with a fear of life, transparent, hardly existing, chests breathing with the force of a steel trap, defending themselves against invisible aggressors.

And the face. What can be said about a human face? What a small word, *face*. How little it says by itself. But what about the sensations that surge into it, all the feelings behind it that never get out because of frozen eyes, jaws, or lips.

I look at a face smiling. Lips pursing, reaching, denying, accepting. Sometimes playing games. Sometimes refusing all compromise. Sometimes a face is smiling, but the eyes are crying or pleading and the cheeks are doubting while the lips try to convince.

I see eyes with veils over them wishing they were not there, others sitting there matter-of-factly. Eyes, eyeballs, eyelids, and brows all speak of someone.

What else is there to see in a body? Everywhere I look I hear someone speaking. What can a shoulder say as it moves or refuses to move? What can it say by its contour, by its form and muscle, by its fleshiness and boniness? What can it say by the way it moves out of the chest into the arm? Does it say yes or no? Maybe it says, *I don't care.*

The evening air was warm, and people were wearing light shirts and blouses. I watched all the dancing shoulders. There goes a sassy shoulder. There's a shoulder trying to make a point. Everywhere I looked on a body, I saw something being said.

*   *   *   *

Decroux's insistence on weight and gravity, the basic principles of his technique, gave me a way of seeing the body I had not known before. Attending concerts of the Chinese opera and the Japanese Kabuki theatre sensitized me further to body movement that reinforced the act of being on the ground. That's when the ballet struck me as being odd. It never looked odd before, wrapped in its associations of elegance, sophistication, even spirituality. But now, seeing it alongside other dance and movement that was so earthy and grounded, the ballet's upwardness looked, well, odd.

Decroux once said that the questions we ask are often more important than the answers we find. A good question can lead us on a journey for years. I didn't know it then, but that was my case here.

My question was simple: Why this mania for getting off the ground? Where did it come from? Could the ballet have developed an aesthetic that emphasized the body being on the ground? Conversely, could a dance with this upward aesthetic have come out of, say, Africa or Japan? Are these things random, or was there something else at play?

Unwittingly, Decroux had placed a box of wonders in my lap. This question would preoccupy me for years, leading me from one field of study to another. In time I saw connections between things I never thought possible. Who would imagine a historical arc connecting Louis XIV and Elvis Presley? They were both kings, sure, but there is more. Ask a good question, be open to where it leads you, and you are never bored.

Questions have always driven me. When I was a little boy I had to walk down a long, dark hallway to get to the bathroom at night. I was always afraid of encountering a burglar in the house and wondered what I would do if I ever did see one. I concluded that I would ask him why he became a burglar. Alexander Pope was right: "Just as the twig is bent, the tree's inclined."

I brought up my question about the ballet to Richard, who lived across the hall from me. Richard was an American photographer, about thirty-five, and had been in Paris for years. He drove a big Mercedes-Benz and sucked his thumb at the wheel. Richard's insecurities were a driving force in his life. His constant need to prove himself to others made him a master at weaseling into impossible situations in order to bolster his lack of self-esteem. His talent and imagination at picking up women anywhere—sitting at a café, in the movies, even on street corners—was nothing short of amazing. His boyish good looks, beguiling charm, and shy demeanor made an immediate opening that led to a long list of phone numbers. But he rarely called any of them. The phone number itself was the conquest. Stranger yet, he lived with his Dutch girlfriend, Saskia, and she put up with this.

We sat in the kitchen. I sipped a cup of espresso coffee while Richard percolated a cup of Maxwell House he had shipped to himself from America. He hated French coffee. "The museums are the best place to pick up women," he assured me. "It's perfect. You've got a civilized atmosphere with no commotion. If you know anything about the paintings, the girls think you're educated with good taste. If you like a girl, you can walk away and then conveniently bump into her somewhere else in the museum. And where's the one place everyone wants to go after the museum? The café. It's perfect."

I stood in awe of Richard's talent. I had accepted my fate as a shy person. I told him about class with Decroux and my questions about the ballet. "I heard that Louis XIV started the ballet," Richard said. "In fact, that he was crazy about dancing. They called him the dancing king."

"Yeah, but what's that got to do with the ballet getting off the ground?" I said.

"I don't know," he said. "Maybe it's because he wore high heels."

"He wore heels?" I didn't know anything about the French kings.

"Haven't you ever seen paintings of him?" he said, reaching out the window for the milk carton on the ledge. "High heels are a good starter for getting off the ground, aren't they? Just think: if Louis had worn flats, the history of French art might have been totally different."

And then I committed a cardinal sin. I cut a piece of Camembert cheese, put it on a slice of baguette, and, yes, I salted it. Richard burst out laughing. "Oh, God! I don't believe it! That's great, just great. The French would love it. Pouring salt on Camembert!"

How was I supposed to know? Cheese was not a major food group in Detroit. Whenever my mother put a few slices on a sandwich, my brothers and I would salt it in order to get rid of the cheesy taste.

The next morning I woke up with Louis XIV on my mind. Did he really wear high heels? I walked to the Louvre and found Hyacinthe Rigaud's painting of the Sun King. With his long wig, bouffant sleeves, and layers of brocaded material, Louis looked more like the king of the drag queens. And yes, he was wearing high-heeled shoes. This man started the ballet? Well, he had the posture for it, with his chest held high, feet turned out. My curiosity was piqued.

I left the museum and walked over to Shakespeare and Co. on the Left Bank and found a book on the history of dance tucked away on the shelves. I went to the café, took a table by the window, and began reading.

Richard's oversimplification contained a grain of truth. Louis XIV didn't invent the ballet, but he did play a crucial role in helping get it off the ground, so to speak. In 1669, he established the Royal Academy of Music, with a dance school to train dancers for the opera, the first institution of its kind in Europe. Before Louis there were no such thing as professional dancers. All the dancers in the court ballets were the courtiers themselves—noble amateurs. The king's new school took the dance from an amateur pastime to a professional art form practiced by dedicated students attending full-time classes.

Dance in the seventeenth century had none of the elevation, lightness, speed, and virtuosity we know today. That was years off. Men paraded around like Roman generals with heavy swords and shields. Woman wore floor-length dresses padded with layers of petticoats, along with large wigs and hats decorated with elaborate flower arrangements. The dance was slow, like elegant walking or marching. To make things worse, dancers—men and women alike—wore heavy-heeled shoes. There was no possibility of leaping or jumping, much less running. Yet despite these obstacles, the dance's evolution over the years was towards greater and greater elevation, culminating in the Romantic Ballet in the 1830s with prima ballerinas flying in the air. What brought this about? I wanted to know.

*   *   *   *

After four months of classes with Decroux, he asked me to join a new company he was creating. This meant an extra hour of technique in the morning plus rehearsals in the afternoon, not to mention the endless trips back and forth on the Métro to his house just outside of Paris in Boulogne-Billancourt. With a quick calculation, my friends and I figured out that every year we spent a total of two weeks, twenty-four hours a day, in the Métro going back and forth to his house.

*   *   *   *

Some people discover Paris by going to nightclubs or museums or by shopping. For me it was bookstores and cheap restaurants. Day after day I searched through the bookstores and the bookstalls along the banks of the Seine looking for works on dance, all kinds of dance from all over the world. My French was improving but was far from perfect, so I struggled through. It didn't take long for my tiny room to fill with books. They were stacked high on makeshift shelves, in piles on the floor, all over my desk, on my bed.

*   *   *   *

I enrolled for French lessons at the Alliance Française on Boulevard Raspail. Here was high school all over again. Decroux often said that the most interesting people on stage are those who are interested in what they are doing. "He's interesting because he's interested," "Il est intéressant parce qu'il est intéressé." The opposite was true of my French teacher, Monsieur Crapard. He was boring because he was bored. I couldn't keep my eyes open. I failed everything and never got beyond the first level. I quit after six weeks.

*   *   *   *

After class, my friends and I often stopped at the café next door. Sitting with our cups of espresso or Viandox, we puzzled over what seemed to be the hybrid nature of Decroux's mime. His posture and attitudes of the body were identical to the ballet. His zero position had the spine extended and gut pulled in like the ballet. The feet were turned out in first position. Beyond this his work was like an obscure form of Yoga or Asian martial arts. Unlike the ballet, where the dancer melts in and out of every movement, Decroux's mime was full of impulse and punctuation—muscular explosions that set the body in motion or brought it to an abrupt stop. While demonstrating movements, he looked like a French Toshiro Mifune. We tried to figure out how he could have devised this renegade movement system.

In the 1960s, there was no dance in Europe or America that used weight and gravity as a major organizing principle. No one talked about what is known today as "grounded" movement. Decroux never studied dance of any kind. He knew nothing about the martial arts and had only seen Asian theatre once in the 1920s. While the modern dance of the 1960s had rejected the elevation of the ballet and was more on the ground, Decroux had gone further. He demanded that the body be firmly on the ground. The legs provided a fixed base, continually pushing and pulling on the ground to give control and artistry to the movement. Like a spider spinning a cobweb, Decroux had spun his creation out of himself.

*   *   *   *

One day at the Louvre I stood in front of *La Grande Odalisque* by the French painter Ingres. I had seen this work many times in art history books. But now the real painting before me encapsulated my experience of being in Paris. It was like standing on a mountain peak and seeing the world laid out before me. I knew that living in Paris was the right thing.

*   *   *   *

One night I had a dream. I was nine years old and was in the middle of a school gymnasium full of kids. Small booths decorated with colorful crepe paper lined the walls. Each booth had a game for us kids to play, a simple game like throwing rings on bottles. But the stakes were high. If we didn't do well at the first booth, we couldn't move on to the next booth. We had to get it right. And each game was more difficult than the last. The gym was crowded with chatty kids standing in line. Teachers directed us from one booth to the next. I stood in line and was worried. I'd never learned the easier games at the first booths. How was I going to get the tougher ones? I wanted to go back and do the easy ones over again, but the teachers wouldn't let me. Suddenly I was in the middle of the gym with people milling around. A teacher grabbed me by the collar and growled at me, "Hey, Pitt, how come you're outta line? You trying to pull something?

Where's your pass?" I dangled on my toes as he yanked me high in the air by the collar. I pleaded with him. "Mrs. Dexter said I could go to the bathroom without a pass, sir!"

"You're lying, you little twerp. Aren't you?"

*   *   *   *

One day, I entered my building and bumped into Madame Ragout in the elevator. We chatted on the way up. I could see something in her now that I hadn't seen before—a brittleness that gave her an age far beyond her years. Maybe that counted for the distance between us and the fact that I never got beyond thinking of her as the landlady. She invited me in for a cup of coffee. I'd always wondered what her apartment was like. There was everything you'd expect—a sofa, comfy chair, record player— but something was off. The place was not terribly clean, nor was there any great disarray; there was just a strange feeling of disconnection, as if none of these things belonged to anyone. "Please seet down," she said, "I'll make a *café*."

The French are very good at the formalities of social interaction. You always know where you stand with them. The difference between addressing someone with *vous* or the more familiar *tu* immediately defines a relationship (this subtlety can easily be lost on anyone who hasn't spent enough time in France to know the difference). *Vous* maintains a distance; *tu* implies a degree of intimacy. Many relationships begin with *vous* and stay there. Neighbors can live next door to each for years and never get beyond *vous*. Others begin with *vous* and over time move on to *tu*. The shift is significant and is always noticed by both parties. Like many Americans, I had once committed the error of addressing a store clerk with *tu* and then tried to figure out what all the embarrassing looks were about. Madame Ragout and I were on a *vous* basis. There was no reason for it to be any different. She was the landlady.

She brought in a silver platter with demitasse cups and saucers and set it on a small table. She poured two cups. "Merci, Madame," I said. She smiled. "Please, do not call me *Madame*. Call me *Berthe*. It is my, how you say, my neekname for *Albertine*." She opened the lid to the Hi-Fi and put on a record of Georges Brassens.

"*Tiens, tu veux du sucre*," she said, holding out the sugar bowl. *Tu!* I lurched inside. She sat down on the sofa, one of those long low sofas you'd expect in a Freudian shrink's office with worn-out velvet and tattered fringe running along the bottom. She leaned back, put her feet up, and lit a Gauloises cigarette. Her shoes slipped off and fell to the floor. The venetian blinds cast a filtered light on her as she reclined in the shadows. She looked like a figure out of a 1940s film noir.

"So you like leeving in Parees?" she said.

"Oh, yes," I said. "America is too materialistic. Everything is so commercialized there. But you French, you know how to live."

She smiled a faint smile. "Perhaps. But, I am tired of Parees. I would like very much to go to your country, *l'Amerique*. I would love to see New York, Sheecago, Holy-wood. And also, you Americans are so *symphatique*. Not so formal like zee French."

"You think so, really?"

"*Mais oui*. You Americans are so free. Much more than zee French."

"Free? How?" I asked. She crushed her cigarette in the ashtray and lit up another.

"Some years ago I was watching zee *télé* [television] and I remember seeing Eezen-over walking—"

"I'm sorry," I interrupted. "You remember seeing what?"

"Eezen-over," she repeated, "Your president, Eezen-over!"

"Oh, you mean Eisenhower?"

She nodded. "I saw him on the *télé* walking with a man, and this man, he slapped your president on zee back. Oh, that was so shocking! In France you would never see anyone do that with De Gaulle. You Americans are like *des grands enfants*, big children. Very *symphatique*. And sexually too. You are not so, how do you say, not so . . . held back."

Suddenly, the room shifted.

"Is that so," I said. I felt awkward. "I always thought it was the opposite, that the French were a lot freer than us. You'd never see Americans kissing on the street like you do here."

She threw off my comment with a shrug of the shoulders. "Oh, it means nothing," she said. "You follow your desires more than us. It is a good thing. Don't you think?"

"Yeah, sure," I said.

Wait a minute . . . is she coming on to me?

"It is better to not be so . . ." she searched for a word, ". . . *paralyzé*. That way we enjoy things more."

She is coming on to me. Holy shit! I never thought about her sexually before, but now . . . what the hell. I looked at her sitting over there, her knees drawn up to her chin. She held the coffee cup to her lips with her eyes peering over the top. *Not bad . . . not bad at all.* A flood of racy possibilities ran through my mind. She leaned back on the sofa and took a drag on her cigarette as she stretched out. I glanced at her breasts for a second, then back to her face. My heart pounded. I glanced at her legs, back to her face. I glanced at her breasts again, back to her face. What if she saw me looking at her like this? I'd be dead. My eyes became uncontrollable. They bounced all over her body: shoulder, face, legs to face, breast to face. She kept talking. My mouth was on automatic pilot saying I don't know what while my brain was somewhere else. I sat there calmly sipping my coffee with a full erection. She was across the room, so far away. *How the hell do I get over there?*

I snapped out of my sexual trance. "Who are those pictures of?" I asked, pointing to the photos on the wall behind her. I walked over and looked at a picture of a man standing in front of an old car, his foot on the running board. She threw a look over her shoulder. "Oh, that is my father, a vacation in the Midi."

"Really? Looks like the 1940s," I said, looking closely at the photo. I glanced over at her.

"No, I think it is the '50s," she said, smoke puffing out of her mouth with each word.

I wanted to make a move, but there was that damned cigarette. *Better wait until she's done. But what if I'm wrong? What if I'm imagining all this? No. Impossible.* My heart was pounding.

I leaned down and kissed her. Her cigarette fell to the carpet. We both fumbled to pick it up. She grabbed it and crushed it in the ashtray. "*Ca va, ca va!*" she said hurriedly. She took my arm and pulled me down. I fell awkwardly onto the sofa and wrapped my arms around her. Her mouth was all over my face. I reached under her blouse and ran my hand over her stomach. Her skin was incredibly soft. She unbuttoned my shirt. *Christ!* She pressed her crotch into my thigh. *Christ!*

She tugged on my arms. "*Viens, viens en moi!*" We were screwing. I couldn't believe it. This was like screwing mother superior. It was great but it was awful. Our bodies jerked and bolted. She took in large gulps of air. Her skirt was bunched up around her waist. I tried to kick off my shoes but couldn't get the damn things off. My eyes were closed. I was too embarrassed to open them. *She might see me.* I peered through my lids hardly believing what was happening. She looked like she was a million miles away.

We lay still for a moment without speaking. Suddenly she rose up and scurried off to the bathroom. I heard the bidet turn on. I sat up on the edge of the sofa, my pants down around my ankles, and looked around the room feeling like I had been dumped out of a hurricane. The bathroom door opened. I jumped up and pulled up my pants. There was an awkward silence as she came back into the room. She lit a cigarette.

"Here, let me get this," I said, picking up the tray of cups.

"No, no, it's OK," she said. "You have things to do, I am sure." She barely looked at me.

"Yeah, right . . . I do," I said, walking to the door. "Thanks for the coffee." I closed the door and walked down the hall to my room.

Our misguided interlude did nothing to eliminate the distance between us. Seeing her again would be unbearably awkward. What would I say? "Bonjour, Berthe, how are things?" *Is that what I do? And what does she expect? Should I invite myself over to her place for another cup of coffee?* I had no real interest in her even if my penis did think she was the greatest thing in the world. Because of the proximity of my room to her apartment and the layout of the floor, I could hear her coming and going, her door opening and closing; I could hear her phone ringing and her answering. Given that situation, I did my best to avoid her.

*   *   *   *

I woke up on a chilly Saturday morning with the covers pulled up to my chin. I hated the cold. After months of no heat, Berthe bought me a butane gas heater, but it was too dangerous to run during the night. So I slept in the cold. I had a technique for dressing in weather like this: Before going to sleep I'd arrange my clothes on the chair next to my bed in the order I was going to put them on in the morning. I made sure the rug was in place so I wouldn't have to stand on cold tile. I set the box of matches next to the heater. In the morning, I'd jump out of bed, light the heater, turn the flame to high, hold my clothes over the fire to take the chill out, and dress as fast as I could.

Go! I jumped out of bed, lit the fire, grabbed my T-shirt, held it over the fire, and . . . oh no, the flame petered out. The tank was empty! Resigned, I dressed quickly and then heaved the empty butane tank onto my shoulder and took the elevator downstairs to buy a new tank of gas. The coal-gas vendor on the Rue Thérese was a gnarly unkempt little man who barely spoke above a mumble and never looked anyone in the eye. His dark matted hair fit in well with his dirty surroundings stacked high with burlap bags of coal and tanks of butane. I gave him my ten or twelve francs, heaved the full tank onto my shoulder, muttered, "Tanks a lot," and trudged home.

*   *   *   *

I made photocopies of pictures from different periods of dance and plastered them on the walls of my room. I lay on my bed looking at pictures of Louis XIV and the dancers from his court, as well as photos from the Noh theatre. The costumed Noh actors standing with knees bent were most compelling.

A classmate at Decroux's, Yves Lebreton, was also interested in these same questions. One day at the café he pulled out a book by the fifteenth century dramatist and theoretician of the Noh theatre, Zeami. The next day I bought my own copy—perfect reading on the Métro to Decroux's.

Zeami was a Japanese Decroux from centuries past. Stillness, he wrote, is the flower of Noh. Some Noh actors were famous for their stillness, called *mie*, and audiences came to the theatre anticipating these moments. The actors' movement, in fact, was only a prelude to their stillness. The stylized nature of the body in the Noh theatre was in direct opposition to the ballet. Each illuminated the other. The ballet goes up; the Noh goes down. The knees are bent in Noh, and the body is held low. The actor stomps on the stage. In traditional Noh theatre, clay pots are placed under the stage to amplify the sound of the feet hitting the ground. In ballet the dancer seeks to reduce contact with the ground and walks on the ball of the foot.

Sitting in the front row of a ballet concert, the sound of the dancers' footsteps across the stage is almost offensive, an intrusion into a world where friction and contact are only tolerated. Everything in the Noh strengthens the actor's connection to the physical world. The Noh actor is embedded in nature. Everything in ballet diffuses that connection and seeks to take the body out of nature.

What was going on in the seventeenth century that produced something as bizarre as the ballet? If the dance came out of the court, then wouldn't there be a connection between the dance and the court body, how the courtiers held themselves, how they moved? I wondered about the court body. I went to the Louvre and walked through the galleries, this time looking at paintings depicting court nobility to see what people looked like. I read about life in the court.

Court life was a world of vanity, competition, and one-upmanship. Every action, every move was calculated for its political gain. Effect was everything. Women pointed their toes to show off their ribbons, buckles, and fine leather shoes. Men practiced the turnout to show off a well-turned calf. Bodily affectation was developed into a high art form. In this milieu of intrigue and contrived elegance, an intense political agenda sapped the human body of its intrinsic nature. There was no conception, in fact, that the body even had an intrinsic nature. The court body was little more than a cultural artifact, a canvas on which the mind could paint beautiful pictures in the field of art and politics. Dancing, like everything else, became a political statement. Who danced with who, a person's proximity to the king or to his favorites while dancing—everything spoke of social position, hierarchy, and power. This was the breeding ground for early ballet.

*   *   *   *

One day, Decroux told us that the first original thought he had as a young man was when he realized that if he wanted to become intelligent, he must not be afraid to appear unintelligent. I took his advice to heart and plunged headlong into the French language. I never hesitated to ask questions. A

French-English dictionary became part of my anatomy. Someone once said that you only know a language when you begin thinking in that language. One chilly night I was walking home from the movies. I had been in Paris for only three months and said to myself, "*Il fait froid.*" Eureka! *I can speak French!* I stopped in a café and with utter confidence ordered a hot chocolate and a chocolate pastry. The waiter returned with two hot chocolates. I went slinking home.

*   *   *   *

I woke up one morning and lay in bed looking at the books stacked up around me. I loved the sight. What an irony. For years books had been my nemeses. Now I was surrounded by them. That's when I realized that I liked having books for the sake of having books. I was becoming a bibliophile. That was dangerous. I couldn't afford it.

One weekend I travelled to London with a couple of friends. I went off on my own for a while and came upon a small bookshop near Pall Mall. Peering inside I saw a prim young woman seated at a desk, typing. The walls of the shop were lined with wooden cabinets full of leather-bound books. A rush of excitement came over me. I wanted to go inside but was afraid. This was alien territory. Besides, I was only wearing a beat-up jacket and jeans.

The bell on the door jingled as I walked in. The young woman left her typing and asked if I needed any assistance. "Well, I'm interested in the history of dance," I said. She showed me to a case in the rear of the shop and apologized for having only a couple of items. The books were from the 1930s and were on the "new spirit" of the dance. Not my period. "Please feel free to browse," she said, smiling. I was taken aback. I hadn't expected that. I walked along the aisle looking through the glass doors of the cases. *I wonder if she'd mind if I opened the case on my own. I'd better not. She might think I'm trying to steal something.* I glanced at her. She looked up and nodded as if to say, *Please, go ahead.*

In the old insane asylums, mental patients were kept chained to the walls inside their cells. When reforms freed them from their manacles, I read, they walked to their cell doors and just stood there, free to walk out but too awestruck to do so.

I opened the door of the glass case and stood looking at all the leather-bound volumes. I never knew books could be so beautiful. I scanned the shelves and took a book out—*The Irish Rebellion of 1641*, published in 1646. My mind stopped dead on the spot with incomprehension. The oldest thing I had ever seen was the pendulum clock on the wall of my grandfather's fish market in Detroit. This book was over three hundred years old. The title page was in beautiful hand-pressed type. The uneven letters evoked the presence of a human hand, not a machine. I sat down with the book at a large mahogany table. The worn binding and the soiled pages spoke to me in a language that was beyond words. Holding this book in my hands was like grabbing a fistful of soil from seventeenth century Ireland. That was the moment I went from being a bibliophile to a bibliomaniac.

*   *   *   *

Some of life's best moments happen quietly and are almost too ordinary to mention: A ripe fruit that sings of summer. Sunlight pouring through a window onto a breakfast table set with fresh bread and steaming hot coffee. The perfect look from someone who cares. These are delicious moments. And so is a walk through an outdoor market. A great outdoor market is as much fun to adults as eating pizza is to kids. Kids love pizza not only for the taste but because they can eat it with their hands. Both the outdoor market and eating pizza blur the edges between order and chaos and have a healthy dose of messiness. Shopping in a supermarket is like eating with a knife and fork. Neat, clean, efficient, orderly. The rational mind has triumphed. Life needs places where the edges blur. When edges blur, things connect. There is more room for feeling. The body is invoked. Sensuality grows. Life becomes delicious.

*   *   *   *

The Métro screeched into the station. I raced upstairs. Decroux didn't like tardiness, and I was late. I ran across the courtyard and burst into the kitchen. Madame Decroux was sitting at the kitchen table slicing vegetables. "*Mon Dieu*, who put the fire to your pants?" I threw off my shoes and slid them under the potbelly stove. I ran upstairs to the dressing room, changed, and zap, down to the studio. Everyone stood in silence working on counterweight movements as Decroux walked among them. "Ah, here is Lor' Pitt," he said, with a wry smile. Favorite pupils were given nicknames, and mine, because of my apparent British demeanor, was *Lord Pitt*. "Bonjour, Lor'. I'm so glad that you've taken the time out of your busy schedule to join us today." I took a place in the corner and worked alone.

In the mirror I caught a glimpse of a new girl at the end of the studio. Long dark hair, almond-shaped eyes, high cheekbones, alabaster skin . . . hmm, very attractive. I kept glancing at her during class. We chatted on the Métro afterward. Her name was Penelope, and she was from England, was sixteen years old, and lived as an au pair near the Luxembourg Gardens.

We saw each other every day in class. We went to the movies and to restaurants together. We learned how to smoke cigarettes together. We spent whole afternoons talking about nothing. I'd like to say that Penelope and I became lovers, but it wasn't that easy. We talked about "doing it," but at sixteen, she wasn't ready. I didn't want to rush things either.

We were lying in bed in my tiny room. Penelope had her back to me. "C'mon, let's do it," I said. "It's not going to kill you. You'll like it, really. It's not that bad." We had been through this a dozen times. Penelope had all her reasons why she didn't want to, and I had my arsenal of reasons why we should.

"What's the big deal?" I said. "People do it all the time. It's like brushing your teeth." She groaned. "You have to be more casual about these things," I said. I put my arms around her and tried to turn her towards me, but she refused. We fell asleep.

CHAPTER 5

PURSUING THE DANCE

THE NEXT MORNING PENELOPE AND I got up early and walked over to the Left Bank for breakfast in the Latin Quarter. We sat at a table outside with our *cafés crème* and buttered baguettes. Shafts of sunlight cut through the clouds and set the streets, just washed down by the street cleaners, glistening. In those days the Paris street cleaners were tall, long-limbed Africans. They made their own brooms out of tree twigs that they tied to the ends of long wooden broom handles. It was early, the city was quiet. Good for reading. Penelope was in the middle of Flaubert's *Madame Bovary*. I pulled a book out of my bag and plunged into the dance.

I wanted to find the first signs when ballet began its ascent into the air. In the 1720s, the young ballerina Maria Camargo invented the entrechat quatre, where the dancer springs into the air and crosses her feet rapidly four times. Camargo was of a younger generation and rebelled against the older "noble" style known as "horizontal dancing." Instead of the traditional heeled shoes, she wore light slippers and shortened her dress to just above the ankles so audiences could appreciate her innovation. The crowds loved her jumps but cried "*Scandale!*" at the shorter dress. The academicians protested, "Once there were dances, now only jumps."

In the 1770s, ballerina Anna Heinel was described as entering the stage "on stilt-like tiptoe." Toe slippers had not been invented yet, and the only support dancers had was a little wadding stuffed in their toes. What motivated these dancers to endure such pain to go on point? This seemed as uncanny as salmon swimming upstream.

Wait a minute, what's this? In 1796, French choreographer Charles Didelot staged the ballet *Zephyr and Flora* in Paris and rigged his dancers to a system of wires and pulleys so they could fly though the air. This man was ahead of his time. Technique or not, he would get his dancers into the air. I turned to Penelope. "Hot-air balloons! Penelope, weren't they invented by the French?" The waiter was bringing us our second round of coffee and *tartines*. "What? Oh . . . I'm not sure," she said, without looking up from her book.

"Stay here, I'll be right back." The stores were just opening, and I went off to a bookshop around the corner. I was right. The Montgolfier brothers began experimenting with air hot-air balloons in Paris in 1783. The first human ascent was made by Messrs. de Rozier and d'Arlandes from the Tuileries Garden, and it drew a crowd of more than eight hundred thousand spectators! Ballooning and toe dancing at the same time in the same place. Was this a coincidence?

I walked back to the café. "Don't you get it?" I said. "Here's the ballet dying to get off the ground, and right around the corner these men are sending up hot air balloons. What's going on? Everyone was thinking, *Up!*" Penelope looked at me with an air of exasperation. "Why do you always have to figure things out? Why not enjoy things more instead of always picking them apart?" She reached into her bag and pulled out a book—the poetry of Gerard Manley Hopkins. "Why don't you read something like this; you'd have a much better time of it." I opened my notebook and began writing.

*   *   *   *

By 1820, the notion of elevation had fully entered the dance. That year, teacher and theoretician Carlo Blasis codified the ballet technique and established a rigorous method of instruction for every part of the body in his book *An Elementary Treatise Upon the Theory and Practice of the Art of Dancing*. Of the "bodily machine," he wrote: "Be as light as possible, bearing in mind that the public looks for an aerial quality in a dancer and feels dissatisfied when this is lacking. Study ballon [lightness]; I would like to see you bound with a suppleness and agility which gives you the impression you are barely touching the ground and may at any moment take flight." His training brought a new lightness and aerial quality to the dance by developing greater strength in the body—in the ankle, knee, and back. He also took the turnout to a full opening of one hundred and eight degrees.

With Blasis the body began to take flight with a new and more rigorous method. A few years later, ballerinas were dancing on point, but it was only a tour de force with no real interest. That would change.

In 1831, the Paris Opera staged Meyerbeer's *Robert le diable*. The production was uneventful enough until the third act. Set in the ruins of a medieval cloister, a group of dead nuns rise from their tombs and dance a wild bacchanal in the moonlight. As one writer reported, "the audience woke up with a start."

Here was history in the making.

A tenor in the opera, Adolphe Nourrit, stood in the wings and noticed the audience's excitement. He paid a visit to the famous choreographer Filippo Taglioni with an idea. Taglioni's daughter, Marie, was already a renowned dancer with an adoring public. She had been trained by her father, who worked her mercilessly for greater elevation. "If I ever *hear* you dancing," he exhorted. "I'll disown you!" By 1831, she had taken the technique of toe dancing to perfection.

An American saw her in Paris that year and wrote:

> *I went last night to the French opera to see the first dancer of the world. "Have you seen Taglioni?" is the first question addressed to a stranger in Paris, and you hear her name constantly over all the hum of the cafés. No language can describe her motion. She swims in your eye like a curl of smoke, or a flake of down. Her difficulty seems to be to keep to the floor.*

But something was missing. For this virtuoso technique to come alive with meaning, it needed the right dramatic context. And Nourrit had the key.

He told Filippo an idea for a new choreography, and the following year on March 12, 1832, *La Sylphide* debuted at the Paris Opera with Marie dancing the role of the sylph. Opening night was momentous. That night, the earth shifted. The Golden Age of the Romantic Ballet was born.

In the scenario, James, a Scottish woodsman, is engaged to marry his sweetheart Effie. On the day of the wedding, he takes a nap. A sylph-like creature appears in a dream and kisses him on the lips. James awakens to find the sylph hovering before him. Entranced by her beauty, he pursues the creature as she flies off to her forest abode. An evil witch waiting in the bushes calls out to James, "Here, use this to catch her." She throws him a scarf, but the scarf has been cursed. James throws the scarf around the sylph's waist. As he takes her into his arms, her wings fall off, and she dies. Just then James hears church bells ringing in the distance. Effie has married his best friend.

Here was a scenario with the psychological lynchpin to give toe dancing its life—a deep yearning for the unattainable. The disembodied sylph, forever out of reach, was a perfect match for the ethereal quality of toe dancing. Here was the perfect merging of dance technique and dramatic narrative that carried the illusion of flight to its logical conclusion. A centuries-long dream had been realized.

Years later, in 1890, Charles Dickens made a journal entry of his memory of seeing Taglioni dance:

> *The best dancer I ever saw was Marie Taglioni . . . her danc-ing was the "poetry of motion," for anything more graceful and ethereal than her slight figure, as it seemed to float across the stage, could not possibly be imagined.*

As I watched this slow ascent of the body in dance, I was puzzled. I always thought that dance was linked to nature. But now the opposite seemed true. The Romantic Ballet now looked like the apogee of disembodiment, the body divorced from nature. Wasn't this a contradiction? Wouldn't dance be about embodiment, not the opposite? The ballet's connection to nature was all about inverting the natural order, in dominating nature. Ballet was a reversal of the natural order. In 1760, pedagogue and theoretician Jean-Georges Noverre wrote:

> *To dance elegantly, to walk gracefully and to carry oneself no-bly, it is imperative to reverse the order of things and to force the limbs, by means of an exercise both long and painful, to take a totally different position from that which is natural to them.*

*   *   *   *

Scanning the history of dance was like witnessing an aviation of the human body. From the courtiers wearing cumbersome costumes and clunking around in high-heeled shoes in the seventeenth century to the Romantic Ballet of the 1830s, the body had been in full ascent. The progression was clear. Slowly the dance gathered its forces and developed its technique until it finally gained enough momentum to lift off and fly. The whole process took about a hundred and fifty years. But why up? Why this obsession with flight? How did this evolution take place? There was no firebrand manifesto declaring a philosophy about going up. Yet, with no overt acknowledgment, people labored for years all going in the same direction. How did this happen? I looked for clues.

*   *   *   *

As the Métro hurtled along, I reread my notes. Sometimes it pays to review the obvious: the classical ballet evolved out of the European courts, and the courtiers had a deep aversion for the physical world. It reminded me of my experience with English cooking. In the 1960s, the English could not accept a fresh vegetable on its own terms. They had to do something to it: fry it, boil it, steam it, bake it. In a similar fashion, the courtiers could not accept the body on its own terms. It had to be mediated through the filter of the mind.

The Church, in its abdication of the flesh, had a strict hierarchy of values. Everything good is up. God and his retinue of angels reside in the heavens. Everything evil is down. There is no spirituality or inherent value in the body or in nature. Only the Devil lurks there. This explains why monarchs are addressed as your highness, not your lowness. The Church was still driving this message home in 1981, when Pope John Paul II declared that "the shame people feel about their sexual organs helps them maintain holiness and honor."

The dance had plenty of encouragement to go up. But I wanted a smoking gun, something that would illustrate this cultural bias for getting off the ground. And I found it. Lincoln Kirstein's book *A Short History of Classical Theatrical Dancing* had been lying on my shelf for some time, and that's where I found a key to the puzzle.

But first some background. The raised proscenium stage, so common today, was developed in Italy during the Renaissance. The early court ballets took place in large ballrooms, with the audience seated on bleachers looking down on the dancers in what resembled a glorified basketball court. The scenic effects featured in these lavish productions were created by an intricate system of ropes, hoists, and pulleys arranged overhead. The Italians wanted to conceal this machinery in order to increase the magic of the effects and so invented the raised stage. Now all the machinery was hidden behind the proscenium arch framing the stage.

This change cannot be underestimated. In the ballroom arrangement, the dominant feature of the dance was the horizontal movement of the dancers weaving intricate patterns across the floor in something resembling an early version of Busby Berkeley. With the invention of the proscenium stage, the audience sat opposite the dancers. This was crucial. Viewing the dance head-on instead of looking down on it retrained the choreographer's eye to see the body in relation to a vertical instead of a horizontal axis. Verticality in the dance was born.

Given this new visual orientation, the choreographers could have accentuated the downwardness of the body movement, but they went up. This was a foregone conclusion. A value system already present in the culture of attributing goodness and spirituality to up—and evil to all things natural and down—would find its way into the human body.

That's why no one had to make a grand declaration about going up during the dance's early evolution. Cultural bias took care of everything.

And here we arrive at Lincoln Kirstein. He recognized the innovation of the proscenium stage and wrote, "there opened up the possibility of *verticality* . . . and also of elevation. A dancer could now also inhabit the *vertical* province of the air . . ." (The italics are mine.) In a later passage he speaks of toe dancing as the "final realization of the body's inherent *verticality.*" This is odd. Verticality is only a plane at right angles to the ground and includes up and down. Kirstein equates the term with up only, "the *vertical* province of the air," as if down did not exist. Is this a misuse of a word, or does the association reveal a cultural bias?

Years later, I read *Theatre and Playhouse*, by Helen and Richard Leac-roft. They too noted the evolution of the raised stage and its effect on the-atrical performance. "Raised stages," they wrote, "not only made the ac-tors visible above the heads of a standing audience but also provided the mechanics of a *vertical* movement." (Italics mine.) Once again, *vertical* is equated with up only. They could have said *upward movement* or *eleva-tion*. That would have been more accurate.

I sat in my room examining photos of the Japanese Noh actor and the ballet dancer. Both perform within the same vertical axis, yet they made different choices. The ballet dancer goes up; the Japanese actor goes down.

Japanese theatre did not evolve out of the court but out of the martial arts, and the underlying principle of all martial arts is the body's connec-tion to the ground. The downward orientation in their movement was in keeping with the traditional body language of their culture, just as ballet was in keeping with the body language of the court and the values per-petuated through religious belief. The Japanese traditionally eat, sleep, and sit on the floor. The Japanese and the French were faced with the same choices of body orientation on stage and went in opposite directions.

I looked at photos of the Noh actor and the ballet dancer and won-dered, wouldn't each have a different experience of being on the ground? The realization that people can differ in how they experience being on the ground was a thunderous thought. Just because we're all standing on the ground doesn't mean we all experience being on the ground in the same way.

I ran downstairs to that great laboratory across the street, the café. From the perfect vantage point of my sidewalk table, I watched the crowds stream by. I saw differences in how people walked now that I had not seen before. Some people moved as if they had no idea that the ground was be-neath them. Others had more freedom as they walked. I could see energy passing through their bodies.

I left the café and walked to the Tuileries Garden and sat on a chair near the large fountain. Little children played with sailboats in the water. The older folks sat chatting nearby. An infant on the ground crawled over to a chair and worked her way onto the seat. I watched her negotiate the complicated moves as she made her way up. Each part of her body knew exactly what to do, hands reaching, taking hold, feet and knees pushing and supporting, the spine bending to accommodate the limbs, the head taking its cue from the spine, moving left and right. What beautiful intelligence.

I looked at all the people around me. I looked at these bodies, a head jutting forward here, a slouched, sunken spine over there. A short, chunky body with no neck walking next to a longer wispy body with legs like an exotic bird. I looked at the ankles and feet to see what was going on down there and what they mirrored of the upper body. I kept going back to the feet. Feet turned in, feet turned out, some people walking on the inside of the foot, others on the outside of the foot. Look at the sole of the shoe and notice how it wears. What a story is told there. Someone once said that a martial arts master can look at the soles of your shoes, see how they are worn, and will know how to defeat you.

*   *   *   *

Everyone is on the ground differently. Years later, a student in my school in California brought this home clearly. During an exercise I had every-one walk around the studio and accentuate the downward action of their steps. While I stood on the side beating a drum, I noticed something odd in Rosie's walk. She stepped on the beat, but something was off, and I couldn't tell what it was.

The next day I repeated the exercise. Rosie walked around, on the beat, but that something was still off. Then I saw it. When the average person walks, the heel touches the ground first. Try it. Rosie, I saw, was walking ever-so slightly on the ball of her foot. When the exercise was over, I watched her walk around the studio and saw that she walked like everyone, heel touching the ground first.

The next day we repeated the exercise, and once again she walked ever-so slightly on her toes. Afterwards I asked her if she was aware of walking this way. She was not. I suggested that when we did the exercise again, she try stepping on her heels first. "No problem," she said. I began hitting the drum and watched her as she walked with the others. She was having a hard time of it.

I stopped the class and gave the drum to a student to give the beat. I took Rosie by the hand and walked around the studio with her to the drumbeat. I told her to imitate me. I exaggerated the action of my heel and angled it into the floor when I landed on each step. I exhorted her, "Angle your foot into the floor!"

She went into what looked like a mad dance as she tried desperately to get her heels on the floor, but couldn't. "Feel the heel!" Her heels and toes flicked and jerked as she struggled to get her heel onto the floor first. Then she got it! She walked around the studio with the downward accent of the heel on the floor first. Now she and the drum were together.

Her appearance changed immediately. I felt like I was seeing Rosie for the first time. Students often make leaps of progress with no awareness that anything has happened. So I asked her if she felt anything different. "I don't know if you'll understand this," she said, "but it felt opaque rather than transparent." I understood perfectly. She found the ground, was present, was *here* in three dimensions, occupying space. That's opaque. Walking on her toes diffused her presence and made her transparent.

The next day after class, Rosie took me aside and told me why she thought the walk had been so hard for her. As a young girl she was desperately unhappy at home and dreamt of escaping. One day she discovered that she could make her pain go away by imagining that she was walking on the ceiling. And from then on she imagined that she was walking on the ceiling.

What ingenuity. Here's how I see it: When Rosie was a little girl in pain, she struck a deal with her body. "Please, I've got to get out of here," she pleaded. "Can't I walk on the ceiling?" "That's impossible," her body said. "But if you want, I can move your center of gravity high up in your body. That way you'll *feel* like you're on the ceiling, but you'll look like you're on the ground. That's all I can do. What do you say? Deal?" She went for it.

Now that she was in my class and I had her accentuating the downward action of her body, I upset the bargain. She had spent years getting off the ground, and now I was doing everything to get her back onto the ground. This threw her into a panic. "Hey, body," she exclaimed. "This wasn't the deal! I'm not supposed to feel like I'm on the ground! Forget it. I'm getting outta here!" And up she went onto her toes.

We all have a different relationship to the ground. This varies from culture to culture as well. We saw how the French and the Japanese treat the body differently within the framework of their performances. The French go up; the Japanese go down. A greater example of this can be seen in the South Pacific.

In 1976, a group of Satawal islanders sailed their outrigger canoe twenty-five hundred miles from Hawaii to Tahiti with no instruments of navigation. They carried no maps, no compass, no radar or depth finder on board. Piailug, the captain, understood the winds, the currents, the swells of the ocean. He also knew the star coordinates and the distances between islands. All of this information essential to the voyage he held in a chant, which he memorized and sang to himself to keep the canoe on course.

Young boys on Satawal are taught how to navigate by lying on their backs in the ocean for hours until they grow sensitive to the subtlest swells. This refined kinesthetic awareness of the sea can at times prove more important to survival than eyes. Some of the most famous navigators in this part of the world have been blind. Seamen from the nearby Gilbert Islands report that when sailing at night, their keenest sensitivity to the ocean is in their testicles as they squat to feel tiny vibrations coming from the ocean.

Accompanying Piailug on his journey was an American colleague, a traditional navigator. In a film recording the voyage, we see the two men next to each other leaning on the outrigger, each presenting a different image of their cultural inheritance. Piailug is relaxed, his eyes are half closed, his jaw hangs loose, his motions are slow and deliberate. The American is alert, ferret-like, tense, and searching. His countenance suggests an intellect engaging nature, processing data. Piailug looks like a sponge soaking up information through his senses.

Here are two opposing ways of knowing, two different ways of being in the world. Piailug gains knowledge through the body, physical sensation, through a feel for things. This knowledge is in his body. The American on this voyage processes knowledge primarily through books and mechanical devices and retains information in his mind.

Piailug defies Western science. No explanation on his method of navigating the sea can be offered within the framework of Western thinking. This is an example of gaining precise knowledge through vague means.

CHAPTER 6

THE FABULOUS GARDEN OF THE PALAIS-ROYAL

WHEN THE SOLITUDE OF MY ROOM became too much, I'd often walk around the corner to the garden of the Palais-Royal to read. Most tourists miss this place. The happy traveler who stumbles upon it will find one of the most beautiful places in any city in the world. Among those who know this urban gem, few know the extraordinary history that played out here. Not one, but two world-shaking revolutions took place in this garden. This is impossible to gloss over. So follow me while I digress. You'll be the better for it. To get the full effect, the best place to read this is in the garden itself, on a bench, or at a café there.

*   *   *   *

The first revolution that took place in this garden happened in 1786. While nearly nobody knows about that revolution, everyone has enjoyed its fruit. The second revolution is better known—the French Revolution of 1789—for the spark that ignited that social conflagration took place here in this garden.

First of all, picture the garden. It is seven hundred feet long and three hundred feet wide and is enclosed on three sides with shops, cafés, and restaurants under handsome vaulted arcades with three stories of apartments above. The fourth side gives onto what was originally a palace, hence the name Palais-Royal. Today this wing of the garden houses offices for various city agencies. One of the most famous residents of the garden was the novelist Colette, who lived in an apartment on the north side.

The garden was created around 1630, as part of the palace built here by Cardinal Richelieu. Those living in houses on the garden had a fine view of a bucolic setting, a happy respite from the noisy, crowded city. Richelieu died in 1642 and left the palace to the king. When the king died the following year, the palace passed into the hands of the king's cousins, the Orléans family, and that's when things become interesting.

The young Duke de Chartres took ownership of the estate in 1781, but the duke had a character flaw. His extravagant lifestyle brought him to the edge of ruin. In a distraught state while facing bankruptcy, he listened to advice from a friend: enclose the garden, and build shops at ground level with apartments above. Real estate. Income!

For a member of royalty to engage in a real estate venture was unheard of. Before the duke could proceed, he needed permission from his cousin, King Louis XVI, the same king who would lose his head on the guillotine twelve years later in 1793. At the request, the king famously said, "But my good cousin, if you become a shopkeeper we'll only see you on Sundays!" Permission was granted.

The news that the garden was to be enclosed created an uproar in the neighborhood. People living on the garden were going to lose their priceless views and find themselves on a dark, narrow street with plummeting property values. They gathered petitions arguing for preservation of the garden and presented these to the king. Handbills of protest went up all around the neighborhood, but to no avail. The duke proceeded.

His original plan was to enclose the garden on all four sides. Three sides would have arcades filled with shops and restaurants with sumptuous apartments on the floors above. The fourth side adjoining the palace was to have an open colonnade with a floor above.

The three sides were completed, and that is what we see today. The fourth side got no further than the foundation. For, no surprise, the money ran out. When work came to a halt, the duke's architect suggested that a temporary structure be built to protect the foundation from the elements until more money came in. And here was the first revolution in the Palais-Royal.

In haste, a wooden arcade was constructed over the foundation and was known as the Galeries de Bois. This was the first arcade in Paris with three rows of stalls featuring a variety of merchants: book sellers, clothiers, jewelers, hat makers, etc. The success of the arcade was immediate and spawned the growth of arcades around Paris, and later all of Europe. Anyone who has enjoyed any of the arcades in other cities like London, New York, Brussels, or San Francisco owes a debt of gratitude to the duke and his debauched lifestyle. The great arcade in Milan, the Galleria Vittorio Emanuele II with its enormous dome, was inspired by the Galerie Colbert in Paris.

Arcades lined with attractive shops provided Parisians with a new shopping experience that changed the landscape of the city. Paris in those years was not the pleasant walking city we know today. Rather, it was a labyrinth of narrow streets strewn with garbage and encumbered by pushcarts, wagons, buggies, and carriages of all kinds. On rainy days these streets became impassable rivers of mud. In effect the arcades were the first malls. Shopping became a relaxed, unhurried, pleasurable experience free from inclement weather, passing carriage axles that could break a knee, or garbage thrown onto one's head from floors above.

The Galeries de Bois, along with the vaulted arcades surrounding the garden with all the cafés, restaurants, shops, and gambling houses, made the garden the most popular spot in Paris. Its success went beyond anything the duke could have imagined. And because the garden was owned by royalty, the Paris police had no jurisdiction there. This meant anything goes. And go it did.

At a time when Montmartre was still a village outside of Paris and the Champs-Élyssés was only a wood, the Palais-Royal was the center of Parisian social life. Day and night the populace flocked there to indulge every taste and fancy in an atmosphere as lively as a Middle Eastern bazaar. Imagine Rodeo Drive with its exclusive shops combined with the Mustang Ranch with its prostitutes, plus Las Vegas with its gambling casinos, and for flavor throw in a rich assortment of luxury shops, cafés, and restaurants to appeal to every pocketbook and political persuasion. This was the Palais-Royal. Food, drink, sex, gambling, political discussion, or shopping, nothing was wanting. The sheer variety of humanity crammed into this small property was unlike anything anywhere in the world. Aristocrats and con men shared the same promenades. Elegant women of the upper classes strolled under the same arcades as the prostitutes, who brazenly paraded around practically nude. Princes and pickpockets eyed the same crowd but for different reasons.

Englishman John Carr wrote in 1802 in *The Stranger in France*:

> *This place presents a scene of profligate voluptuousness not to be equalled upon any spot in Europe. Woman of character are almost afraid to appear here at noon day.*

Prostitution was a cottage industry in Paris and was accepted and regulated by the police. Pamphlets with names of popular prostitutes along with addresses, personality traits, and fees could be purchased at booksellers. One of the most popular cafés in the Palais-Royal was the Café des Aveugles—the Café of the Blind. The musicians who played there nightly were blind, which left room for the most unrestrained expression of sexual desire among customers.

At the height of the garden's popularity there were thirty-one gambling houses, each with a Hall of the Wounded (*Salle des Blessés*), where a just-ruined person could be seen lying on a divan trying to regain their composure or sanity. Pawnshops on the garden were frequented by those on the losing end of the roulette table, and it was not uncommon to hear a pistol shot as some poor formerly rich person blew their brains out.

The prostitution and gambling alone were enough to guarantee the garden its notorious reputation. Imagine travelers from button-downed England, America, or Germany visiting Paris and viewing this breathtaking spectacle. Read this account by an English traveler in 1819:

> *Visit the capitals of other European states, repair to London, to Amsterdam, to Berlin, to Vienna, and you will meet with novelty, with magnificence, but with nothing to compete with the Palais-Royal. Nothing that delights the eye, provokes the appetite, inflames the passions, and excites the sense of enjoyment is here wanting. The Palais-Royal exhibits a sink of dissipation, a vortex of profligacy, an abyss of vice, of ruin, and corruption. It most questionably merits to be seen.*

An American visiting Paris in 1835 wrote:

> *If you wish to know where is the centre of the earth, it is the Palais-Royal. Ask a stranger, when he arrives, "Where will you go first?" He will answer, "to the Palais-Royal." Or ask a Frenchman, on the top of the Caucasus, "Where shall I meet you again?" He will give you rendez-vous at the Palais-Royal.*

Those living in houses facing the garden who had protested construction now found themselves on the doorstep of the most popular spot, not just in Paris, but in all of France, and celebrated the duke for his vision.

Legendary Paris chronicler Jacques Mercier wrote, "One could spend a whole life in the Palais-Royal, and a long life at that, in a perpetual state of enchantment, and at the end say, 'I've seen everything, done everything.'"

By the summer of 1789, the garden was in full stride. Any visitor to Paris only had the feeling of having arrived in the capital after visiting the Palais-Royal. As social unrest grew in the early months of 1789, the crowds flocked there to hear the latest news and rumors or simply to vent their spleen. Interestingly, while much of the aristocracy fled France, the duke stayed behind and sided with the revolutionaries. Despite his wealth and lineage, he had strong Republican leanings and favored a more democratic government in France. He was a follower of Jean-Jacques Rousseau, believed in Enlightenment ideas, and supported a freedom of expression that was thought by some to be dangerous.

With the garden beyond the jurisdiction of Paris police, it was also free of government censorship, which meant radical ideas of every persuasion were freely expressed there. The Palais-Royal became a center for revolutionary ideology. The cafés and restaurants were ablaze with rhetoric as the social conflagration gained momentum.

Then on Sunday, July 12, 1789, a Rubicon was crossed. And this brings us to the second revolution to take place in this garden: the French Revolution. In 1789, in the Galerie Montpensier arcade at about number 58 stood the Café de Foy, the only café allowed to have chairs in the garden under the trees. A young lawyer, Camille Desmoulins, was engaged in a heated discussion at one of those tables, and in a moment of excitement, He said:

"They just fired Necker! [Necker was the finance minister in favor of taxing the rich.] We're next! Now they'll come after us. It'll be a massacre! We must defend ourselves. If not, we're finished. We need something, a color to identify ourselves with. What shall it be? Blue for the liberty and democracy of America, or green, the color of hope?"

Green for hope was chosen. The men pulled off leafy sprigs of tree branches and affixed them to their caps. This was the first call to arms that lead to the Revolution. The crowd, whipped into a frenzy, went marching off to arm themselves and to spread the word. Two days later the Bastille was taken, and history took a terrible turn.

Because we know where the Café de Foy was located, we know within a few feet where that historic table stood. For many years there was a marker commemorating the spot, but it was removed in 1926. In a city so full of plaques commemorating so many historic events, it is remarkable that there is nothing to mark this spot where modern France was literally born.

There are many ironies in this history.

All titles of nobility were abolished with the Revolution. The duke became Philippe Egalité (Philip Equality). The Palais-Royal became the Palais de l'Egalité (Palace of Equality).

The duke might have fled France along with the other nobility, but he chose to stay. To convince the public about what side he was on, he even signed the death warrant for his cousin the king. In the end this maneuvering did him little good. On November 6, 1793, ten months after the king lost his head, the Duke d'Orléans made the same trip to the guillotine. Many believed his repositioning was only posturing to gain favor so he could reestablish the monarchy with himself on the throne.

He might have escaped his end on the scaffold. It is said that a high member of the Revolutionary court wanted to marry his sixteen-year-old daughter and was willing to make a trade, the duke's life for her. On the way to the guillotine, the cart carrying the condemned duke reportedly stopped in front of the Palais de l'Egalité to give him one more chance to change his mind. But he was resolute. The cart continued on its way, and one more head fell at Place de la Concorde.

The young man who gave the spark to the Revolution, Camille Desmoulins, lost his head on the guillotine too in 1794. And a few days later his young wife Lucille made the same tragic journey. Irony of ironies: in 1830 the Duke d'Orléans' son, Louis-Philippe I, became King of France. He was a more sober man than his father and looked poorly upon the libertinage that the garden exemplified. He rid the garden of the prostitutes, and on December 31, 1836, he closed the gambling casinos. This was the death knell for the garden. The crowds, seeking new fields of pleasure, migrated up to the Grand Boulevards, leaving the Palais-Royal to fall into a state of somnolence that lasted for almost a hundred and fifty years.

In 1867, as the Palais-Royal lay dormant, Paris chronicler Auguste Villemot wrote:

> *Cleaned up of its vice, the Palais sleeps the sleep of the virtuous. One could write over the entrance, "Here once stood Paris. Today it is the provinces."*

By this time, the covered passageways in Paris began to lose their appeal as well. One reason was because of Baron Haussmann's rebuilding. With his new thoroughfares crisscrossing the city, Parisians could stroll along clean, broad sidewalks in the open air with plenty of sunlight, safe from traffic, and with the added enjoyment of a continuous spectacle of endless large shop windows. Window-shopping was born! By the mid-1860s the passageways of the Palais-Royal had become empty, dark, and quiet.

And then there was the invention of the department store in the 1820s and '30s. La Belle Jardiniere (1824), Aux Trois Quartiers (1829), and Bon Marché (1838) grew into the new palaces of consumerism exhibiting an abundance of goods never before seen under one roof. This alone would have been enough to draw the public away from the passageways. It didn't take long for the once-popular arcades to become old-fashioned, "umbrellas for the poor," as they were called. Many fell into a dilapidated state and were torn down.

By the early 1900s the Palais-Royal was a doleful place. Nobody went there anymore. It was still hauntingly silent when I lived in Paris in the 1960s. Few Parisians wandered in, and most of the shops under the arcades were empty. Except for the occasional nanny pushing a stroller or the bent figure of the old birdman shuffling along with a handful of breadcrumbs, this was a striking stage set where nothing happened. The only remnant of the garden's former glory was a restaurant tucked away in the north corner, Le Grand Véfour, opened in 1784 (and still there today). For years, the restaurant's curtained windows and lackluster facade matched the dour atmosphere of the garden and had the look of an octogenarian who had turned his back on the modern world.

Then in the 1980s, the garden began showing signs of life again. As if on cue the public began frequenting it more, lounging in chairs around the fountain to take in the sun, strolling under the arcades, or finding shade under the trees. Cafés and restaurants began opening up, bringing a liveliness to the garden that had not been seen in over a hundred and fifty years. Today the Palais-Royal is thoroughly reintegrated into the city, and we can see how a once-shunned place rediscovered a splendor no one would have imagined possible a few years before.

Chapter 7

THE ENGLISH LESSON

A DULL, GRAY DAY IN PARIS WAS made brighter when a friend told me about a French businessman looking for an English teacher. I could make as much as $6 an hour. I made the phone call that day. Monsieur Merdouille was director of the largest wine company in France, *vin ordinaire*, that is, and he needed to learn English because of plans to do business in America. He suggested that we begin that evening at his place, dinner with him and his wife. Great. Two birds with one stone—free dinner while earning money. "Bring one of your English books," he said over the phone. I was late getting out the door, so I grabbed a book off my shelf and ran down to the Métro.

I arrived at his apartment in the east of Paris and felt immediately uncomfortable. First of all Monsieur Merdouille was wearing a suit and tie. Did he expect me to show up in a suit too? But also because he was trying so hard to make me feel comfortable. "Please, would you like a drink? Here, sit down. May I show you around? Do you like the view? Can I get something else for you?"

Monsieur Merdouille lived in a thoroughly boring apartment in a thoroughly nondescript building in the epitome of what the French middle class thought of as *le moderne*. Like many French, Monsieur Merdouille sought distinction by putting as much distance between himself and what he thought of as French provincialism, or anything that smacked of old-fashioned.

Monsieur Merdouille was going through a stage that Americans had gone through about ten years earlier. In the United States the arrival of the Atomic Age brought not only a new technology, but also a new look that changed the aesthetic of the country. A strong feeling of having entered a more modern era pervaded the nation. Like the twelve-year-old who disdains the things of a ten-year-old, America rushed into the future looking upon the world it left behind as hopelessly old-fashioned and out of date. Ballpoint pens, Formica-top tables, and cars with fins changed the way we saw the world. It was a good time for garage sales. It takes at least twenty years before a combination of nostalgia and scarcity give the cast-off objects of the bygone era a new, more appreciated look. Wait a few more years and they become sought-after collectibles. Objects have a life. France was now turning that same corner. Monsieur Merdouille was definitely part of an avant-garde rushing headlong into a modernity made up of blandness and mediocrity.

He showed me around his apartment with obvious pleasure. There were plenty of clean lines everywhere. At least he got that right. Clean lines were definitely part of the new aesthetic. But a line is only a line. What counts is what emanates from that line. What was manifestly lacking here was Life. Japanese design has a long tradition of simplicity too. They know clean lines. But their clean lines convey spirit and aliveness. Their lines wake you up. No such luck here. Monsieur Merdouille's clean lines put you to sleep.

An evening that started out as merely uncomfortable became most awkward when Monsieur Merdouille opened the cupboard to discover that he was out of wine. "No problem," he said. All he had to do was go down to the wine cellar and get a few more bottles. "Dear!" he said to his wife. "Where's the key to the wine cellar?" "I don't know, dear, I thought you had it." And that was the end of that. The rest of the evening was spent in a frantic search for the now-vanished key to the wine cellar. If one can imagine controlled panic, this was it. All the while trying to convey that everything was fine, that dinner would be along in a minute, Mr. and Mrs. Merdouille went through every drawer in the kitchen, scoured the floor, looked behind the refrigerator, searched under the sink and through every pocket and everywhere else they could think of trying to find that damned key. This was a matter teetering on national disgrace. Indeed French honor was at stake. Here is the director of the largest wine company in France entertaining an American, and he has no wine to serve? They had no children, so that was out. They had no dog, so no animal ate the damned thing. How about the bathroom, maybe the bedroom? They moved from room to room, opening and closing drawers, shuffling things around, muttering under their breath, "*Enfin . . . ça alors . . . c'est pas possible!*"

I tried to reassure them that it was OK, that I didn't drink that much wine anyway, that alcohol made me sleepy and that I actually avoided it. This was true, and I was gladdened by the prospect of dinner without wine. The last thing I wanted was to be yawning during my first evening as an English teacher. This made no difference to Monsieur Merdouille. The hapless look on his face was memorable.

Finally the dreaded moment arrived. We sat down at the table with the elegant but empty wine glasses in front of us. Monsieur Merdouille sat stock-still staring at them. The ignominy of it all. We ended up drinking orange juice.

After dinner Monsieur Merdouille and I moved into the living room for the English lesson while Madame busied herself in the kitchen. I could still hear her rummaging through the drawers. He offered me an after-dinner drink of brandy—an attempt to salvage an evening of dishonor. In a matter of minutes I was feeling tired from the alcohol and struggled to swallow my yawns. I pulled the book I'd brought out of my bag and handed it to him. "Here, let's start with this," I said. "Pick any page and start reading." It was a copy of Henry Miller's *Tropic of Cancer*. I'd bought it a few days earlier and hadn't read it, but I knew it took place in Paris and thought it might be fun. Monsieur Merdouille began reading, and my mind wandered. I knew this was not the job for me. I wasn't even listening.

After a minute or so he stopped and asked me, "Varum coont, vat eez zees, varum coont?"

Varum coont? What's the hell's he saying? "Read the whole sentence and we'll see," I said. He held the book closely and read slowly, trying to give his best pronunciation.

"O Tania, var now eez zat varum coont uf yours . . ."

Warm cunt! Jesus Christ! I gingerly snatched the book out of his hands. "You know, that's not really what I had in mind tonight! Actually, let's look at this." I pulled a copy of *The New York Times* out of my bag. Lucky I had one with me. "Here, this is much better for a start." We spent an hour reading the newspaper, and I did my best to look interested. Then I was happily in the Métro on my way home with thirty francs in my pocket.

What I needed now was a good dose of the café, so I headed to Montparnasse to La Coupole. In the Métro a group of young boys came striding down the corridor arm in arm. They had been drinking and were singing the classic bawdy French student song, "*Les Filles de Camaret.*" The song is all about screwing. It goes on forever with the same melody repeating over and over again with dozens of imaginative verses added on by generations of students: "Oh the girls of Camaré, they say they're all virgins. But when they're in my bed, they prefer my dick to the candle, the caan-dle, the caan-dle, the ca-an-dle!" Each verse ends with riotous laughter, and then someone starts another equally bawdy verse, and so on.

It was a warm evening with Boulevard Montparnasse bustling. I sat down at an outdoor table at La Coupole with a great view. By now I had fully discovered the enjoyment of the Paris café and the simple pleasure of doing nothing but watching people. Here in a public place surrounded by people, you can be totally alone. But there is more. One goes to the café not just for a drink. The café is a way of life, an organizing principle in the lives of those who make it their home away from home. At a table near the window sat a large rotund man impeccably dressed in a tuxedo with a cherubic face and curly blonde hair. This gentleman, they said, was the longest-standing (or should I say longest-sitting) regular at La Coupole. He'd been coming every night since 1926. He sat alone at his table with his cup of espresso, his hands folded on his big belly, and every night he fell asleep. All the waiters knew him, exchanged social niceties, and would never think of rushing him.

As the crowds walked by I watched all the shoulders, knees, chests, spines, thighs, and hands do their little dance. But there was more than the bodies. There was the space around the bodies. I watched the people as they moved and looked at the space between them. I saw how it changed shape and moved like a giant invisible organism shifting before my eyes.

Certainly the café ranks as one of the greatest of institutions. And the most democratic too. For the price of a cup of coffee you can witness all of humanity passing by: happy humanity, toiling humanity, bored humanity, sleazy humanity, humanity in love, humanity down in the dumps, pretentious humanity, dumb fucking stupid humanity, lost humanity, humanity looking for a warm body, humanity of every ilk. It's all there.

How is it that a city full of monuments and plaques celebrating artists, writers, politicians, and fallen resistance fighters has no monument to the man credited with inventing the café? Someone had to invent this institution. And it wasn't easy. It took time to catch on. The inventor of the café was a Sicilian—Francesco Procopio. He opened the Café Procope in 1675 on Rue de Tournon near the Luxembourg Gardens on the Left Bank. In 1686, he moved the business a short distance away to the Rue de l'Ancienne-Comédie, and miraculously this café still stands in the same spot, the oldest café in Paris. At that time the popular theatre Comédie-Française was across the street, and no doubt many Parisians developed their taste for both the drink and the ambiance of the café during a night out at the theatre.

Procopio was not the first to sell coffee in Paris. Others tried before him, but the Parisians weren't ready for the imported drink. The first cup of coffee was reportedly sold in Paris in 1643 by a man from the Middle East. He eventually gave up and moved to London. A couple of Armenians then tried selling the brew, but they too failed. By the 1660s doctors were praising coffee for its medicinal qualities. By the early 1670s coffee was sold on the streets of Paris from walking vendors who dispensed the drink from large spigoted metal tanks strapped to their backs. Procopio came along at the right time and made the best of a primed public. Soon the café was an institution. In 1723, when Paris was still a relatively small city, there were already 380 cafés. By 1792 the number had reached 1,800 cafés. By 1813 the number had risen to 3,000.

*   *   *   *

Richard and I sat in the kitchen while he made breakfast. Saskia was away in Holland, and Richard was enjoying his freedom. I never understood why these two were together. Richard was like a little boy with a bother-some mother he couldn't live without. When he and Saskia were together, he was impatient for her to leave. A few days by himself, and he couldn't wait for her to return. Richard rattled off a long list of his latest female exploits—nothing racy, simply an accounting of ever-more-creative ways of picking up women.

"So I meet a women," he said, "and the first thing I do is check her out. But I have to be careful because I don't want her to catch me in the act.

That can be embarrassing. If you see her from a distance, fine. But if you're in close talking to her, you can't just look at her boobs. That's too gauche. So what I do is while I'm looking straight at her, out of the corner of my eye I'm looking at her boobs."

"You mean you glance at her boobs?" I said.

"No, that's the whole point. She might see you. The trick is to look her in the eye while she's talking, but out of the corner of your eye you're checking her out."

"Oh, so you're using your peripheral vision."

"Yeah, right, that's it. Here, I'll show you. Imagine we're at a party. You're a looker, and I want to check you out. See, I'm looking right in your eyes, but at the same time I can see down to about here." He passed his hand over my upper chest while looking at my eyes.

He went to the stove and poured another cup of coffee. "Of course, the closer you are, the harder it is to see, so it's best to be a few feet away to get the best view. Now, if it so happens that you're too close, there's a way around it. What you do then is bring your gaze down to her shoulder. But don't do it while you're talking. That looks weird, talking to her and looking at her shoulder. You can only do it while she's talking to you. She's talking, you look at her shoulder, and it looks like you're thoughtfully listening to what she's saying. It has that pensive look. But really you're just checking her out. See what I mean?"

Just then Takazu came into the kitchen. He and Yoshi had moved into the room down the hall a couple of weeks ago. They spoke little French or English, so we didn't talk much. They were in the habit of leaving the kitchen in a terrible mess. One of them dropped an egg on the floor a couple of days ago and it was still there. Takazu put a pot of rice on to cook and went back to his room.

Richard pulled out a handful of scraps of paper from his pocket, each with a different name and phone number scribbled on it. "Look at these," he said. What do you think?" Next each name were notes: *Arlette, small, brunette. Cute.* "Richard, you're sick," I said. He began searching through his pockets. "I met this great redhead at the café, big gazonkers. I wrote it on the back of one of my own cards. Where the hell is it?" he said, searching his pockets. He went into his room. I glanced at the pot of rice. The water was coming to a boil, and there was no sign of the guys.

"Found it!" Richard yelled out. He came back to the kitchen. "It was in my jacket." He sat down and sipped on his coffee. "Genevieve . . . she was really good. Maybe I'll call her tonight."

The rice was boiling now. I looked down the hall. No one in sight. The water was overflowing. Richard looked at the mess and then at me. "Hey, what's this? What's going on? Do they always cook like this?"

"Yoshi, Takazu!" I yelled out. They came running into the kitchen. I jabbed my finger at the pot. They muttered something incomprehensible and emptied the steaming rice into a bowl. They didn't even notice the mess. They threw some sliced vegetables into a frying pan and started for their room. "Wait a minute!" I yelled out. I pointed to the mess on the stove and the egg on the floor. "How about cleaning this up!" They muttered more incomprehensible French and moved towards the door. "Hold it! Hold it!" I shrieked. "You're not walking away from this. Clean up this mess!" I took the sponge and made wiping motions around the stove. "Like this!" I pointed to the egg on the floor. "And that too! Yoshi's face flashed with anger. "In Japan," he said, in halting English, "woman clean up!"

Just then Berthe came into the kitchen. She had been drinking and was a little tipsy. "What is it, what's going on?" Yoshi and Takazu walked back to their room. I shrugged and pointed to the mess. Berthe pulled out a cigarette and lit up. Richard grimaced at the cigarette smoke and waved his hand to clear the air. "I'm going to make a few phone calls at the café," he said. He stuffed the names into his pocket and left.

Berthe sat down and offered me a cigarette. I lit up, and we talked about I don't know what. We were alone now. My pulse rate increased. I lit up another cigarette. Berthe had a way of dressing that many men would find enticing. Not that she dressed in a particularly elegant or sexy way. It didn't matter what kind of clothes she was wearing. It was the way she wore them. Her blouse never seemed to hang quite right and was off to one side, exposing a little shoulder. Her skirt seemed too loose, a little off-center and not quite square on her hips. This disarrangement made it look as though her clothes could fall off her body at any moment. In other words, it gave her a certain je ne sais quoi.

We chatted as I tried to decide what to do. *Should I make a move seeking a few minutes of pleasure knowing that I'll feel terrible later? Or should I avoid the whole situation by getting out now? I could look at my watch and say, "Oops, gotta go now."* We smoked our cigarettes, drank coffee, and kept talking. *If I'm going to make a move, I'd better do it. But where? Here in the kitchen? In my room?* I surveyed all the possibilities. Thought usually precedes action. In my case, thought would precede, precede, precede, and never move to action. I'd become paralyzed by shyness, insecurity, and an all-around feeling of not knowing exactly what to do. Rhythm is everything in the game of seduction. I'd spend so much time thinking about what to do that the moment would come and go and I'd still be pondering my first move.

Just then I did something that surprised even me. I took Berthe by the hand and led her to my room. She didn't say a word. I could hardly believe what I was doing. I closed the door behind us and brought her to my bed. I kissed her and unbuttoned her blouse. We had a very steamy fifteen minutes. Lying naked in the semi-darkness with only a sheet over us, Berthe dozed off. I looked at her. I had never really seen her this close before. In her relaxation I could see an attractiveness behind a fatigue that I knew she would never sleep off. *How do I get out of this?* I would have given anything to be anywhere else in the world. She and I could have great sex for a hundred years, and it still wouldn't bring us any closer. I didn't want to wake her, yet I didn't want her to lie there all night either. Suddenly she stirred and opened her eyes. She glanced around the room and stood up, wrapping the sheet around her toga-style. She grabbed her shoes and clothes, muttered something, and stumbled out of the room without saying a word. "Oh no," I groaned.

The next day I went shopping on Rue Saint-Honoré and saw Berthe coming down the street. I ducked into a butcher shop to avoid her. The place was full of people, and I pretended to be looking in the meat case. I waited a few minutes and then moved for the door. It swung open, and there I was, face-to-face with Berthe. "Bonjour!" we both said, as gaily as two old friends who hadn't seen each other for ages. "How are you today?" "Fine!" "Good!" "Well, I'm off now, see you, bye!" That was enough clumsiness for one day. How was I going to get out of this?

My deliverance from this painfully awkward situation came a few days later in the form of a balding, middle-aged, bucktoothed, overweight, low-level bureaucrat who worked for the Paris bus company and who was pleased as punch with his new mistress. His name was Hubert, and he was what the French call "*un petit fonctionnaire*," a bureaucrat of the lowest order. Hubert was married and had a nine-year-old daughter.

I never learned how he and Berthe met, but in the ensuing weeks, a routine emerged in this new relationship that made everyone happy—above all, me. Hubert took to spending his weekends with Berthe, arriving every Friday after work and leaving Monday morning. Berthe seemed happy to have a man, and an older man at that, who looked after her. They ate out at restaurants, went to the movies and cafés, shopped in the market Saturday mornings, and generally led a life with all the appearance of normalcy for two days out of the week. Hubert, for his part, had fallen into a plum of a situation that no doubt made him the envy of his male friends.

Now whenever I ran into Berthe she seemed genuinely happy with her new life, and in time our passing hellos had no trace of the tension we had formerly known. I considered myself a free man.

*   *   *   *

Sunday morning Penelope and I woke up early, had breakfast, and decided to go to the Musée de l'Homme, the Museum of Man. We took the Métro to Trocadéro station and walked around the grand esplanade with the spectacular view of the Eiffel Tower across the Seine. Hitler walked on this very spot after the Nazis took over Paris in 1940. From this wonderful vista he looked upon the city he had just conquered, full of satisfaction at his latest possession.

Inside the museum we walked through room after room viewing Stone Age tools, dioramas of early man "at home," etc. But it was the small wooden sculptures of standing African figures that caught my attention. Their stance puzzled me. *Why do they stand with bent knees?* They weren't squatting, but they weren't totally erect. People don't stand this way naturally. *What does this posture mean? Is this how they walked? Is this part of their "primitive" aesthetic?*

Years later I figured it out. The bent knees were not an aesthetic choice, but rather were a representation of how the people of that culture felt in their bodies. It was an artistic rendering of their internal energetic state.

The bent knee promotes an energetic connection in the body and in turn a connection of the whole body to the ground. Observe a Tai Chi or martial arts master, and you will notice that in all of the basic poses and movements, the knees are bent. The shape we give to our body sets up patterns for how energy moves in our body. Standing with locked knees shuts down the energy and renders the body stiff. The center of gravity moves higher in the body and promotes a feeling of disconnection. The bent knee encourages connection in the body and connection of the body to the ground. Giving this structure creates a physical dynamism and vitality that is typically non-Western.

*   *   *   *

A good stationery store has all the tools one needs for an ordered desk, hence an ordered mind. Going to a good stationery store is like visiting with a Buddhist monk or a sagely vegetarian. It's like seeing the image of my most highly evolved self. A good art store has the same effect on me. It's a place of peace and calm where my mind can spread out. An art store in the Passage Choiseul was my source for Japanese rice paper. I loved all the elegant pencils, paintbrushes, sketch pads, and watercolor paper. It was all so beautiful.

*   *   *   *

A few days later, I bumped into Simson as he came running out of the Métro. It was four in the afternoon, and he was in a hurry to drop off a package. Simson was in his early thirties and had a short, wiry frame barely visible underneath his large overcoat. He was Canadian and had been living in Paris for years working for the French state radio delivering the news to the French colonies abroad. I knew it was time for his afternoon pastis and talked him into a quick stop at the café.

Sitting low in his chair, he twiddled the red curls circling his balding head. In the early 1960s, long before anyone had heard of altered states of consciousness or alternative anything, Simson stood on the margin of society sure in his belief that the conventional understanding of the world was flawed. With a mind like a ferret, he had spent years studying ancient traditions of knowledge from cultures and religions from around the world and was part of a Gurdjieff group that met weekly in Paris.

I told him about my interest in the ballet and my search to understand why it went up. "We take it for granted, but there's nothing like it anywhere in the world," I said. "There must be a reason." I sat quietly, seeing pictures in my mind of ballet dancers flying through the air and Indian dancers stomping on the ground.

"Context," Simson said, sipping his pastis. "I'm getting to be just like all the other old French farts. I just can't go without my afternoon pastis."

"What do you mean, 'context'?" I said.

"Context is everything. If you want to understand anything, you have to look at context. People are too atomistic in their thinking. All they see are bits and pieces. But on a deeper level, everything is plugged into everything else. *Toute est dans tout, et reciproquement.*" (The translation, "All is in all, and vice versa," is close, but doesn't do full justice to Simson's intent.)

Simson was sitting up in his chair now and was going for the last drop of pastis in his glass. "It's like scientists who study animal behavior in a laboratory. Reductionist thinking with a vengeance! Can you imagine someone thinking that taking an animal out of its natural habitat and putting it into a sterile laboratory would not have a profound effect on its behavior? It's the old mechanical thinking that says animals are simply instinct machines, and no matter what happens they'll go on instincting in the same way. It denies that animals have feelings and can respond to situations that are not prescribed by humanly contrived mechanical laws. We're terribly specio-centric!" Simson was on his soapbox now.

"Everything exists in a context. When the French describe a person, they'll often say he is beautiful by his features but not beautiful by his expression, or vice versa. The French make a distinction that we Anglos don't make. After you've known someone for a while, their features don't change but we see them differently, their expression changes. That's because you've got more emotional information about them. Their appearance is embedded in an emotional, psychological context. All this meshes together and they look different, not in their features but in their expression. The context is different."

Simson was articulating my first thought, that the dance was part of a larger social picture. "But where do I go from here?" I asked, "What do I look for? I don't know anything about anything."

He shrugged. "I don't know anything about the ballet either." His face grew pensive. "Well, if you're talking seventeenth century, you're talking Scientific Revolution. I'd look at that if I were you. If you have any trouble finding stuff, let me know. I may have a few things for you to look at." He glanced at his watch. "*Merde*, I gotta go!"

"Hold on, hold on!" I said. "One last thing. African statues. Why do you think the knees are bent?"

Simson stopped. "Don't know. Good question, but I don't know." He ran off. The next morning I started making the rounds of the bookstores, this time looking for books on the history of science.

The books I found all seemed to say the same thing. Modern science began in the late 1500s and went into full swing by the mid-1600s. Out of this period came what is known as the mechanical worldview. The intelligentsia—people like René Descartes, Francis Bacon, and Robert Boyle— were reconceiving the human body, nature, and the universe in mechanical terms. They likened the world to a clockwork mechanism made up of weights, pulleys, and pumps, all put into motion by a transcendent God. Animals too were seen as soulless machines devoid of sensation, feeling, or consciousness. In 1662, Boyle, one of the founders of the Royal Society in London, conducted experiments before his colleagues in which live dogs were crushed to death in order to study their nervous systems. These men were not sadists; they simply didn't think that animals could feel pain. The animal's shrieks were thought to be mechanical reactions, like a bell ringing in a clock when the spring is tripped. Descartes's new philosophy split mind from body and sent both of these aspects of humanity reeling off into separate spheres.

The new metaphor for the human body were automata, exquisitely crafted mechanical figures with a magnificent precision of movement. All functions of human physiology were in fact reduced to mechanical principles. In 1651, Thomas Hobbes wrote, "For what is the heart, but a spring; and the nerves, but so many strings; and the joints, but so many wheels . . ." Feelings of connection with the natural world were slowly ebbing away. Connection with nature was being superseded by separation; organism was giving way to mechanism. Years later, historian Carolyn Merchant referred to this era as "the death of nature" in her book of the same title.

What if these seventeenth-century thinkers had been choreographers and devised a new kind of dance? What would be its aesthetic? Earthy and connected to the ground? Unlikely. The ballet made perfect sense. Both it and the new science were two sides of the same coin: dislocate humans from nature.

*   *   *   *

Decroux stood at the entrance of the studio and greeted each of us with his ritual handshake and an air of mock seriousness, as if we were members of Parliament arriving for a secret convocation. We took our places across the blue linoleum floor and assumed the zero position as he walked by and looked us over. Some had tension in the shoulders, others the head off-center. He talked about the finer details of the posture. "The zero," he said, "is the attitude of the body that represents the apex of human evolution. Before humans stood up, when they were still at the stage of quadrupeds, the angle of the hip joint was very closed." He leaned forward and drew his knee up, imitating a four-legged animal. "As man grew more vertical over time, this angle opened up." He straightened up and extended his leg behind him. "The straighter we stand, the more open this joint," he pointed to his hip, "the more evolved we are." Then he bent his knees and stuck his butt out. "Standing like this," he said, "this is vulgar." Decroux's idea was clear and logical—and also wrong. But I didn't know it then. For all my years in Paris, I walked around sucking my gut in with my spine as straight as possible, convinced that I was at the pinnacle of human evolution.

*   *   *   *

While my French was improving, I still preferred reading in English. One afternoon I was upstairs at Shakespeare and Co. looking through the dusty shelves and came across *An Englishman in Paris* by Albert Vandam, published in 1892. Vandam lived in Paris for close to forty years, knew everyone, partook regularly in the café life, and witnessed the major political and social upheavals of the time. This was not the historian writing from a lofty distance but rather was a personal account of Paris from the streets. I parked myself at a café.

Vandam had met the ballerina Marie Taglioni and had actually dined with her. He'd also known the director of the Paris Opera, Dr. Louis Véron, one of the most colorful characters of the period. Here were anecdotes about personalities of the period that no history book would ever recount.

Véron was the opera's first director in 1831, when it became independent of the court. In his hands the opera reached a new level of popularity. He created the first star system by pumping large sums of money into advertising to make his dancers full-fledged celebrities. Vandam compares him to P. T. Barnum and attributes him with the invention of "newspaper puff."

Véron also introduced the greenroom to the opera, the room backstage where the audience meets the artists. (Invite wealthy gentlemen backstage to meet the dancers. Once the heart, or some other organ, is engaged, the pocketbook will follow with contributions to the opera.)

Vandam writes about a dinner he attended where Marie Taglioni was also a guest and recounts a story she told about her Russian tour of 1824–

25, a combination of danger and romance that could fill the pages of a dime-store novel. After a triumphal run in Saint Petersburg, Taglioni decided to take a short vacation to the country. Her Russian friends warned against the idea because of bandits on the road.

The name of the notorious highwayman Trischka came up. Before embarking on his career as an outlaw, Trischka had been a steward to a prince. He could speak French and German and was even known to be an excellent dancer. He never harmed his victims or took all their possessions, but he could ruin an otherwise fine day. Despite these warnings Taglioni left for a holiday in the country, accompanied by her father, her maid, and two German violinists.

She recounted how one night, "In the thick of a dense forest, our road was barred by two men on horseback, while a third opened the door to our carriage. It was Trischka himself." The bandit took off his hat, bowed, and apologized to the ballerina for not being able to see her perform in Saint Petersburg. "I hope you will do me the honor to dance for me here," he said. After a brief protest, Taglioni consented. The alternative was to have all of her goods taken. Trischka's men unrolled several of Taglioni's rugs that she had brought with her. The German violinists tuned their instruments while father Taglioni stood on the side, brooding. "I danced for about a quarter of an hour, and honestly believe that I never had a more appreciative audience either before or afterwards." Trischka led her back to the carriage, tipped his hat, and bade her adieu. "I keep the rugs, mademoiselle. I will never part with them."

*   *   *   *

Part of my Paris routine consisted of regular trips to the Louvre. My first visit there was disorienting in the extreme. This was my fault because I failed to take the simplest advice: don't try to see everything all at once. Shamelessly, I went through room after room with the zeal of a glutton.

I had spent years in school studying art history and had seen only tiny black-and-white reproductions of the great masters. Here were the real things. Even though I lived down the street and knew I could return to the museum whenever I wanted, I saw no reason to stop after . . . *how long has it been, an hour?*

Before the installation of the glass pyramid (designed by I. M. Pei and unveiled in 1989), the old smaller entrance set you up to be even more overwhelmed by the art treasures inside. Moving up the wide marble staircase in the first hall and through the galleries full of Delacroix, Rubens, the *Mona Lisa* was impressive enough. The real shock was to pass through a small doorway and into the Grand Gallery. And by *Grand* I do mean *Grand*. Here was a single room over twelve hundred feet long, the length of four football fields. The narrow width of the room heightened the effect of its length. Walking along I passed all the Italian masters: Mantegna, Botticelli, Titian, da Vinci, Giotto, etc. At the end of the Grand Gallery was a small room with Michelangelo's *Slaves*.

By the time I finished my quarter-mile trek past endless great art, I had had enough. *Please, not another masterpiece.* Then something unexpected happened.

I was looking for the exit when I passed through a room of eighteenth-century French paintings and saw Watteau's *Pierrot, formerly called Gilles.* It hit me like a whack on the head. Bang! I stopped short and gazed at this romantic, melancholic figure wearing his oversized white costume with big buttons and large fluffy collar and sleeves staring straight at me with arms hanging limp. It was the face that was so shocking. It shimmered with a dozen different emotions at once.

I don't think anyone could put a word to that face. The eyebrows and the forehead looked empty and forlorn. But the eyes. *Are they questioning, or are they resigned? The mouth looks like it's about to burst into tears . . . or is that a timid smile?* I couldn't tell. If this were a photograph and not a painting, I could understand. *People do have complex emotions like this, but this is a painting!* Watteau's mastery to create such subtlety through artifice was almost too much to take. I looked at it for a few minutes and then had to look away. "Damn, I don't believe it," I muttered under my breath. I turned and looked at it again. I went home.

*   *   *   *

Immobility. Stillness. Not moving. This was the most interesting aspect of Decroux's lexicon of movement, in part because it was so surprising. Who would think that not moving could be so interesting? Over time, stillness became part of my way of seeing the world. Just as I'd heard that Eskimos had seventeen different words for snow, stillness, I found, had at least as many different shades and subtleties. I began to watch people while they were still in order to notice their different qualities, the qualities of their stillness. Some people are empty when still. Some are bubbly. Some are thick and opaque. Some are clear and transparent. Others are full, bursting with potential. On rare occasions I have seen people with a stillness that contains infinite space.

I thought one such person was Monsieur Bougepas—at least, that's what I called him; I never learned his real name. I often saw him at La Coupole sitting alone. This man exuded a feeling of stillness and silence that made the sphinx look like a fussbudget. With my newfound appreciation for stillness, Mr. Bougepas was very interesting to me. I could watch him for a very long time. Whenever he did move, it was an event. He didn't have to do much—reach for his coffee, turn his head, shift his weight. But each movement, no matter how small, came from a place of such stillness that it was, what can I say, it was an event. When he reached into his pocket to pay, that was something big, an upheaval of movement and activity that seemed almost out of character. Having completed this colossal operation, he would quietly slip back into his stillness.

Monsieur Bougepas had a small goatee and wore a fez. This, in combination with the farawayness of his person, made him a prime candidate to be a sage. But upon deeper observation, I knew better. Mr. Bougepas's quiet was not because he had followed a spiritual path that had helped him burn through the layers of his person to get to a core from where he could hold himself with equanimity. No, Mr. Bougepas's stillness was a terrible stillness, a stillness with a history. Monsieur Bougepas was not quiet because he had emptied himself, but rather, it seemed, because he was too full, as if the totality of his life experience, an experience of hardship, was too great for his small frame to contain, and in order to hold everything inside, he had to compact it, and now he was this dense mass of concentrated experience, and it was so dense and so concentrated, and there was so much of it, that he could hardly move.

CHAPTER 8

RICHARD'S TURTLE

RICHARD KNOCKED ON MY DOOR. He and Saskia were going to England to do a photo shoot of philosopher Bertrand Russell. He had photographed virtually all the great artists of the twentieth century: Picasso, Braque, Dali, Miró, and Giacometti. Saskia had a little sketchbook, now priceless, with each page featuring an autograph or sketch done for her by these artists. Unfortunately Richard had little appreciation for their work and seemed only to enjoy rubbing shoulders with the famous—important food for the undernourished ego.

Now and then he would set up an easel in his room and put paint on a canvas. That's all you could call it, putting paint on a canvas. It wasn't really painting. He didn't have enough intention to be an artist. One day I came into his room and found him painting a copy of one of his own paintings. He told me how the assistant Minister of Culture had admired this painting and rather than give him the original, Richard was painting a duplicate.

"That's outrageous," I said.

"He'll never know the difference."

Richard held a cardboard box in his hand, delicately, as if it contained a birthday cake. "What's in the box?" I asked. "A turtle," he replied. He set the box on my desk, opened it up, and inside was a very large turtle with a beautiful spotted shell. "I'm going to give it to Russell," he said. "I thought it would be an unusual gift."

"C'mon, you're crazy!" I said.

"Why not?" he said, grinning. "How many turtles do you think he gets?" I couldn't wait to hear what happened.

Richard and Saskia were sitting in Russell's study along with his secretary. In the middle of the conversation, Richard opened the box, plunked the turtle on Russell's lap, and said, "This is a gift for you." Without flinching, Russell picked up the turtle, handed it to his secretary, and with utter deadpan said, "Would you take this turtle and put it in the next room with all the other turtles."

*   *   *   *

One day Richard took me to an art gallery on Rue du Faubourg Saint-Honoré to attend an art opening where Salvador Dali was to make an appearance. As we entered, Dali came striding in with the press following close behind. To please the TV cameras, he devised a scene where he would look intensely straight into the camera spouting rapid-fire gibberish while a beautiful woman in net stockings, high heels, and a tuxedo jacket with martini glasses pinned all over the front walked slowly behind him blindfolded.

The gallery director wanted to enhance the setup for the camera and disassembled a large metal sculpture made by a German artist and rearranged it as decor for Dali and the TV camera. When the sculptor arrived and saw how his work had been manhandled, he went into a rage. Standing nose-to-nose with the gallery director, he vigorously made his point.

The gallery director, the picture of culture and refinement, stood his ground, and in the best tradition of French disdain, he treated the man as a mere trifle with a derisory sneer. A smug crowd gathered behind him and mirrored this contempt. Suddenly, and with no provocation, the gallery director slapped the artist in the face. The artist was stunned. The director, ever cool, said to him, "In France, sir, when one is slapped, one answers." The German artist, refusing this invitation to violence, grabbed his sculpture, threw it in the back of his pickup truck, and drove off.

*   *   *   *

Paris in the 1960s was many cities rolled into one. A person or a place could evoke a whole other era, like catching a whiff of a scent that sends you reeling to another time and place. On Rue du Faubourg Saint-Denis, a working-class eatery called Restaurant Julien was a step back into the 1900s with richly hued wood paneled walls, bentwood chairs, ceiling fans, and turn-of-the century light fixtures. A plate of coq au Vin cost 60¢. Veal chop, 48¢. Lifetime waiters wearing black uniforms and long white aprons stepped out of a Toulouse-Lautrec lithograph. Every night an enormous woman sat alone and devoured a plate of boiled cabbage topped with a quarter kilo of butter that she mashed into the dish with gusto. Today this restaurant has gone terribly upscale. For a beautiful café of the 1900s, there was La Frégate on the Seine at the corner of Rue du Bac and the Quai Voltaire. Sitting at the tiny booths in the window you could almost hear the clip-clop of the horses and carriages passing by. Amazingly, this place held out until 1999, when it too fell victim to the wiles of fashion and a facelift.

In Les Halles, an obese man worked in the meat section. His bulbous, pickled nose sat on his pulpy face as if it had landed there by accident. His jaw hung open in a perpetual state of not knowing. His small eyes with thick, heavy lids seemed to have no memory of a smile. He looked like a figure out of a Hieronymus Bosch painting dressed in his long dirty apron spattered with blood and his tight-fitting cap with earflaps pulled down tight and tied under his chin.

Everywhere in Paris I found pockets of the 1920s and '30s. On the Left Bank a small restaurant on Rue de l'Université had a large wooden chest with about a hundred little drawers, each one with a brass number on it. These drawers contained the cloth napkins for the regulars.

An old woman on the bus hobbled about on two canes dressed in the elegant fashion of the 1910s—a large, wide-brimmed black hat with a veil, a black ankle-length dress, and delicate black gloves reaching up to the elbow. Talking to anyone who would listen, she made sure that everyone knew about "*mon accident*" of 1926. Studying with Decroux in an intense master–disciple relationship was a taste of the Renaissance. For a glimpse of the future with its faster, glossier rhythms there was Le Drugstore on the Champs-Élysées. Today the past is harder to find in Paris, but it's still there.

*   *   *   *

I picked up my newspapers at the *New York Times* office on Rue Lafayette and was told I had a new beat. For months I had been in Montmartre at the Place du Tertre, the small square crammed with artists trading in on the myth of Paris as the art capital of the world. Now I was going to Notre Dame—much better for sales and within walking distance of home. Twice a day at 10 AM and 3 PM, I'd wait for the tour buses to pull up alongside the cathedral and disgorge crowds of tourists with cameras dangling around their necks.

One day, I stood on the Rue du Cloître-Notre-Dame alongside the cathedral waiting for the tourist buses to pull up when I noticed a man walking by hurriedly with a large sketchpad under his arm. He walked quick, stopping to glance up at the cathedral, puffing away on a cigarette. I recognized him right away. Alberto Giacometti. This was an OMG moment. I resisted saying anything. He was busy.

*   *   *   *

My lips, my mouth, and my tongue—what must they do to learn French? Speaking French is a different way of moving the face. The language not only sounds different but also moves differently than English. I was in the Métro one day and my train pulled into the Franklin Roosevelt station on the Champs-Élysées. Two women stood on the platform across from me waiting for a train. They were fashionably dressed and had that typical French allure. I couldn't hear them speaking, but I knew they were American. Their mouths gave them away. The mouth moves differently with English. Maybe that's why chewing gum is so popular in America and not in France—because the motion and rhythm of chewing is closer to how we Americans move our mouths when we speak.

One day in Paris I was walking with a young French fellow who casually pointed to a group of people across the way. "There's a bunch of Americans over there," he said. How did he know? We couldn't hear them speaking. What was the giveaway? My friend was at a loss to explain. He just knew. In time, as I became integrated enough into French culture, I too could spot an American from a hundred yards away. What is it? Dress, sure, but to a large extent it's the body. We have a different combination of tension and relaxation in the body. American women had a tension in their behinds, a constriction in the thighs and legs as they walked. The men had a looseness in their knees as they walked. Their feet seemed to throw forward with each step. This is not to say that all American men and women walk this way, but whenever I saw this walk, I knew it was an American. You would never see this among the French. No doubt about it. Cultures have bodies.

If we are shaped by our experience, then how does that experience shape our body? Can we say that experience shapes the character but does not shape the body? Do we really think that our body has a life of its own and develops separately from our experiences? Everything is in everything. And if that's true, things can get messy. How do you make distinctions if everything bleeds into everything else? Where's the order in this salad?

Look at the face. I would not say there's an American face, but there is a face that only Americans have even though not all Americans have it. Milton Berle is an example. He has a face you'd never see among the French. Look at his mouth. It's a quintessentially American mouth. There's an unmistakable youthfulness there, in its softness and fleshiness. His is not a cynical mouth, a mouth hardened by experience, nor is it blasé and cool. It's a young mouth with a naiveté, an openness, a readiness to experience life. A mouth that wants to drink in the world. Another example is the TV marionette Howdy Doody. Remember him? His mouth has these same qualities. And those eyes on both Berle and Howdy Doody—they're ready to drink in the world. You'd never see a puppet or marionette in Europe with a face like that. They all have thin lips.

Do cultures have a body? What do the French see when they think of Americans as "*les grands enfants*," big children? Do cultures have a character?

During World War I the U.S. Army sent a jazz band to Europe to represent the United States in public ceremonies, parades, etc. The man assigned to assemble this band was an African-American who was coincidentally named James Reese Europe. Jazz was new, and the French had never heard it before. An outdoor celebration was held in Paris with military bands from England, France, Italy, etc., playing the usual marching music as people listened politely. Then the American group came on with their herky-jerky syncopated rhythms, and all hell broke loose. The pristine ears of the French had never heard anything like it before. They loved it and couldn't get enough. The French musicians were so astonished that they demanded to see the musical instruments the Americans played. Certainly they had been altered to get those impossible sounds.

The next day, the French band director called on Europe and asked if he could borrow the American sheet music for his musicians. They were dying to play this new music. Europe agreed. A few days later, the French director returned the sheet music. Try as they did, his men could not get the same sounds out of their instruments. Why not? The reason is simple. The French were too stiff in their bodies. The Americans were looser in their joints and spines than the French. They had a give-and-take foreign to the French body. Jazz is full of diphthongs and slides. It's a curvy music with a swing to it, and this is the antithesis of the angular, predictable, metronome-like rhythms of military music. The American body and its particular kind of relaxation was conducive to playing jazz. The French didn't have the physical basis to understand the jazz rhythms.

Americans even relaxed differently than the French in the 1960s. Nothing irritated the French so much as seeing Americans sitting in chairs with their feet up, or, worse yet, sitting on the ground. I was in a café once with friends and was reprimanded by the waiter for sitting too low in my chair. "Out of politeness to others," he said, "would you please sit up straight!" I rose from my chair with a grimace on my face and pointed to my back, explaining in deliberately poor French that I had an injury and could not sit any other way. His apologies were profuse.

A key to understanding this difference between Americans and the French about relaxation and control was Jerry Lewis. Lewis enjoyed a popularity that few movie stars have had in France. In those days there was always a festival of his films going on somewhere in Paris. This adoration is mystifying to Americans, but it makes sense. Lewis's physical awkwardness flies in the face of the French need for Cartesian rationality and control. When the French buy a piece of property with the idea of building a house, the first thing they do, or at least the first thing they would do in the '60s, is build a wall around the property. They have boundaries for everything. The world is made up of separate and distinct entities. Jerry

Lewis, stumbling around, annihilates all boundaries. His anarchy is a respite for the French caught up in their world of hyper-rationality.

Jazz filled the same need for the French at an earlier time. So did the Marx Brothers. Decroux's son, Maximilian, told me of the revelation he found in the Marx Brothers the first time he saw them as a young boy. His world had been joyously exploded apart by their anarchy. Cultural blind spots often create the biggest idols, just as Elvis's stardom needed the sexual uptightness in America in the 1950s. Without it he might have been popular but would never have reached his level of superstardom.

*   *   *   *

In time, Berthe and Hubert reached the end of their conjugal bliss and ran hard cold into reality. Far from resolving her problems, Berthe's new affair was only a new way of obscuring them. Eventually the veneer peeled away, exposing the many pustules of unresolved conflict. Hubert for his part was perfectly happy with the arrangement and saw nothing wrong with anything. He was content to let things go on exactly as they were. And they would, but only after a fashion. The first sign that a congealing of sorts was taking place was when I saw Berthe and Hubert on the street. I was at a distance, and they did not see me.

Silence speaks. The silence of two people who are comfortable together and feel no need to speak for long periods is different from the silence of two people leading a clumsy existence built on bottomless need and unreal expectations. This was Berthe and Hubert. Together they conveyed an awkwardness of two people who were thrown together by the fates.

The quiet evenings at home that marked the beginning of this liaison soon became punctuated with loud shouting matches accompanied by an occasional glass or plate shattering or door slamming, around nothing more than misplaced Métro tickets or who paid what portion of the food bill. Things trundled on like this for some time.

*   *   *   *

My plan for the morning was to build a small low wooden table for my room that could fit under the sloping eave of the roof. I had about an hour before the stores opened, so I lit a fire, made some breakfast, and put on a record of Bach's Mass in B Minor while I went through my notes. I discovered Bach in Paris. It was a long journey from Chuck Berry to Johann Sebastian Bach. I wasn't introduced *to* classical music as much as I was seduced *away* from it. George Gershwin did this with his Concerto in F. It's not classical, but it is orchestral—enough to open my mind to a music other than rock and roll.

I took the elevator downstairs and walked out into the bright sunlight. I headed down the avenue to the department store Magasins du Louvre (now transformed into an antique mart) to buy some wood. On my way, I scanned the panorama of the dance in my mind. At one extreme was the ecstatic dance. This is all internal. The dancers have no concern for who is watching or how they look to an audience. Those watching are not relevant to their experience. The dancers become egoless and lose any sense of self in the Big All of everything. The cosmos is still a big soup; nothing has been separated out yet. The individual dancers count only in as much as they fulfill the group ritual or complete a process of inner experience. Ballet is at the other end of the spectrum—the ecstatic dance turned inside out. All attention is directed to an audience and the thrust of the movement is away from the earth. This is the dance of display. Internal experience doesn't count. It's all about the look. The personality of the dancer is everything.

I thought about how ballet uses space. Because the early dance came out of the court, everything was choreographed with the king in mind. No one dared turn their back on the monarch, and because of this, the dancers always danced facing the audience.

This created a hierarchy of values to the space. Not all directions are equal. The direction out front is of supreme importance. The space behind the dancer is less important. This also conditioned the dancers' experience of their bodies. The front of the body has greater value; it takes on a different quality of focus than the back of the body. That thought sent me reeling.

I sat down on a bench at the bottom of the avenue. I had met several dancers in Paris, and after a while, I began seeing light emanating from their bodies. Not that I saw real light, but I did see it in my mind's eye. I saw light, and it varied at different parts of the body. Lots of light emanated from the front of the body, and none emanated from the back. The intensity of the light on the front of the body varied depending on where it was located. The upper body put off a lot of light. Lower body, no light. The topside of the hands gave off light. The palms less. The forearms some light but less. The upper arms even less. The forehead was very bright, and so were the cheeks. Chest very bright. Waist, no light. Neck, no light. What was I seeing? Was it the person's psychological energy? Was this where a dancer's personality was most invested?

Highly skilled movers in other disciplines of the body that were more grounded—African dancers, Chinese acrobats, Japanese Noh actors—did not have this unequal distribution of energy in their bodies. To the contrary. Every part of the body was equal to every other part of the body.

When searching for an answer to a question, one might have all the pieces of information needed to solve the problem, but if these pieces of information are not in the right relationship to each other, the picture can't come together. Or perhaps the one thought needed to make everything fall into place is lacking. So one keeps working.

Understanding is the knowledge of relationships.

Knowledge is the understanding of relationships.

I thought of a young ballet dancer I had met in Paris. One day as we walked through a doorway, I placed my hand on her back and was surprised. I lurched inside, like one does when one expects a step at the top of a flight of stairs that isn't there. It was as if she had no back.

Years later, I met a physical therapist who had done a lot of work with dancers who said that typically, ballet dancers have no back. I asked him to explain. In the classical dance, he said, the back of the body is continually working to support the front of the body. The back has no life of its own and has been usurped of its power. There is no back there. The back's value is measured only in how well it supports the front of the body.

I walked to the store to buy the wood. By the end of the day, I had made a low table for my room.

*   *   *   *

In time I became a professional people watcher. Someone once said, "A pickpocket sees a saint, and all he sees are pockets." I look at bodies. I see expression. That's what I do. It's not only seeing but also feeling, taking in the whoosh of someone's physical presence. No thought, no judgment. Just take it in.

CHAPTER 9

THROWN OUT OF THE CAFÉ

IT WAS ABOUT 11 PM. I WAS TIRED, hungry, and depressed. I sat in my room staring at the bag of unsold newspapers lying in the corner. My last chance to make any money today was to catch the crowds as they left the opera house up the street.

I slung the bag of newspapers over my shoulder and trotted up to the Place de l'Opéra just as the crowds were pouring onto the boulevard. To my surprise I was besieged. People descended upon me, all clamoring for a copy of *The New York Times*. I was taken aback. Within minutes my bag was empty. As people walked away I saw their disappointment after looking at the front page. Then I found out why. Kennedy had been shot. My paper was the earlier edition and didn't have the news. The French loved Kennedy and took his death as if he were one of their own. The next day a pall fell over Paris as the city went into mourning. Many merchants put pictures of Kennedy with a strip of black cloth across the corner in their shop windows.

In times of great crisis a sense of common disaster pulls people out of their isolation and strangers actually talk to each other. As I walked past the Café de la Paix, one of the ritziest cafés in Paris on Boulevard des Capucines, a man seated at a table asked for a paper. I didn't have any more, but we started talking. The man was from Philadelphia and was engaged to be married and thought he needed one last fling before getting tied down, as he put it, so he was on a trip to Europe by himself! Now he was desperately lonely and wanted to talk in English to someone, anyone, and that was me. He invited me to sit down and join him for a drink.

As I sat there anticipating a coffee in this swanky café where I could never go on my own, an elegantly dressed waiter in a black vest, a black tie, and a long, white apron approached and informed me that he would not serve me and that I had to leave the café. I was taken aback. "Leave? Why?" "We do not serve news vendors," he said, with utter politeness. I folded my empty paper bag and placed it under the table. "Now I look like everyone else," I said. "Now you can serve me." This made no difference; I was still a newsboy. He insisted I leave. My Detroit began rising fast (take no crap). I walked inside to find the maître d', or as we Americans say, the "mayder dee." When this slimy gentleman in a tuxedo confirmed what the first slimy gentleman outside told me, I began raising my voice, gesticulating, and throwing glances left and right. He quickly acquiesced and muttered under his breath, "Very well. This time, yes. But never again!" Little did I know what a minefield of history I had fallen into when I sat down at that table. I should have known better. Every inch of Paris has deep layers of history each with a rich story to be told.

In fact, a stunning example of this is on Avenue de l'Opéra, right where I lived. Back in the fifteenth century, long before the avenue was created, there was a large hill known as Windmill Hill situated across from my building. At that time, a young Joan of Arc, with an army behind her, stood on this hill looking into the walled city of Paris below her, contemplating an attempt to retake the city from English occupiers. Legions of tourists, as well as Parisians, walk by there every day with no idea of the history under their feet.

There I was sitting at the Café de la Paix with no idea of the thick history I had fallen into. The waiter's reaction was part of the history of these Paris Boulevards. And it's a history worth knowing.

*   *   *   *

Boulevard des Capucines, home to the Café de la Paix, was one stretch of what are known as Les Grands Boulevards that cut across the Right Bank in a two-mile arc east to west from the Place de la Bastille to the Place de la Madeleine. Anyone who has been to Paris knows that most streets change name every block, and this long boulevard is no different. It changes name eleven times as it crosses Paris.

Walk the length of the boulevards from east to west, and one traces the distribution of wealth in Paris: east is poor, west is rich. Begin your walk at Place de la Bastille in working-class Paris. By the time you reach the Place de la Madeleine, you're among the moneyed. The Café de la Paix sits comfortably in the western wealthier boulevards.

These Grands Boulevards were laid out by Louis XIV in the 1660s on the site of old fortifications built in the 1500s that no longer held any strategic value under his peaceful monarchy. Imagine a high crenellated stone wall snaking across the Right Bank with towers, moats, ditches, and sloping escarpments. Imposing gates with drawbridges stood as entries into the city.

In a desire to embellish Paris, Louis dismantled this old fortification and laid out a broad promenade 120 feet wide with four rows of trees and built two triumphal arches in place of the old city gates. And they still stand today: Porte Saint-Denis, 1671, and Porte Saint-Martin, 1674.

While this new boulevard was a striking addition to the city, it took time for it to grow on the public. This was still the edge of town, a rural and rustic repair where few dared to tread. Aside from the few who tended gardens or played a game of *boules*, this was largely a gathering place frequented by prostitutes, thieves, and other shady characters. But the boulevard's most obvious feature, its width, was an irresistible draw to the Paris social elite. Seeing and being seen was essential, and this was not easy in the congested streets of Paris. The broad expanse of the new promenade was like a vast, empty stage waiting for the actors and décor to arrive. And it wasn't long in coming. The boulevard became a grand concourse of ostentation and display, the *American Graffiti* of its day, as the wealthy took to riding up and down in their fancy carriages to demonstrate their status and wealth.

An unexpected development from this new pastime of the rich was the growing popularity of the carriage. For years, carriages were shunned by men because they were taken as a sign of effeminacy. They were only used by children, the very old, or the infirm. A man demonstrated his manliness by riding on his horse. Now with the broad new boulevard the carriage became the new status symbol to flaunt with men behind the reins. Be it a Berlin, Landau, or Phaeton, the different models spoke as strongly as today's Aston Martin, Lexus, or BMW.

And this popularity of the boulevard brought growth. Entrepreneurs set up drink stalls that became the first cafés to cater to the crowds. This drew street entertainers: strolling musicians, jugglers, singers, ropewalkers, trained animals, all creating the atmosphere of a carnival sideshow. The new boulevards became *the* place to be in Paris, and this brought the construction of fashionable estates for the wealthy. During the Revolution these choice properties were confiscated by the State and sold to land speculators who tore them down to lay out new streets and erect the first apartment buildings in the neighborhood.

One of these abandoned estates to survive the Revolution stood on the corner of Boulevard des Italiens and Rue de Richelieu and was transformed into Café Frascati, that became famous throughout Europe for its perfumed ices. A visit to Frascati's after an elegant saunter down the boulevard made for an exquisite day in Paris.

Over time, each stretch of boulevard took on its own personality, with the east/west, poor/rich divide holding true. The line of demarcation for this economic divide was Rue de Richelieu. Everything west was classier. Everything east was more working-class.

The Boulevard du Temple in eastern Paris was known as the Boulevard du Crime because of the many theatres there catering to the working class with melodramatic productions full of murder and mayhem. The cheap seats in the upper balconies were known as "paradise." The patrons sitting up there were the "children of paradise," from whence comes the film of the same name. Most of these theatres were obliterated when Baron Haussmann created today's Place de la République in the 1860s. One of the most popular, the Ambigu, stood until 1966.

As one strolled westward along the boulevards—from Boulevard Saint-Martin to Boulevard Saint-Denis, Bonne-Nouvelle, Poissonniere, to Boulevard Montmartre, getting closer and closer to Rue de Richelieu—the feeling of imminent luxury was palpable. Just short of this intersection was the Théâtre des Variétés, opened in 1807, a step up from the working-class theatres of the Boulevard du Crime. If anyone wrote the soundtrack for nineteenth-century Paris, it was composer Jacques Offenbach, and a number of his popular operettas had their debut at the Variétés.

Next door to this theatre was one of the great attractions of the day, the Passage des Panoramas, built in 1799 and still in place today. The entrance to this passageway was flanked by two large rotundas, each one three hundred feet in diameter and sixty feet high with eye-popping panoramic scenes painted in stunning detail. One of these vistas depicted a breathtaking 360-degree view of Paris seen from on top of the Louvre. The other was a view of the French military victory over the English at Toulon.

Spectators paid a franc and a half admission to mount onto a platform in the middle of the rotunda and watch the panorama revolve around them under specially designed illumination. The effect of a painting so large that it seemed endless in all directions was startling and drew a huge public.

One name connected to these panoramas is American Robert Fulton, the inventor of the steamboat. Fulton saw the attraction in England, bought the patent, and imported it into France but then ceded the patent to Robert Thayer, who built panoramas around Paris for a thrilled public. One of his close associates was Louis Daguerre, who was a very able painter before he invented the photographic process carrying his name.

The Café Frascati on the corner of Rue de Richelieu and Boulevard Montmartre marked the end of one world and the beginning of another. Cross this intersection, and you enter onto the boulevard of all boulevards, the Boulevard des Italiens. If Paris was the capital of the nineteenth century, this short stretch of cobblestoned boulevard was its headquarters. The French elite played out their lives in public, and this was the stage on which they chose to strut their wealth and larger-than-life personalities. To stray beyond a block or two in either direction was like wandering off into the desert. Curiously the north side had all the draw. The south side of the boulevard, despite its fine restaurants, never attained the mythic level of the north side.

The Opéra-Comique, opened in 1783, was on the lesser side of the boulevard and had a curious feature that reveals the intense snobbery of this classy boulevard. At the actors' request, the opera house was built with the rear of the building on the boulevard instead of the entrance because the king's actors wanted to distinguish themselves from the common actors playing in the low-class theatres on the Boulevard du Crime.

In the first block of the fabled north side were two covered passageways: Galerie de l'Horloge and Galerie Baromètre, constructed in 1821. These lead to the opera house around the corner on Rue Le Peletier, where the Romantic Ballet exploded onto the art world in 1832 when Marie Ta-glioni danced in *La Sylphide.*

Another draw on this boulevard were the Chinese baths, built in 1792. Because indoor plumbing was a rarity in Paris, public baths were a necessity. And these were the most elegant of all the baths in Paris. A multi-storied pagoda with fanciful minarets and gilded balconies on a set-ting of artificial rocks served as a backdrop to steamy mineral baths set in grottos. An elegant café, restaurant, beauty salon, and reading room added to the splendor. Charles Dickens wrote that the Paris Chinese baths are "a specimen of the most fantastic taste, which proves that extravagance is not confined to England."

In this rarefied world of the Boulevard des Italiens, an unparalleled spectacle played out. A typical summer evening became a parade of elegance and ostentation as the Beautiful People strolled, sauntered, and ambled along looking like upholstered furniture with their ruffled collars; rolled-up sleeves to show off expensive cuff links; silver-buckled footwear; artistic buttons; jeweled rings; flowing muslin; single, double, and triple vests; elaborate silk cravats with elegant stickpins; spotless leather gloves; monocles; gold-handled walking sticks; decorated fans; an array of expensive bracelets, pins, and necklaces; top hats with fanciful brims for men out to make a statement; women's hats of every design; and any other accoutrement that the imagination could conjure to spell out high fashion and wealth. Summer evenings were so crowded that one observer of the period noted, "One doesn't walk. One is carried by the crowd and moves no faster than a few inches in a minute."

The attention to detail in men's dress would astonish people today. Read this advice from "The Art of Tying the Cravat Demonstrated in Sixteen Lessons and Thirty-Two Different Styles," published in London in 1828:

When a man of rank makes his entrée into a circle distin-
guished for taste and elegance, and the usual compliments have
passed on both sides, he will discover that his coat will attract
only a slight degree of attention, but that the most critical and
scrutinizing examination will be made on the set of his Cravat.
Should this unfortunately, not be correctly and elegantly put
on—no further notice will be taken of him; whether his coat
be of the reigning fashion or not will be unnoticed by the as-
sembly—all eyes will be occupied in examining the folds of the
fatal Cravat.

The outdoor cafés filled up as these *Fashionables*, *Élégants*, *Incroy-ables*, and *Merveilleuses*, as they were known depending on the period, did not hesitate to spread themselves out across three chairs at a time. The anointed sat on one chair, their feet went up on another, and their dog occupied the third. The carriage stood nearby, attended to by their valet wearing a powdered wig. With nothing meaningful to fill the days of the wealthy, boredom and ennui were a way of life. Affected yawning was part of the social vocabulary. Some of the most elegant women never left their carriages and had their tasty sorbets brought to them by their valets, known as "tigers," so they could sit perched on high, queen-like, and watch the crowd hustle and bustle by.

In this closed world where eccentricity and caprice were common, the most bizarre behavior played out. Gérard de Nerval, out to "*épater le bour-geois*," to shock the bourgeoisie, reportedly walked down the boulevard with his pet lobster on a leash.

As a nightly regular at the Café de Paris, Monsieur Saint-Cricq al-ways ordered two scoops of ice cream—one vanilla, the other strawberry. He took off his boots and scooped the vanilla into the right boot and the strawberry into the left. On the occasion when he put a flavor into the wrong boot, he ordered two more scoops and then repeated the action, crying out, "Vanilla, right boot! Strawberry, left boot!" During a meal he always ordered a large salad and sprinkled a little tobacco onto it from a small pouch he carried. After turning the salad energetically, he then called the waiter and asked for a jar of cold cream he kept at the café. He then smeared this onto his face and threw pinches of tobacco onto it. Mr. Saint-Criq ended his days in an asylum, where he died of boredom.

The status of the boulevard grew again when King Louis-Philippe closed the gambling houses and ended prostitution in the Palais-Royal in 1836. A pall fell over the garden and brought a fifty-year reign to an end. The wealthy gravitated north to the Boulevard des Italiens. The streets had been cobblestoned, oil lamps had been installed, and the first buses for public transportation had been introduced. And out of this world of the crème de la crème evolved a social type that became an icon of the boulevard—the flaneur.

A man of demonstrable wealth with no need for employment, the flaneur took strolling to the level of an art form. Appearance was everything, and it was not uncommon to have several hats or pairs of boots held at different hat makers or boot makers on the boulevard in case an errant bit of mud or a drop of rain might obscure their perfection. The right witticism—*bon mot*—at the right moment was a powerful social weapon, and it was common for a particularly trenchant witticism to make the rounds in gossip circles.

During this prime period of the boulevard, Honoré de Balzac wrote:

> *Every capital has its poem, that one place where it expresses it-self best, where it sums up its nature, where it is most assuredly itself. The boulevards are to Paris what the Grand Canal was to Venice, the Corsia de Servi is to Milan, the Corso is to Rome.*

Gastronomy was an essential part of this world of refinement. In 1839, an American from Kentucky, John Sanderson, travelled to Paris and wrote of the extravagant culinary scene:

> *I have not the courage to describe our gorgeous banquet. I have an excessive headache. Though I ate of nothing but the soup and the fish, and game, and of the roasts and ragouts and side dishes, and then the dessert, drank scarcely anything but burgundy, medoc and champagne, and some coffee, and liqueur, yet I feel quite ill this morning. If one should die of the stomach-ache by eating a gooseberry pie, I wonder if it is suicide?*

Comparing French dining to American dining, he said, "The French dine to gratify, we to appease appetite. We demolish a dinner, they eat it."

As the boulevard flourished, the seeds of its decline were already in place. The introduction of public transportation was the first fissure into this hermetically sealed world. The horse-drawn omnibus ran at fifteen-minute intervals and committed the sin of delivering outsiders into this exclusive world of the wealthy. More insidious yet was the invention of the railroad. For the first time, tourists— provincials and foreigners alike— began wandering the fabled boulevard and frequenting the sacrosanct cafés and restaurants to the utter dismay of the staff and regulars. As one observer wrote with disdain, "This was the beginning of the democratization of the Boulevard." Another observer did not mince words. A trip to Paris that once took days now only took hours and brought with it "an invasion of barbarians."

For generations these establishments had been the private domains of the super rich. Everyone knew everyone, and everyone knew exactly what to expect at every hour of the day or night. Imagine the hapless English tourist walking into say, the Café Tortoni on the corner of Boulevard des Italiens and Rue Taitbout. This was one of the most exclusive cafés in Paris, an icon of its age with habitués like Victor Hugo, Alexandre Dumas, and the Rothschilds.

Like clockwork the waves of regulars arrived every day at their appointed times. Mornings it was the stockbrokers and banking crowd. At noon they disappeared, and on cue the café filled with dandies and flaneurs. In the evenings it was the crowds going to and from the opera.

And here is our starry-eyed tourist gazing in wonderment at a scene they heard about for years and dreamed of visiting. Everyone present, customers and personnel alike, immediately notices the violation. Everyone except the tourist. The waiters glance at each other in bafflement as they witness the dissolution of their world. This café could only take so much progress and closed its doors on July 3, 1893. One observer suggested placing a sign on the door that read, "Closed due to the death of the Boulevard."

Worse yet were the World's Fairs—boons to the economy but disasters for the boulevard. The first *Exposition Universelle* held in Paris (in 1855) lasted an excruciating six months and brought over five million people to the city. And high on everyone's list of places to visit was Le Boulevard. For the first time tourism became an industry in Paris. Cafés and restaurants had to adapt to the flood with changes in their menus. Merchants had to rethink their buying strategies. Those who resisted change risked disappearing. The Café de Paris refused to budge, not even for the invention of gaslight, and kept their interior illuminated by candlelight. But the World's Fair was too much, and they closed their doors in 1856.

In these years before Paris was transformed by Baron Haussmann, everything to the west of Rue de la Chaussée-d'Antin was still largely unbuilt. The south side of the boulevard was lined with single-story buildings, but the north side had nothing but a steep drop of about twenty feet, a vestige of the old rampart that ran along there. At the bottom of this drop, a street had been laid out in the early 1700s, Rue Basse-du-Rempart

(Lower Rampart Street). The second floor of the buildings on that lower street were at the level of the boulevard. Leveling along here was begun in the 1850s and was not completed until after 1900.

Baron Haussmann's work in this neighborhood in the 1850s and '60s, including the construction of the Garnier opera house, brought a new dynamism to the quarter and moved the center of animation away from Boulevard des Italiens towards the Boulevard de la Madeleine.

This westward migration of modernity was reinforced by Felix Nadar, who practiced the new art of photography in his studio at 37 Boulevard des Capucines, where the first exhibition of Impressionist painting was held, in 1874. Across the street was a café where, in 1895, the Lumière brothers projected moving images onto a wall for the first time in history. The brothers offered the café owner a percentage of the daily receipts in place of the exorbitant rental. Unconvinced that this new invention had a future, he declined.

By the early 1900s, the Boulevard des Italiens was fading into history. As described by American writer Orlo Williams in 1913, it was "dowdier and more workaday." The boulevards with "the most distinguished and luxurious appearance" were now west of the Garnier opera house.

This movement westward was reinforced by the new department stores on Boulevard Haussmann—Au Printemps (1865) and Galeries Lafayette (1896). Émile Zola's *Au Bonheur des Dames* chronicles the rise of the department store and how this changed Parisian life.

World War I created a psychic rupture that changed the landscape of Paris and sent the richer classes looking for new fields of pleasure. And they found them on the Champs-Élysées. The Boulevard des Italiens, once the heartbeat of Paris, had faded from view. But worse was yet to come for this boulevard—complete obliteration.

In the late 1850s, Haussmann began laying out a boulevard in his name in the western Paris. Over the years Boulevard Haussmann was progressively extended eastward block by block with the idea of ultimately connecting it up with Boulevard Montmartre. This was finally achieved in 1927. But the completion of this last stretch of boulevard entailed the demolition of fourteen buildings on the north side of Boulevard des Italiens. For days the sidewalk was littered with handbills protesting this destruction, but to no avail. The pickaxes arrived, and the boulevard passed into the ether.

The juggernaut of progress did not stop there. A handsome building stood at the corner of Boulevard des Italiens and Rue Le Peletier. When it was constructed in 1899, it was known that the final extension of Boulevard Haussmann would eventually be cut through and that the other buildings next to it on the street would be torn down. This would place this building's north facade on the new boulevard. For this reason, that side of the building was built with an elegant facade in the expectation of its eventual prized position on the boulevard. But cruel irony ensued: this facade saw the light of day only long enough for the demolishers to tear the whole building down around 1929.

The myth of Boulevard des Italiens lived on into the early twentieth century and was one of the most photographed streets for the growing phenomenon of the picture postcard. Endless photographers mounted ladders in the middle of the street to shoot the boulevard from every angle east and west or walked up six flights of stairs to shoot from rooftops. In keeping with the myth of the boulevard, all of these views featured the north side. Studying these postcards closely reveals fascinating details lost to the cursory view. Upon close observation one notices a marquee with large letters reading *Robert-Houdin*. This was a popular theatre operated by the legendary French filmmaker Georges Méliès and featured in the film *Hugo* by Martin Scorsese. Houdin is known as the father of modern magic. One of his followers, Erik Weisz, changed his name to Harry Houdini.

When I sat down for that leisure cup of coffee at the Café de la Paix in 1963, I had no idea of the history that I had stumbled into. The glory of the boulevards had faded, but the illusion lingered on, and it did not include the likes of me, a simple paperboy.

CHAPTER 10

THE SPECTACULAR RISE AND IGNOMINIOUS FALL OF NAPOLEON III

KNOWN BY MANY AS THE EMPEROR of France, as well as the man who orchestrated the rebuilding of Paris, few know the real story behind Napoleon III's rise to power. True, he doesn't have much to do with my own story, but as the broad strokes of his life appeared during my research on Paris, I saw a remarkable story that needed to be told. This is all part of my Great Meander.

Few people came from so far behind to achieve so much and then lost it so spectacularly as Napoleon III. Were someone to concoct a story such as his, no one would believe it. His ascent from the ultimate outsider to Emperor of France challenges credulity. Twice he tried to usurp power, and twice he failed. The third time was his charm.

The odds of his ever becoming emperor were insurmountable. Even though he was born in Paris and was nephew to the great Napoleon, he was banished from France at age seven along with the rest of the Bonaparte family after his uncle lost the famous battle at Waterloo in 1815. No Bonaparte was ever to set foot on French soil again. Consequently he grew up in Switzerland and Germany and hardly knew France at all.

To make things worse, if France were to have an emperor again, Napoleon III was last in the line of succession as established by his uncle. Before him was his father, brothers, a cousin, and an uncle. To make things more difficult, he lacked the bearing of an emperor. He was short like Napoleon I but was also ill proportioned with legs too short for his torso. His eyes were half closed in a perpetual squint, and he spoke French with a German accent.

And by 1840, he was in prison serving a life sentence after his second failed coup to grab power. What possibly could have led him from that jail cell to the throne as Emperor of France in 1851?

The prince had several advantages in his favor. First of all, he had a circle of devoted followers who believed in his rising star as much as he did. They helped him plot, lay plans, and carry out the groundwork. And he had money, enough to buy anything or anyone to accomplish his end.

His first attempt to usurp power was in 1836, at age twenty-eight. It lasted about three hours. The plan was elegant in its simplicity, but flawed. Entering France from Switzerland in the early hours of an October morning, he was to meet up with a group of co-conspirators, cross the border into Strasbourg, and with all the right bribes paid off, he would gain the support of the military garrisoned there in three army barracks and go marching off to Paris with thousands of armed troops behind him all pumped up on the myth of a Bonaparte ruling France again. Along the way thousands more were expected to join in, soldiers and citizens alike, all riding on a grand wave of enthusiasm until at the gates of Paris, with a swelling population behind the prince, King Louis-Philippe I would have no choice but to hand power over to France's new leader. And all this was to be carried out without spilling a drop of blood. Things did not go exactly to plan.

The prince needed an insider in Strasbourg, someone high up in the military to help implement his plan. The commander of one of the army barracks in Strasbourg, Colonel Vaudrey, was perfect. He had one weakness: in the hands of the right woman, he was putty. So the prince arranged for him to meet a popular singer of the period, Madame Gordon, a devoted follower of the prince. She laid the bait necessary for Vaudrey to pursue her, and when the moment of truth arrived, she told him she would only give herself to a man who swore allegiance to the prince. Done. Good start.

To ensure success, hundreds of people in Strasbourg were paid off so once the coup was underway they would all cry out, "Long live the emperor!" This would stir the soldiery and give the impression that the populace was in support of the uprising.

In a touching note, the prince concealed his plans from his mother. The day he set off for Strasbourg, he told her that he was leaving for a short hunting trip and would make a stop along the way to take care of some political business. It is believed that she knew what was afoot, for she slipped a ring on his finger as she said good-bye, a ring given to her personally by Napoleon I. She meant this as a talisman.

At the appointed hour in Strasbourg, Prince Louis and his small band, decked out in striking military uniforms, entered the garrison with trumpets blaring, carrying a French flag with the imperial eagle mounted on top, all orchestrated to stir emotion. Vaudrey assembled his men, gave a short speech introducing the nephew of Emperor Napoleon I, spoke of the glory of France, etc., and on cue the soldiers drew their swords in the air and cried out, "Long live Napoleon, long live the emperor!"

Buoyed by this reception, the prince and his men marched off to take a second garrison in Strasbourg while several of the prince's men took over the local telegraph office to stop messages from being broadcast about the revolution in progress. They also arrested the local prefect of the town and ran off to the local printer to print up proclamations declaring that a great revolution was underway. One wonders why the prince didn't bring printed proclamations of his own to save himself the trouble.

Arriving at the second barracks, the prince addressed the soldiers and got the expected enthusiastic response: "*Vive l'empereur!*" But then he ran into a problem. The commander was nowhere to be found. Along with a contingent of men, Prince Louis marched to the commander's quarters and found him in a state of surprise—in fact, in a state of undress. This man was a great sympathizer of Napoleon I and was expected to fall in line, but his loyalties to the king were stronger, and he vehemently refused to support the prince. The prince ordered his troops to sequester the man in his quarters, but he escaped out the back door.

Not expecting this setback, the prince hurried off to a third barracks with hundreds of men behind him. Unfortunately he took a wrong turn along the way and found himself in a narrow lane, cutting himself off from the bulk of his followers. With only a few of his troops behind him, his entrance into the garrison was less than grandiose. And from there things devolved.

Unbeknownst to the prince, his advance man had not showed up to inform this garrison commander of the events that were about to unfold. Everyone there was caught by surprise. The prince entered the yard expecting to find troops assembled and ready for action, but instead he found everyone in their rooms preparing for inspection. A loud declaration on his part brought the troops running into the yard. A sergeant of the guard ran up to the prince and, swelling with emotion, kissed his hand. Shouts of "*Vive l'empereur!*" went up all around. The prince was encouraged. Then came the debacle.

The commander arrived and refused to believe that the man standing before him was a real Bonaparte. "This man is an imposter!" he yelled. "Arrest him at once!" Pandemonium broke out. Napoleon tried frantically to organize his men, but they were too confused to do anything useful. Men who moments before were ready to follow him anywhere were now coming at him with bayonets. Confusion was total. No one knew what to do. The camp soldiers ran around arresting everyone in sight. In desperation, Napoleon tried to escape but was caught. For the ultimate humiliation, the garrison commander stood Napoleon at attention in the yard and ripped everything from his chest that was meant to impress; the sash for the feigned Legion of Honor, his fake military epaulettes, his decorations—everything was trampled under foot for all to see. The prince had committed an act of treason and expected to be shot on the spot. Instead he was locked up for several days and then carted off to Paris.

When his mother heard the news, she entered France under an assumed name and made a personal appeal to the king to spare her son. But the king was one step ahead. Summary execution or a trial would only give power to the Bonaparte cause. The best solution was for the prince to quietly disappear. So he was granted an unconditional pardon and sent into exile to that far-off exotic land, America.

His co-conspirators did not get off so easy and were held for trial in Strasbourg. The populace harbored a deep resentment towards the king, and despite the almost-comical attempt to overthrow the government, they looked upon the Bonaparte cause with sympathy. In fact, as the insurrectionists were rounded up in the melee, the townsfolk pelted the soldiery with stones.

People cued up at the courthouse hours in advance to get a seat for the trial that went on for twelve days. The jury deliberated for a full twenty minutes. Their entrance into the courtroom was taut with suspense. "Not guilty!" they declared, and the crowd erupted into applause and gave the jury an ovation. The prisoners were released and that evening were treated to a banquet by the townspeople. Failed as this coup might have been, it inadvertently served the prince well. Eight thousand copies of his biography were sold during the course of the trial.

In exile, the prince landed in New York, but six months later, upon the news of his mother lying on her deathbed, he returned to Switzerland. When she died, he moved to London, and by the summer of 1840, he was plotting his next coup. This time he would enter France from the English Channel into the coastal town of Boulogne-sur-Mer.

The date of August 5 was chosen because it was known that the barracks commander in Boulogne, a man unsympathetic to the Bonaparte cause, would be away on a hunting trip. The Lieutenant in his place had been well bribed and could be counted on to join the prince in his grab for power. With the troops from this garrison behind him, the plan was for everyone to go marching off to Paris with the same groundswell that was supposed to happen in Strasbourg.

The prince hired a band of old French soldiers living in London to join him on his coup and dressed them up in military uniforms with muskets so that when they entered the barracks in Boulogne, it would look like the coup was already underway and that other troops had been won over to the cause.

The operation got off to a bad start. The prince was under heavy surveillance in London by both English and French authorities alike, and it took him a whole day to lose them. This delay put him in France a day late. Some of the prince's co-conspirators advised him to scuttle the operation. The unsympathetic commander, it was thought, would have returned from his hunting trip, and this would upset everything. Others urged the prince to press on. "We'll take care of him when the time comes!" They proceeded. Bad idea.

The prince chartered a steamer and sailed the Channel. Once debarked and approaching the garrison in Boulogne, the prince's men threw money into the air to gain support from citizens milling around the entrance. Once inside the garrison, Napoleon gave assurances to anybody and everybody. To one soldier he yelled, "I'll make you captain of the grenadiers!" To another, "I'll make you a captain!" The unfriendly commander suddenly appeared. One of Napoleon's men approached him and exhorted, "Captain, join us, and your fortune is made."

"Treason! Out of my barracks!" he retorted.

Chaos followed. Soldiers came running from everywhere with swords drawn. Napoleon and his men ran from the barracks throwing money at anyone on the street in a desperate attempt to gain support. The town police joined in the pursuit. The prince and his band of revolutionaries ran to the water's edge and jumped into a rowboat, hoping to make it back to the steamer, but they capsized. For a grand finale, Napoleon was left hanging on to a buoy until he was picked up, brought to shore, and put in jail. End of coup. It lasted a little less than three hours.

This time Louis-Philippe thought twice about a pardon and put the prince and his co-conspirators on trial. Unlike the outcome of Boulogne, everyone was found guilty. The prince received a sentence of prison for life. His incarceration was to be served in an impregnable fifteenth-century medieval fortress in the town of Ham, about ninety miles north of Paris.

Located on a flat, open plain, the fortress was surrounded with a moat and drawbridge and heavily guarded with armed sentries posted everywhere. Additional security came from four hundred soldiers housed in barracks on the fortress grounds. There was such a fear that soldiers might harbor a blind devotion to the Bonaparte cause, hence the prince, that no one except the fortress commander was allowed to speak a word to the prisoner. His correspondence was read in detail. This was the perfect place for incarceration. Escape was impossible. Six years later, the prince escaped, and he walked out the front door in broad daylight.

Here is a study in cunning, daring, and ingenuity. Repairs were being carried out on the building housing the prince, so workers were entering and exiting the fortress all day. A carpenter named Badinguet smuggled a set of work clothes into the fortress for the prince.

The prince shaved his beard and moustache, applied makeup to give him a ruddy complexion, put on a black wig and a cap, donned the work clothes, and with a dummy figure in his bed made to look like he was sleeping, he walked out the front door of the prison, hiding his face from the guard behind a plank of wood he carried on his shoulder. Mack Sennett before Mack Sennett. Once out of the fortress, the prince mounted a waiting carriage and fled to England. For the rest of his life the name Badinguet stuck as his nickname.

To help with this impossible escape, the prince had two inside men, two followers so devoted that they chose to live at his side during his captivity: his personal physician Doctor Conneau and his valet Thélin. Both these men carried out the distractions needed as the disguised prince made his way along the labyrinthian pathway out of the fortress. Nerves were high because all the guards had orders to shoot on the spot.

Because the fortress was so heavily guarded, no one thought a daytime escape was even possible. The greatest danger, it was believed, was that a band of the prince's supporters would try to overpower the fortress at night. Armed sentinels on the ramparts covered all approaches. No one was allowed near the fortress without prior consent, and anyone who approached was immediately taken into custody.

Because the fortress commander never got out of bed before 8 AM, 7 AM was chosen as the hour of escape. Plus, with an early departure, the prince could catch the 4 PM train for Belgium. This was on Saturday, May 23, 1846.

But that morning held a surprise. Visitors from England arrived to visit, a couple the prince knew from his time in London. And apparently they thought nothing of arriving early in the morning. Imagine the scene with the prince forcing smiles as he sat hearing about the children, Mr. and Mrs. so-and-so, etc., yawn, yawn. The escape was put off until Monday. But this presented a problem. By Saturday the workers would have nearly finished their work, and it was not guaranteed that they would return on Monday. No workers, no escape. Damn those nice people from London! But Thélin saved the day by requesting additional work on the building, and this was granted.

The most crucial part of the prince's disguise was shaving off his moustache. That done, there was no going back. Putting that razor to the face was a Rubicon, the last thing to do before stepping out the door. If the escape were aborted and the commander saw him clean-shaven, this would arouse suspicion and security would become draconian.

Imagine the tension as the prince contemplated the gauntlet he had to run that morning. His quarters were on the second floor of the building. At the end of the hallway was a staircase leading down to the courtyard with two armed guards posted at the bottom. Crossing the large, open courtyard, he had to face armed guards, soldiers, and sentinels everywhere. And an armed guard was posted at the Big Exit.

At 6:45 AM, Thélin and Conneau distracted the workers on the floor, offering them wine to drink and peppering them with questions about the repairs, while the prince slipped out the door, hiding behind the plank on his shoulder. Thélin continued his artful distractions, aiding the prince down the stairs, past the guards, and across the courtyard.

Thélin followed close behind, playing with the prince's dog Ham to draw attention. The prince walked up to the gate and was only feet from freedom when either by accident or calculation he lost control of the plank so that it swung towards the sergeant guarding the exit, who pulled away just in time while pulling the bolt on the gate to allow him to pass.

Finally outside, the prince saw two workmen approaching on the side of his exposed face. They looked at him quizzically. "Who's that guy?" one said to the other. "Dunno, never saw him before!" The prince heaved a feigned sigh of fatigue and transferred the plank to the other shoulder. The two men walked directly towards him, and his heart sank. Only feet away, one said to the other, "Oh, it's Berthoud!" and they walked on. The prince kept walking.

It wasn't even 8 AM, and the impossible had been accomplished. The fortress commander was still in bed, oblivious to the bad day before him. As the morning got underway, he wondered why he hadn't seen his charge and went to check on him. The prince was sick today, said Doctor Conneau. He was resting in bed and must not be disturbed. As part of the charade, the doctor had arranged a table in the room with glass bottles and vials of medicine.

"Wait here, I'll look in on him," said Conneau. He entered the prince's room, and in the ultimate ruse, downed spoonfuls of a purgative to induce vomiting and began loudly regurgitating in an impromptu performance of The Sickly Prince. Moments later, the doctor reappeared holding a basin with effluent to convince the commander. "Where's Thélin?" asked the commander. "He's gone out to buy more medicine." The commander peeked in the door to see the prince sleeping and quietly left.

Hours later, he returned and inquired again. "The prince is much better," Conneau said. He crept into his room and called his name but received no response, of course. "He's still sleeping," Conneau whispered. "Well, he can't sleep all day," said the commander. "I'll just wait here," he said and sat down.

Conneau distracted him with conversation until the commander grew impatient and said, "I think I heard him move. He must be up now!" Conneau tiptoed to the door to listen. "I don't hear a thing. We must let him sleep." The commander, at the end of his patience, entered the room and approached the bed. He touched the dummy and was startled. "He's gone?" "Yes, early this morning," replied Conneau. And all hell broke loose. Imagine the pandemonium, everyone yelling, "*Quoi! Comment! C'est pas possible!*" Everybody in the fortress was arrested—all the guards, the workmen, Conneau. When the commander's wife heard the news, she fainted. The poor commander was a ruined man and died not long afterward. Conneau received a three-month jail sentence.

The prince had one more fright before making it out of France. While waiting for the train in Valenciennes, Thélin heard someone call out his name. He turned around and was face-to-face with one of the gendarmes from Ham dressed in plain clothes. "What are you doing here?" Thélin asked, feigning coolness with the disguised prince sitting only feet away. "I left the gendarmerie and am working for the railroad now. And how's the prince?" "Oh, he's fine," said Thélin. And they parted.

Safe in London, the prince watched the gradual unraveling of the monarchy under King Louis-Philippe I. Attempts on the king's life were so common that he was nicknamed the "target king." Public appearances became impossible for fear of assassins.

Louis-Philippe's undoing came in February 1848. A demonstration near the Grands Boulevards turned bloody when government troops opened fire on unarmed civilians. The crowd of demonstrators became a mob and descended on the Tuileries Palace. Abandoned by his court, the king abdicated, donned a disguise, and along with his wife made it out of France for England.

Hearing this news, Prince Louis returned to Paris. One might ask here, given that Louis was an escaped convict, why wasn't he thrown back into prison? The reason was the total confusion in Paris after the abdication. No one knew what to do with the prince once he arrived in Paris. As one observer wrote, "No two people are agreed on the policy of the new government." Some wanted him arrested and sent back to prison.

Others wanted exile, while some argued that any action at all would only invigorate the Bonaparte cause. The public was enthralled at the news of his return, and print sellers did a brisk business selling his portrait.

In the confusion, the new government asked him to leave France, and Louis wisely returned to England. This took place in February. The following May, to the dismay of the government, Louis's supporters made him a write-in candidate in the election of representatives from France's 101 states, or "departments," as they are called. And he won in four departments. The following September he returned to Paris to take his seat in Parliament, and one can imagine he did this with no small sense of satisfaction. But this was only the beginning of his rise.

The following December, in 1848, presidential elections were held. Louis was on the ballot and won by a landslide. President of the Republic at last! But his sites were set higher yet. The constitution limited him to a four-year term with no possibility of a second term. His arguments against this prohibition were unsuccessful. So Louis staged a coup d'état on December 1, 1851, and in effect overthrew himself.

He dissolved the National Assembly, threw opposition leaders into jail, and had edicts drawn up declaring the rule of Emperor Louis Napoleon. The empire was back. Thousands were arrested and deported to the French colonies. Resistance erupted all around France. Demonstrations on the Grands Boulevards turned violent when government troops opened fire indiscriminately on men, women, and children, slaughtering hundreds. Victor Hugo, a staunch resistant of the coup, described this bloody scene in his work "Napoleon the Little." He fled France and lived in self-imposed exile on the isle of Guernsey for the duration of Napoleon's nineteen-year reign.

Napoleon III reigned until September 3, 1870. His fall from power was quick and ignominious. On September 2 he was the grand emperor of France. Two days later he was ex-emperor, a broken man. The reason was the Franco-Prussian War, the war that never should have happened.

Enmity between France and Prussia had been longstanding, and France was itching for a fight, certain it could not lose. In truth it was a fight that France could never win. The events leading up to this war are so preposterous that at every moment one wants to yell, "Wait! No! This must not happen!"

The catalyst for this sorry war was the situation in Spain. In 1870, the Spanish throne was vacant, and the main candidate to take over the monarchy was a Prussian prince. A Prussian on the Spanish throne would disrupt the balance of power in Europe, and the French protested with much saber rattling. Amazingly Prussia withdrew. That should have been the end of the story. But France was itching for a fight.

On July 13, 1870, while the king of Prussia was on his morning stroll in the town of Bad Ems, followed by his entourage, the French ambassador Benedetti approached and conveyed the message that while the French government was pleased at the withdrawal of the Prussian prince, they needed an assurance from the king that Prussia would never again consider presenting one of their own as a candidate for the Spanish throne. The Prussian king was ruffled at the request and put off giving an answer. That afternoon he communicated to Benedetti that he had nothing more to say. The exchange was polite, cordial. Voices were never raised. As Benedetti later said, "No one was insulting or insulted." Yet it was this interaction that lead to the Franco-Prussian War.

Dispatches of the exchange were sent to respective governments and foreign embassies, with each side slightly altering the dialogue to make the other side look worse. The French dispatch portrayed the Prussian king as insulting. The Prussian dispatch described the French as more demanding. On a background of previous hostility, these false dispatches inflamed the French public, who foolishly called for war.

Napoleon was actually more sober in the matter and was not so ready to lead his nation into battle. As one observer wrote, he did not fall victim to "that enthusiasm of the imagination which darkens reason and gives birth to illusions." But still, he was carried away by the delirium. The decision was made to invade Prussia. Enthusiastic crowds confidant of victory gathered at the train station and cheered on departing troops with cries of "Down with Prussia!" and "To Berlin!"

One general, when asked about France's readiness to go to war, replied, "Never have we been so ready, never shall we be so ready. War is inevitable. We don't lack a button."

Hubris. To say the French were unprepared for this war is an understatement. Troops arrived at the front with the wrong maps and no idea of where they were. Supplies and ammunition were short. The French were undisciplined and outnumbered. In a letter to the empress, Louis Napoleon described the scene: "Nothing is ready, the confusion indescribable." Three weeks later, with nearly one hundred thousand troops, he was forced to capitulate.

The scene of the official surrender stands out as an extraordinary moment in military history. The king of Prussia was present and greeted the French emperor with tears in his eyes, knowing the distress his adversary was feeling.

When rumors ran through Paris that the war was going badly, agitated crowds filled the boulevards day and night, stunned at the possibility of a reversal. The news of defeat sent the population into a state of frenzy. Shopkeepers who had proudly displayed insignias on their storefronts reading *Provider to the Emperor* could be seen climbing ladders, hammers in hand, to smash to bits their associations to the empire.

While the empress sat with her advisors receiving a steady stream of dispatches describing the events unfolding, the mob invaded the Chamber of Deputies and destroyed the imperial arms. Deputies defected to the side of the revolutionaries. Throughout the streets the cry "Long live the Republic!" rang out. The empress was urged to flee. Her life was in peril.

The mob was approaching. She grabbed a cloak, hat, and veil and rushed to her carriage, but she was advised against it. Traveling through Paris in a royal coach was a bad idea. By now the crowd was surging outside with cries of "Death!" She raced to a door leading to the Grande Galerie. If she could make it to the other end three hundred yards away and exit through the door, she could escape in a cab. But the door to the Galerie was locked.

With extraordinary luck Thélin happened to appear. The same Thélin who helped the emperor escape from Ham twenty-four years earlier was now Treasurer of the Empire and had the key to that door in his pocket. The door swung open, and Empress Eugenie made a mad dash down the long gallery, rushing by the museum's great collections. Ironically, the last painting she saw in her flight was Géricault's *The Raft of the Medusa*.

Out the door with her attendant Madame Lebreton, the two women mounted a cab to find refuge in Paris. They first went to the apartment of an advisor to the emperor, but no one was home. (No one was ever home in times like this. They were in the street or in the cafés getting the latest news.)

They then went to the house of the empress's dentist, a well-liked American, Thomas Evans. Evans was out, but a servant answered and took the women in. Evans returned and was stupefied to find the empress in his house. He put the women up for the night, and the next day they all mounted in his coach for the long and nerve-racking ride to the channel coast. Eugenie's biggest fear was that she would be apprehended like Marie Antoinette and taken back to Paris for a similar unhappy ending. But the fates carried her through. She made it to England and settled in Chislehurst. Napoleon was released by the Prussians after a short incarceration and joined her. He died a broken man two years later. Eugenie lived another fifty years, dying in 1920 in her native Madrid at age ninety-four.

Often it is the non-historians who write the most interesting works with insight and detail missed by the real historians. Thomas Evans is of this breed. His memoir of saving Empress Eugenie is riveting from start to finish. Of particular interest are his observations on the events that lead up to the Franco-Prussian War. Their parallel to our financial meltdown of 2008 is startlingly similar.

In both instances there was a long period of unparalleled growth and prosperity that created a state of delusion and unreal expectation. During Napoleon III's reign, France experienced the greatest period of industrial growth in its history. Paris had been transformed from a medieval city to a modern marvel that struck the world with awe. Nothing seemed out of reach for the French. Approaching their war with Prussia, they were deluded into thinking they were invincible. Their bubble burst in a matter of weeks with a war of grand humiliation. America was as deluded as the French as it sailed through the buoyant 1990s and early 2000s, until that bubble burst too.

In the weeks leading up to the Franco-Prussian War, Evans describes Paris as "possessed with a species of hysterical insanity, seized with irrepressible enthusiasm and wild excitement." A kind of intoxication made up of "a sordid and incoherent individualism filled people's minds with disastrous consequences." The French nation was "enticed away from all thought or concern for the public welfare by the demands of individual and private interest, the accumulation of wealth, the love of luxury and the display of personal possessions." Had Alan Greenspan been there he would have warned of an "irrational exuberance."

What a grim presage of our own time.

The Aftermath

The victorious Prussians returned the French gesture of aggression and proceeded to invade Paris. They laid siege to the city and for three months lobbed over one thousand bombs into Paris, most of which were ineffectual. The Parisians, cut off from all supplies, fell into a desperate state of starvation. The capital of La Grande Cuisine was reduced to killing zoo animals for food. Dining on sewer rats was not uncommon. When the Parisians could no longer resist the onslaught, the Prussians took the city. As the ultimate gesture of humiliation, the conquering Prussian troops entered the capital by marching under the Arc de Triomphe. This entrance held great symbolic value for the French, for this was the same way French troops traditionally entered Paris when returning victorious after battle. When the Prussians withdrew from the capital, the French poured gasoline over the ground under the Arc de Triomphe and set it afire as a purification.

This military debacle loosened long-standing political enmity in Paris between the ruling class and the proletariat. As tensions rose, the government fled to Versailles, leaving a power vacuum in the capital that was quickly filled by the workers, who took over city hall and declared the existence of a new revolutionary government. Everything was in place now for the bloody events of the civil war known as the Paris Commune. The whole affair lasted only six weeks. As government forces advanced from the west, retaking the city quarter by quarter, their ruthlessness increased. In the final week of May 1871, more than twenty thousand Parisians were butchered by other Parisians, brutal massacres in which defenseless men, women, and children were shot and sabred to death.

In the final hours of the Paris Commune, the rebel communards, facing imminent defeat, put the torch to every symbol of French imperial authority in Paris: city hall, Palais de Justice, and the Tuileries Palace.

Ironically, this palace had been sacked and burned during the revolution of 1848, and reconstruction had been completed only a few years before the Paris Commune. This time the palace was judged irreparable, and in 1882, the entire wing was demolished for good, creating the Louvre as we know it today.

While Paris lost its royal palace, it gained something else in its place that added immeasurably to the beauty of the city: a two-mile vista from the Louvre to the Arc de Triomphe, one of the most spectacular perspectives to be found in any capital in the world.

CHAPTER 11

MY DINNER WITH SIMSON

SIMSON AND I MET FOR DINNER IN Les Halles, the sprawling central food market of Paris, a great carnival of biology. Walking its streets was like taking a tour of the human body. There was the pungent aroma of cheap perfume sauntering by on spiked heels; the clochard's piss wafting out of a dark corner; the thick smell of a huge cheese, big as the wheel of a semi truck, cut open and sitting on the back of a flatbed truck; the smell of squashed fruit and vegetables lying underfoot; the huge cow carcasses hanging on iron hooks; and the wet, dripping fish stalls smelling of the ocean and sex. The *Saturday Evening Post* called Les Halles "The best show in Paris," and they were right.

The food stalls lining the sidewalk were punctuated by dimly lit doorways crammed with sexy young girls wearing tight-fitting blouses, miniskirts, and high-heeled shoes, smiling and gesticulating to the small packs of horny men ambling back and forth on the street, stopping here or there to appraise the merchandise. Prostitutes were all over the place. Any guy who wanted to could screw his mother, his school teacher, the girl next door, the fat lady from the circus, or the Jane Russell wannabe—they were all there lurking in some half-lit doorway or under a streetlamp. On every corner stood a café where the girls, the vendors, and the porters could grab a quick glass of wine or a bite to eat. Every block had one or two restaurants where late-night revelers could end their evening with a bowl of onion soup or a dish of pig's feet.

It was a Thursday night, and the market was in full swing. We went to my favorite restaurant on the corner of Rue Rambuteau and Rue Saint-Denis, Au Deux Saules. Our waiter, Jean-Pierre, was a master of his trade. A slender young man with sharply cut features and a shock of white hair, he moved around the outdoor tables with the grace and elegance of a world-class figure skater. For me he was a teacher. Every movement he made was just enough, never too much, and was performed with consummate grace. Watch him set a table: the large piece of paper, the table cloth, comes flying over head and lands right in front of you. Then, bang, the silverware and a basket of bread appear. One night he came gliding over with six full plates of food on his arm. He passed them out with the speed and precision of an orchestra conductor conducting the 1812 Overture, all the while chatting jauntily with the customers, and at the same time flicking a piece of bread lying underfoot into the street with his toe. I have not forgotten seeing him slice up a whole baguette.

"So how's it going with the up business?" Simson asked.

"I'm getting there, but there's still a lot I want to know." I told him about my reading, the connections I'd made, and gave him my quick version of the ballet as a history of aviation of the body and the few things I learned about the Scientific Revolution.

"Not bad," he said, swabbing a piece of baguette with some mustard. "You know, I've got some books at home you might want to look at. Let's go to my place after dinner."

In all the time I had known Simson, I never saw where he lived. This was typical of that old French formalism. You could know someone for years, live next door to them, and never see the inside of their apartment. They still address each other with *Monsieur* and *Madame*. Parisians meet in cafés and restaurants, they go to the movies or clubs, but hardly ever meet in homes.

Simson lived in Montparnasse on Rue Vercingétorix around the corner from La Coupole in a large, airy studio with a small kitchen tucked in the corner. Tall windows over the sink gave a view onto a courtyard. Best of all, he had his own bathroom with a shower. What a luxury. What caught my attention were the floor-to-ceiling bookshelves loaded with books on history, science, religion, and philosophy. "Simson, you never told me you had all this!"

"You never asked."

The evening grew chilly. We made a fire in the woodstove and settled into a couple of large overstuffed armchairs with glasses of Grand Armagnac. Simson lit up a Gauloises. He sat slouched in his chair, legs crossed, holding his cigarette at the very tip of his fingers. He took in a deep drag and exhaled slowly, blowing smoke rings.

"You know," he said, looking at his glass as if it were a crystal ball, "making connections between the dance and other things can get you in trouble."

"Really? How's that?" I asked.

"I don't know much about dance, but if it's anything like the sciences, you're going to rankle people. A big debate going on right now has to do with the contextualization of science, and that's what you're doing with the dance."

I had no idea what he was talking about.

"There's a group of historians of science, so-called 'purists,'" he said, "who believe that true science is not, and should not be, influenced by social conditions of any kind, be they political, economic, or whatever.

For them, any science that's been influenced by social conditions is con-taminated science. They deny that science even exists in a social context.

"Who are these people?" I asked.

"Oh, guys like Alexander Koyré, Arthur Koestler, Rupert Hall, Harold Baker, Michael Polanyi. The truth is that science has never been free of social influence, and since World War II it's been more obvious than ever. Before the war, the biggest science projects were small potatoes compared to today. All scientific work then was done mostly with private grants. But the war changed everything. Afterwards projects became so big that they had to be funded by the government. The only game in town became State science. The end of the war was the watershed that connected sci-ence to government. Those guys could never have penetrated nature with their long penile masculine atom smashers without massive government subsidies. So science free of government is an absurdity. It doesn't exist anymore. The problem is that science is so embedded in context that they can't see it.

"And who's on the other side of the issue?" I asked.

"Well, the big protagonists are people like J. D. Bernal, Joseph Need-ham, J. B. S. Haldane, Lancelot Hogben. They'd argue that it's impossible for science not to be influenced by external conditions. The only question for them is who's in charge, who's creating what social and economic con-ditions that will exert an influence on the sciences. In fact, Bernal wrote a book about it—*The Social Function of Science*. He argues that science should be rationally planned and democratically controlled in a Socialist state. I agree with the basic idea. It might be intellectually sophisticated to think that 'good' science is autonomous from society, but I think it's naive to think it's even possible. Anyway, my point is this: if Hall, Baker, Koyré, or any of the others were shakers and movers in the dance world, they'd probably give you a hard time and either deny that a connection exists or say it's bad dance. Or else you'll simply get people who'll argue that even if the ballet did come out of the court, that it's irrelevant, and that it had nothing to do with how the dance developed."

I shook my head. "That's like saying that Louis XIV's posture, the way he held himself, had nothing to do with the fact that he was king and never had to work. He could afford to wear high heels because he never had to lift anything. You've got to be very rich and have a lot of people working for you in order to afford the luxury of going up." I poured myself another Armagnac.

"But look," I said, "I'm more interested in the Scientific Revolution and what happened there. It seems to me there's a connection."

"How old do you think that is, the term *Scientific Revolution*?" Simson asked.

"I shrugged my shoulders. "I don't know. A couple of hundred years?"

"Try again," he said, raising his eyebrows. "Barely twenty years."

"You're kidding!"

"Yeah, I think it was Koyré who coined the term somewhere in the late 1930s. But it was Herbert Butterfield who brought the term into the English language in 1949 with his book *The Origins of Modern Science*, and it stuck."

"What took the historians so long to realize that a revolution had taken place?"

"Well, until the 1920s or '30s, there were no real specialists in the history of science. Most of the historians were retired scientists who believed that science was a slow accumulation of facts that led towards building this great edifice of science. This kind of slow and steady growth doesn't allow for a revolution. Besides, *revolution* was a political word, and it was hard to speak it in the same breath as *science*. They couldn't see the connection."

Simson scanned the bookshelves in the dim light. "Christ, can't see a thing." He picked up a flashlight, clicked it on, pulled a book off the shelf, and put it in my hands. It was Francis Bacon's *Novum Organon*. I glanced at the table of contents. He went over the shelves again and came back with a handful of books. "Here, this'll keep you going for a while."

I was overwhelmed and took a couple of generalist books plus one on Bacon and Descartes. That was good for a start. I brought up the wooden African statues with the bent knees again.

"You know, I honestly haven't thought about it," Simson said. "Not that I should have, but it is an interesting question. What do the art historians say? They probably have an opinion."

"I don't know. I've never read much art history, except in high school."

"My bet is that no one really knows, but if they do, you can be sure they've written a paper about it."

"Well, it puzzles me," I said. "You find it everywhere in the world, from different periods and different places. People don't stand that way naturally."

Just then there was a knock at the door. It was Theo, one of the most extraordinary people I knew in Paris. "I was walking in the neighborhood," he said. "I saw the light and thought to stop in." Theo was tall and lanky like a stork. He bore an uncanny resemblance to another more famous Frenchman, Antonin Artaud: the same high cheekbones and deep-set eyes, the same thin lips, the long, fine nose and black hair combed straight back, and that faraway look.

We exchanged greetings. While Simson poured another glass, Theo took off his overcoat and sat down near the fire. He lit up a cigarette and took in a long deep drag that sucked in his cheeks, making his face look like a fearsome mask.

Theo was a mass of eccentricities. He didn't like undressing or changing clothes. So he never took off his pajamas and wore them under his street clothes. He hated public transportation and walked great distances across Paris travelling to his job as a night watchman in a factory or to visit friends.

He disliked bathing. Several friends succeeded in getting him into a bathtub once, but only after bribing him with a bottle of champagne. He liked eating, but he didn't like swallowing. During a dinner his cheeks would puff up like a squirrel's, stuffed with food that he would eventually be forced to swallow.

As if Theo's idiosyncrasies were not enough to put him on the margin of society, he had one quality that pushed him to the edge of the known world. This was his singular talent as a psychic. His ability to read the lines on your hand, your handwriting, or your astrological chart and tell you more than you cared to know was legendary in Paris.

We hadn't been sitting there for more than few minutes when there was another knock at the door, and a few minutes later, another. Because telephones were so rare in Paris, dropping in on people, something seldom done today, was common then. On the rare occasions when a number of people all had the same idea to converge on the same address at the same time, a joyful spontaneous combustion of humans took place creating what can only be called a great old time.

There were Ben and Christine, he a Yiddish folk singer, she a translator. Yael, an attractive Israeli girl studying in Paris. Josh and Vickie, New Yorkers living in Paris—she was Jewish, he was black. Their son Kim and a couple of his friends came too. In Paris, racially mixed marriages were accepted, and Josh and Vickie enjoyed the ease of walking down the street without attracting stares. Within half an hour, Simson's studio filled with chatter, smoke, and the sound of jazz coming from the record player.

Vickie reached over to a basket of fruit on the kitchen counter and picked up an apple. "Look at this!" she exclaimed, holding the apple in the air like a prized find. "A worm hole! I haven't seen one of these in years!" This was to be taken as a sign of the wholesomeness of French living. No pesticides, etc.

One of Kim's friends, someone who had heard about Theo, thrust his hand out and half-jokingly exclaimed, "Read my hand!" He had no idea of the deep water he was treading into.

Theo grabbed his hand and bent forward to look closely. "Don't move," he said, his eyes riveted to the palm as he fumbled through his coat pockets for another cigarette. He lit up and began a description of this fellow's inner life as if he were looking directly into his DNA.

He told him what problems he had dealt with in the past and what he was dealing with now. He knew what cycles he had gone through previously and what cycle he was currently in. He told him about the people who were most important in his life, those who were good and bad for him. He told him about his present relationship, where it was going. He told him what was working in his life and what wasn't, and on and on. What began as a lark turned dead serious. The fellow left looking disoriented.

Theo sat slumped in his chair. "I see too much," he said. "I can't stop seeing. Sometimes I think it's going to carry me away." He grasped my hands and looked upward as if scanning the sky. "It's my fate. I was born like this. What can I do?"

He dropped my hands and smiled. "It's all René's fault. Had I met him, everything would have been different."

"René?"

"You don't know René?" he said. "Of course you do. Everyone knows René." He looked around on the floor, calling out in a singsongy voice like someone looking for their cat, "René, where are you? Renéeee! Come here, my little one!"

"Who's René?" I said. Theo leaned forward and looked into my eyes. "Of course you know René, my dear Leonard. He's your best friend." I shrugged. Theo bolted up from his chair and stood like a general at attention, raising his finger to make a point. He took on a melodramatic air, squinted his eyes, and bellowed, "*Je pense, donc je suis.*" (I think, therefore I am.)

"That René?" I said.

"I live, therefore I fart," he exclaimed. He contorted his body into a comic pose and, pursing his lips, let out a slow squeal of a Bronx cheer.

Everyone broke out laughing. Slightly embarrassed by this success, Theo sat down and lit up another cigarette.

"You're lucky. You know René," he said. "But I never met him. Not like you." He snapped his head back, closed his eyes, and swooned, "Ah, the rational mind is a beautiful thing, is it not?" He heaved a big sigh and sat gazing at his cigarette. "It's so crazy," he muttered.

Then he held his hand up in front of me, fingers splayed. "See this?" he said, pointing to his hand. "Here is the world, all of life! And this, you see this?" He pointed to a freckle on his hand. "This is our little rational mind. It thinks it's everything, that it knows everything. It has no idea that it's on the hand or that the hand is even there. Ha! Funny, no? If you live only on the freckle, all the better. What luck! I'd like to live there. But there's no more room. See the sign? FULL! NO MORE ROOM! It's not my fate. No, I see too much."

Yael had received a letter that day written in Hebrew from an Israeli friend in Italy. She showed it to Theo. He didn't even know that Hebrew was written from right to left, yet he told Yael things about her friend that were astonishing because she knew them to be true. As a kicker, he told her that her friend drove a Vespa, and he told her how he drove it.

Theo took my hand and looked at it intently. "You're going to have a school someday, Leonard, a spiritual theatre school." He also said I would go to Denmark for work and would not like it. Right he was. I spent six months there in 1970 and did not like it. Just then someone called out, "Hey, Theo, why don't you sing something!" "I can't sing," he said, "but because you ask, I'll try." Theo actually had an astonishing voice. Some years earlier he had auditioned for orchestra conductor Herbert von Karajan. That in itself signifies a voice of note. He closed his eyes, brushed back his hair, tilted his head down, and launched into Boris Godunov with a basso profundo voice with all the power of a thunderstorm rolling across an open plain. When he finished, everyone cheered. Theo smiled nervously and lit another cigarette.

In Paris all social gatherings were regulated by the clock. Since no one had a car, everyone had to make the last Métro. So around twelve thirty we broke up. Theo walked me to the Métro station. Along the way I brought up the business about up and down, the bent knees in the African statues, the ballet, etc. "They're both seeking their god," he said. "They both hear the same call, but they go in opposite directions." I stopped still. "Whew! Theo, where do you get this stuff?"

"You're a searcher, aren't you, Leonard? Too bad. You'll need many lives to do everything. At least you'll never get bored." He entered the café to buy cigarettes, and I walked down the stairs to the Métro.

*   *   *   *

One Saturday night Penelope and I went dancing in the Rue de Lappe off the Place de la Bastille. This was working-class Paris, someplace tourists never went and where wealthier Parisians frequented only if they were out for some local color. Today this is one of Paris's trendier neighborhoods, with hip restaurants, cafés, and clubs catering to the young.

One of the more popular clubs on the street, Au Ballon Rouge, had a dance band made up of ageing musicians from the neighborhood playing limping waltzes or raggedy two-steps while the locals let off some steam. Simple tables were arranged in rows, each with a candle for atmosphere. A few cheap decorations hung from the lighting fixtures. The band played on a small stage, poorly lit with a faded backdrop strung on the wall. Penelope and I played at imitating people on the dance floor and then trying to guess who the other was doing. We sat at a side table and ordered a beer that had to last us through the evening.

A thin woman with a ramrod back and an expressionless face twitched and shook her hips like a rattle on the end of a stick while her upper body didn't budge. She wore no makeup or any jewelry except for a large cross around her neck. Here was the Virgin Mary and Fatima the hoochie-coochie dancer rolled into one.

One couple danced a waltz while the man smoked a cigarette. He smoked in that typical French fashion, with the cigarette stuck in the middle of the upper lip. They swirled and turned, dipped and paused. They talked to each other all the while they danced, and all the time his cigarette kept puffing. They must have had glass eyeballs not to be bothered by that smoke. He had pomaded hair combed straight back and sported a handkerchief in the breast pocket of his worn, threadbare jacket. She, in heels and a tight skirt, wore a fancy pin in her hair and a scarf around her neck. They danced a waltz and looked like their heads were on fire.

A very fat man danced with a woman who was even fatter than he. They held each other close with chubby little hands, their big bellies touching; their faces were full of glee.

CHAPTER 12

OCEANS OF BLACK INK

SIMSON'S STATEMENT ABOUT THE importance of understanding the context of the dance was key to my study. The more I read, the more things began to fall into place.

On the surface the Romantic Ballet was a reaction to the staid Greco-Roman classicism that had dominated the arts since the Renaissance. The emotional restraint of a former age gave way to a frank admission of feeling—longing, joy, desperation. But on a deeper level the Romantic Ballet was a response to the onslaught of the Industrial Revolution. *La Sylphide* was like a taproot penetrating to the psychological subcurrent of the era. Look at the context. By the 1830s, the natural world was under assault by an Industrial Revolution that changed the landscape of Europe. Towering smokestacks filled the sky with smoke and grime. Thousands left their farms to seek a better life in cities, only to find themselves mired in the worst that progress had to offer: crowded tenements, rampant disease, and an unrelenting rhythm that told people when to eat, sleep, work, and rest.

One outcome of the Industrial Revolution in America was the creation of large public parks—Central Park, Golden Gate Park—known then as "pleasure grounds." These urban treasures we take for granted today were intentionally created by city planners as an antidote to the crushing experience of living in a thoroughly industrialized and dehumanizing urban environment. When Central Park was created in the 1850s, handbills were posted around New York City advertising the benefits of fresh air and sunlight and recommending that mothers bring their children to the park for health reasons.

Park designers consciously prohibited the building of anything suggestive of the city or the workplace. Roads and paths were curved in order to counter the grid layout of city streets. Craftwork was not allowed in the parks because it was too close to factory labor. The only activities encouraged were those using large muscle groups—rowing, strolling, riding, lawn tennis. This attempt to reintroduce pleasure and physicality into people's lives was to a degree mitigated by the morality of the time. At the musical concerts held regularly in Central Park, the German Polka was not allowed because it was deemed too stimulating and might incite people to dance. Accepted music had to be spiritually uplifting and dignified, either military or classical music.

Early on, writers and artists saw the wave of alienation sweeping over them. In 1829, Goethe attacked the heart of the mechanistic worldview and wrote of Descartes's philosophical system, "It seemed to us so gray, monstrous and death-like that we could hardly stand it. We shuddered as if facing a ghost." Poet Friedrich Hölderlin railed against those rationalists for whom "the earth is a corpse." English writer Thomas Carlyle described this mechanistic universe as "all void of Life, of Purpose or Volition, even of Hostility . . . one huge, dead, immeasurable Steam Engine, rolling on, in its dead indifference, to grind me from limb to limb."

Writer Charles Kingsley praised the exhibitions of landscape paintings in museums where he could take a "country walk . . . beyond the grim city-world of stone and iron, smoke chimneys and roaring wheels." While France did not feel the full force of the Industrial Revolution until the 1850s, by the 1830s it was clear what was in store. The connection between humans and nature was eroding.

The Romantic Ballet sprang from an intuitive recognition of this loss and objectified that loss in the figure of the ballerina. The sylph *was* nature, the object of our adoration forever eluding our grasp. With the advent of the Romantic Ballet, the ballerina became a full-fledged cultural phenomenon commanding unheard-of salaries and the adoration of kings. Nature, at first sacrificed on the alter of progress, was then placed on a pedestal to be worshipped. The male dancer was reduced to a mere porter capable only of supporting the ballerina. Many even despised him. Critic Jules Janin described him as something "so sad . . . He responds to nothing, he represents nothing, he is nothing."

What the Industrial Revolution took away, the Romantic Ballet sought to give back: a sense of connection to the natural world. But there was an irony. Rather than bringing us closer to nature, toe dancing and the ballet only confirmed the mechanistic view that took us out of nature in the first place. Lincoln Kirstein referred to the ballet as an "abdication of the flesh." True enough. How can we reconnect with the natural world while denying the body and turning it into an artifact? How do we feel integrated with nature or the body when we view it as an adversary and seek only to control it?

At best the Romantic Ballet offered the illusion of escape from a world suffering from a surfeit of rationalism and gave us a glimpse of our repressed side, the lyrical, emotional, intuitive. In the end the revolution of the Romantic Ballet was only partial. The real revolution would have been to protest the ballet's disincarnation and to reintroduce the body back into the dance. What the dance needed was an Isadora Duncan: find the ground, feel your body, breathe! But it was too early for anything so radical. The very precondition for the Romantic Ballet, a yearning for the unattainable, demands distance. The effort to reconnect with nature had to fail. A cultural dilemma was made into an art form.

*   *   *   *

Penelope and I left Decroux's and took the Métro over to the Latin Quarter for lunch. There was something different about her, but I couldn't tell what. I told her about my latest finds in the world of ideas, and she told me about the movie she saw the night before with Andrew.

"Andrew! Who's Andrew?" I asked.

"He's a boy from London I met not long ago. Nice enough chap. He reads Ezra Pound all day long. He phoned up and invited me to the cinema. We had a good time, actually."

I bristled. I asked her what movie they saw, and she told me, but I couldn't hear a word. I continued bristling.

"What did you do after the movie?" I asked.

"Oh, we walked around Saint-Germain and then stopped for a coffee."

I could feel my back getting rigid.

"Well, actually, we screwed," she said.

"You what!" I was stunned.

"We screwed," she said nonchalantly.

"You screwed! What . . . how, where . . . when!" I sputtered.

"After the café he invited me to his place. At first I didn't think anything of it. But then he started getting fresh and, you know . . ." She shrugged her shoulders.

"I was stammering now. "B-b-but getting fresh doesn't mean you have to screw!"

"Well, you said it was like brushing your teeth, that it was no big deal. So, I thought I'd try it."

She continued talking, but I couldn't hear. My ears were ringing. Everything around me was dripping with fire—the buildings, the people, everything was in flames. "Are you going to see him again?" I muttered. I could barely hear my own words.

"No . . . it wasn't that great. Besides he's not my type."

"Yeah, but I guess he was enough your type to screw, wasn't he!"

"So we did it. There's no use getting upset. In fact, it was nothing. I think I'm sorry now that I even did it with him. I don't see what all the fuss is about."

I was dying to see who this guy was. I just wanted to know what he looked like. Was he so good looking? Was he so smooth? *Just give me a glimpse of the bastard. Please, I won't kill him. I promise. I just want to see him!*

A few days later Penelope left for England to visit her family. I called her on the phone. We sent postcards. When she returned a couple of weeks later, we met at my place.

We were lying on the bed, arms around each other. We wriggled out of our clothes and got under the covers. She was different now. The hesitation was gone. We hugged and kissed and stroked. I became crazy with excitement as she pulled me closer and kissed me again and again. *My god, this can't be real, I must be dreaming!* I opened my eyes for a second. *Yeah, it's her all right, and we're naked!* Our wet bodies slid all over each other. *Wait a minute . . . what's happening? What! Oh no . . . c'mon. I can't get a hard on. No!* I was on top of Penelope looking down at her beautiful face, her large, full breasts. Nothing happened. I kissed her madly, trying to get turned on. Nothing was happening. Her face was contorted in expectation. She held me tighter. Nothing was happening. I thrust my pelvis. Nothing was happening. *Oh, Christ!*

We lay there quietly. I felt awful, dumbfounded with confusion. Penelope looked at me. "Don't worry," she said half smiling. "It's OK. It's nothing."

"Nothing!" I was devastated. We dressed in silence and took the elevator downstairs to catch the Métro to Decroux's. It took years to get there as we wallowed through oceans of dense, black ink. This had never happened to me. I didn't even know this could happen. *There must be something wrong with me. I must have some deep psychological problem. What a joke. Me, the great movement guy with all the incredible body control, and I can't even get a hard on! Is God playing a joke on me?*

For days I could barely function. My world was caving in all around. I had to rethink everything now: *What am I doing in Paris? Am I with Decroux out of some weird mental compensation for a basic physical disability?* Worse yet, I was sure Penelope would never want to see me again. Damn!

The next day I arrived early to class and took Madame Decroux aside. "I have to talk to you," I whispered. "It's important. Can we go somewhere quiet?"

"Yes, yes, of course," she said, with a look of apprehension. She led me into the tiny bathroom and locked the door behind her. "What is it, my boy?"

"I've got a problem that I can't talk about. It's something psychological. All I can tell you is that I might have to leave the school and return to America. I'll have to see a psychiatrist."

"What! What is it, my boy? What's wrong?"

"I can't tell you, Madame. It's just something I have to work out on my own."

She moved closer. "You can tell me. What is it? What is it, my boy?"

I cringed inside. "Really, I can't tell you, Madame, I can't. It's too personal."

She grabbed me by the shoulders and looked me square in the eyes. "Yes you can," she said. "You must. Tell me, my boy, what is it?"

"I can't tell you. Honest, I can't!" I could hardly look at her.

"I know what it is!" she said. "You can't get it up!"

I was stunned. "How did you know?"

She burst out laughing. "So, that's it? Ha! I thought it was something serious. But that? Oh, it's nothing!" She roared with laughter.

I didn't know what to say. I was totally confused. Madame Decroux sat on the edge of the bathtub and laughed uproariously. I leaned on the sink and buried my face in my hands.

"How did you know?" I said.

She looked at me and shook her head. "You're so crazy," she said. "Listen, it's nothing. It's really nothing. When Maximillien was younger, he couldn't do it with blondes. He'd come home and say, 'Mama, I don't know what it is, but I just can't do it with blondes.' Look, why don't you have a good heart-to-heart with Étienne. It'll do you good." I couldn't face talking to Decroux about something like this. That would be like talking to Winston Churchill about your sex life. "Then go see my doctor, Doctor Venelle. Talk to him," she said. "I'll pay for the visit."

"Let me think about it," I said. "I dunno."

She threw her arms around me. "Don't worry, my boy," she whispered. "It'll be OK. Everything will be fine."

With each day I became more consumed by this contradiction in my life. About a week later, I walked out of the movie theatre on the Place de l'Odéon with a splitting headache. It was around 11 PM, dark, chilly, and drizzling. Good gloom weather. I was lucky I wasn't big on alcohol or I would've been sunk. The thought of trying to start my life over somewhere else seemed impossible. Did I really have to leave Paris? I didn't know what to think or to do. Religion had never been a big part in my life, but now, faced with the hopelessness of my dilemma, I was driven to the wall. "Oh, God!" I cried out. "Give me a sign, something, anything to tell me that I'm not deranged, that there's a way out!" Just then I heard a voice behind me.

"Bonsoir, Leonard!"

I didn't know it then, but here was my salvation.

I turned around. It was Nadia, a classmate at Decroux's. I hardly recognized her. I had never seen her in anything other than tights and leotards.

Now she was dressed up, and what a little eye makeup and lipstick can do. We walked to a café across the street and got a table at the window. Before we knew it, it was past twelve thirty. Nadia glanced at her watch. "*Merde!* I missed the last bus to Châtillon. Leonard, can I stay at your place tonight? I have no way to get home."

I gulped. "Yeah, uh, sure, no problem." *She probably thinks I'm some rich American with a big apartment. Wait'll she sees my little room and my tiny bed.*

The next morning I rushed out of the Métro station near Decroux's and met Madame on her way back from the market. I took her grocery bags, and she heaved a big sigh. "*Mon Dieu*, either I'm getting older or these bags are getting heavier." We entered the house, and she emptied the bags on the kitchen table. "Madame," I said, barely breaking a smile. "Uh . . . I won't have to see your doctor after all." She threw her arms around me. "You see!" she exclaimed, "I told you everything would be OK! I knew it, my boy, I knew it!"

*   *   *   *

My worst fears that Penelope would have nothing to do with me were never realized. We even found ourselves in bed again and with greater success on my part. One day she surprised me with news that she had met a boy, Timothy, and that they were serious. My heart sank. I'd met him once. He was a poet, the romantic type, very serious and intense looking. He was also extremely jealous. Penelope couldn't look at the crotch of a tree without him flying into a rage. They married, had two children, and traveled to Africa, where he had a teaching post at a university.

*   *   *   *

One day Berthe informed me that she would be leaving Paris for several weeks to visit her sister in Switzerland. Saskia told me the truth: she was going to dry out in a clinic outside of Geneva. When she returned she looked better than I had seen her look in a long time. Unfortunately, the one thing she did not learn in Switzerland was how to handle Hubert.

A few days later, I arrived home and found him standing in the dimly lit hallway in front of Berthe's door. Clad in his rumpled raincoat, he puffed furiously on a cigarette. He saw me and blurted out, "She threw me out; it's over! I can't believe it. She threw me out the door!"

"I'm sorry," I said.

"Yes, but now I'm free!" he shrieked. "I'm a free man. It's great! I can do whatever I want. I don't have to stay here any more!" He waved his arms wildly in the air. "I can do anything, go anywhere. I'm free!" For a man luxuriating in newfound freedom, he made little effort to actually enjoy his freedom and instead stalked back and forth in the cramped, dark hallway, puffing away furiously on his cigarette. I walked down the hall to my room while he continued muttering to himself, "I'm free. I don't have to be here anymore. I can go anywhere. I can leave. I'm free. I'm free!"

In a few days Hubert recouped from this setback and began applying his subtle technique of winning Berthe back. "Look at you," he told her, "You're nothing. Who's going to care for you? I'm the only one who loves you. You'll never find anyone." He knew exactly when to pull out the bottle of wine, to offer her a little drink to make her feel better, and that was that. Their relationship dragged on in this truncated fashion for several more years, becoming even more bizarre as time passed.

*　　*　　*　　*

Paris weather was unpredictable. Summers were no longer summers and winters were no longer winters, or so they said. Madame Decroux was certain it was because of "*la bombe*." Often times a day started out sunny and warm and by afternoon turned cold and overcast. I'd go out to sell newspapers and not know what weather to dress for: cold, warm, wet, dry. Other times the weather was predictable, like when it turned gray and stayed that way for weeks. The sky hung over Paris in one mass of gray. Humans then were no different from horses. We all saw in black and white.

*   *   *   *

One summer I found temporary respite from my poverty by getting a job painting the shutters on a large estate outside of Paris in the town of Nogent-sur-Marne. It was a large three-story house with a circular drive in front, tennis courts, a swimming pool, separate servant's quarters, the works. One afternoon I was perched on a ladder in the front of the house when a young woman, the daughter of the owner, drove up in her little sports car. Later that afternoon I bumped into her in the garden, and we struck up a conversation. Her name was Paulette, and she had large hazel eyes with short brown hair and an olive complexion. Her fluent English was very French. I was won over in a second. We talked about nothing in particular, and I could tell she was having as good a time as I was. Then a great downpour struck. "Queek, follow me," she said. We ran up the stairs through the French doors into a large sitting room. I looked around in awe. This was light-years from my little maid's room; I gazed at the elegant plush furnishings, a large brick fireplace, thick carpeting, period cabinets full of old plates and figurines, and delicate tables with small lamps. "Would you like a cup of tea, or a coffee perhaps?" she asked.

"Coffee, sure." What a bizarre picture, me in my cap and overalls covered with paint and her, well, she could put the word *lovely* to shame.

After a while the rain let up, but I never got back to work. We spent the afternoon talking about art, literature, music, and why American coffee was so bad. Paulette was a remarkable young woman. At the age of twenty-two she was already the mother of two children and had a degree in art history from the Sorbonne. By the time I met her she had graduated with honors and was angry. She applied for the position of assistant curator at the Jeu de Paume, the Impressionist museum, and was turned down for no other reason than that she was a mother. Her husband Jacques inherited the family business and had become a wealthy businessman. Paulette was disillusioned. The money meant nothing to her. She'd married a man with spirit and imagination, and now he was only a businessman.

She had heard of Decroux. "Yes, he is one of those famous people unknown to most French. He was the teacher of Jean-Louis Barrault, was he not? Decroux is what we call in French *un monstre sacré*," she said. A sacred monster is admired by everyone, but only from a distance because he can be so difficult. Sounded like Decroux all right. I told her about my interest in the ballet and the court of Louis XIV. "Oh, yes, a very important period," she said. "Can you imagine where France would be without Louis? We would have no furniture!" She laughed.

"Did you ever wonder," she said, "why we French became so fixated on the dance and the Italians on the opera? I have often wondered that."

Now there was a thought.

"But the classical dance, I do not find it so very interesting," she said. "It is beautiful, of course. Elegant, but so predictable. In Louis's time I think the dance must have been abominably boring. The courtiers were such snobs. They were only interested in how they looked. Have you seen the paintings of Brueghel and the scenes of the village folk dance? They are so wonderful. Now that must have been fun. But surely, if you are interested in dance, you must know a lot about folk dancing. It is so different from the dancing of the royalty and the court, is it not?"

"Yeah, sure, I guess so," I said. I had no idea. I wasn't interested in dance history per se. I just wanted to know why the ballet went up, and because of that, I focused on a very small part of the dance. But now . . . hmm. I stood at the door saying good-bye. "Maybe we can get together again," I said. She gave me her phone number in Paris.

The following week we arranged to meet, this time at my place for lunch. I was nervous as hell. *Her in my place?* I straightened up my room, stacked all of my books, and put my notebooks away.

It was late afternoon. We lay in bed bundled up under the blanket. She reached over for some grapes on the table. I jumped out of bed and started dressing. I had to be at Decroux's by 5 PM. "You should be more free with your body," she said. "Huh, what do you mean?" I said, pretending not to know what she meant.

"For someone studying an art such as you, you're not always very comfortable with your body." I combed my hair in the mirror and gathered up some books. "It's OK," she said. "You have a very nice body."

I felt defensive. "It's just that I'm in a hurry, that's all."

"You weren't in a hurry in bed," she said, laughing. She was right. I was never at ease with my body but was too embarrassed to admit it. Just a few days before, I was alone in my room at night getting undressed for bed. I stood naked and felt embarrassed.

*   *   *   *

16 Avenue de l'Opéra. What a deceiving address. Here I was living in what was no more than a monk's cell on one of the fanciest avenues in Paris. I walked into the lobby and found Richard waiting for the elevator. He broke into a wily smile. "What's up?" I asked. He pulled a small piece of paper out of his pocket and held it up. A name and phone number were scribbled on it. "Oh, no," I groaned. He shrugged with a sheepish smile. Just then Saskia arrived, her arms full of grocery bags. Richard stuffed the paper into his pocket. "Hi, sweetie," he said, giving her a peck on the cheek. The elevator squeaked its way down and arrived with a thud. Slow ride up. Two fresh baguettes stuck out of Saskia's shopping bag. I broke off the end of one and bit into it. "Why don't you join us for dinner tonight," she said. Great. I wouldn't have to cook, and it meant company.

We dined in their room, a little larger than my own on the avenue side with a window overlooking the street. While Saskia busied herself in the kitchen, Richard showed me some recent photos he had shot of Salvador Dali at his villa in Spain. It was hard to imagine Richard and Dali together, but there was the proof. After dinner Saskia brought in a tray of fruit. She sat down and began peeling an apple. Saskia must have been a bird in another lifetime. She had a thin, wiry body with quick movements. When she spoke her eyes bulged out and darted around the room, particularly when she wanted to make a point. Her high cheekbones, sharply cut nose, and small mouth, with corners pinched back, put her in the family of eagles or condors.

Saskia loved apples. You could tell by the way she handled the knife—quick, deft, sure. Simple everyday movements were a source of fascination for me. Small movements like peeling an apple when done with economy were beautiful little dances with rhythm and flow, a kind of intelligence where the energy was not too much, but just enough to accomplish the task.

"You must never eat the skin," she said. "Too many poisons."

"Apples, poison?" I said.

"You're just a city boy," she fired back. "What would you know? I was raised on a farm. I know what they do. This apple was once covered with chemicals. Washing isn't enough. You must get rid of it completely." She quartered the apple and bit into a chunk with obvious pleasure.

Richard asked me how the "dance thing" was going. I told him I was still trying to figure out why the ballet went up. Saskia leaned back in her chair and threw her long blond hair over her shoulders as she finished her apple. She lit up an English cigarette. "I hate those French cigarettes," she said, sucking in the smoke. I hate that black tobacco; it's awful for you. Blond tobacco is much better."

"What I don't get," I said, "is why primitive African statues of people standing always have their knees bent."

"Maybe they're gonna take a shit," Richard said, laughing. "Ever think of that?"

Saskia groaned and rolled her eyes. "You always have to make things so dirty," she said.

"Wait a minute," Richard said, "I know. They just *took* a shit. That's it!" He roared with laughter.

Saskia pulled out another cigarette and lit up.

Richard scowled. "Oh puh-leese, Saskia, one's bad enough, but two! How about a little health, is that out of style?"

Saskia smashed the cigarette in the ashtray, grabbed an apple, and bit into it.

*   *   *   *

Paulette's comments about folk dance kept nagging. I pulled a couple of books off the shelf. Curt Sachs's classic work *World History of the Dance* became my book of the month and helped me see through some of the confusion. Some things I was not clear about, and did not know I was not clear about, became clear. Sachs helped me understand the difference between social dancing (dancing for one's own pleasure) and concert dancing (dancing for an audience). Social dancing is probably as old as humans and dancing. Concert dancing originated around the fourteenth century, during the Italian Renaissance, and is an outgrowth of the great balls staged in the courts of the period.

More ancient yet is the ecstatic dance, dating back thousands of years to the earliest human cultures. In the ecstatic dance the dancer enters into a trance and becomes possessed with the spirit of a deceased ancestor, an animal, or a god. This dance springs from the subconscious of a culture, and its fulfillment ties into the psychic well-being of the community. In some cultures, Sachs points out, men stood on the side with bows and arrows to shoot those who performed the dance poorly.

With the rise of Christianity around 300 A.D. the ecstatic dance began to die out in Europe. From then on the dominant form of dance among the peasantry and royalty both was social dancing. The folk dance of the peasantry was sociable and fun. That great chronicler of peasant life, Pieter Brueghel, depicts peasants dancing with exuberance and a total lack of self-consciousness. Paulette was right. People jumped, jiggled, shook, laughed, and tumbled. Because the peasants lived an agrarian life tied into the cycles of nature—birth, death, regeneration— their dance took place as part of communal celebrations marking the passing of the seasons, the planting and harvest, the fertility of the land. The royalty, on the other hand, led a life less directly affected by nature. Good weather or bad weather, their well-being was hardly affected. After God, the greatest power in their realm was themselves. Their dance was more about the stability of their own power structure, its increase and preservation.

For hundreds of years there was a give-and-take between the court dance and peasant dance. The peasants took on the style or manner of a court dance to lend an air of elegance to their own dance. Or the nobility took a peasant dance and dressed it up in order to make it acceptable to the more formal behavior of the court.

The minuet, for example, was originally a peasant dance that was introduced into the court in the early 1700s and cleansed of its "primitiveness." Sachs quotes one observer who wrote in 1728, "What a happy fate . . . that the minuet, ugly, insignificant, and lowly as it was, could become so splendid . . . in the course of time that one entirely forgot its humble birth!" This theme of the upper classes borrowing from the lower classes has played out many times since. Over and over again white America has taken the African-American rhythms of ragtime, jazz, and early rock and roll and "sanitized" them to meet their own inhibitions.

The exchange between the court and peasant dance ended around the mid-1400s, when the first dancing masters appeared in the Italian courts. These men codified the dance, the steps and movements across the floor, and in this way developed the first principles of choreography. Compared to the restrained elegance of the dancing masters, the animation of the peasant dance was disdainful. In 1463, the early dancing master Guglielmo Ebreo described the popular dance as fit for "the vicious and artless common people who frequently, with corrupt spirits and depraved minds, turn it from a liberal art and virtuous science, into a vile and adulterous affair."

Quite a stiff reproach. What was so vile and adulterous? Paulette was right. It was their abandon, their imagination and letting go, that sent shudders through the courtiers. Compared to their calculated restraint, the peasants looked like a band of hysterics out of control.

The drama of the minuet was repeated in the 1770s when the waltz was introduced into the ballroom. Here was a threat to the rigid control and repressed sensuality in the very heart of the court. For the first time a man and woman faced each other while dancing in public. Many cried scandal. Worse yet, they held each other with both hands, and they were turning. Oh, that intoxicating turning! There was no precedent for this close contact between men and women in public. Proper men and women danced side-by-side, touching only the tips of the fingers. There was little eye contact. The waltz exploded the social relations of men and women and drove people wild—not only those who danced, but those who refused to dance. In the Age of Reason losing your mind was not a recommended form of social behavior.

CHAPTER 13

MY FIFTEEN MINUTES OF FAME

ONE DAY I DISCOVERED THE BEAUTY of simple geometric forms—a cube, a sphere, a pyramid. There was something powerful and enigmatic in these forms that were so simple and unequivocal. A sphere has no desire to be anything else than what it is, and it is that. I bought some sticks of balsa wood at a hobby shop and constructed a simple cube that I hung from the ceiling in my room. I cut additional lengths of balsa and fit them diagonally on the sides of the cube. This was the first thing I saw in the morning when I awoke. There was a simple beauty to this pure form as it turned slowly in the air against the silence of my room.

From making this form I learned that I liked the feel of working with wood. I also discovered Japanese rice paper. I bought more balsa wood and made small, flat screens covered with rice paper that could be used as a shade in front of a candle or a lightbulb. I made a number of these screens and sold them to friends for a few dollars. It then occurred to me that if I could construct simple, attractive shapes made of balsa wood—modules of sorts that required less handwork—and could assemble these modules in interesting ways, that maybe I could sell these to friends and make a little money.

One day, as I lay on my bed watching the cube turn in midair I saw the diagonal sticks of balsa instead of the cube itself. Together these diagonals formed a pyramid. I hadn't noticed this pyramid inside the cube before. *Maybe this is the module I've been looking for.* I bought more balsa and began making pyramids that I later learned were called tetrahedrons. A true pyramid has a square base with four sides. A tetrahedron has a triangular base with three sides.

I began looking for ways to fit these tetrahedrons together to make something pleasing, but nothing worked. That's when I learned something important: Back off! Let the work itself take over. Instead of doing, try listening. And that's when the real process of discovery begins.

Playing with the shape of the tetrahedron, I found a way to join the modules that made sense. Soon my room was full of these hanging structures.

I mention this because I bought my balsa wood at a hobby shop on the Boulevard Saint-Germain near Place Maubert. I always took a long time picking out the best pieces, and because I was obviously a poor student, I never elicited the slightest attention from the clerks.

This all changed in early 1968. A friend's father was a TV producer and was producing a two-hour TV special celebrating the hundredth program of the most popular TV show in France, *Les Cinq Colonnes à la Une* (Front Page) with a lineup of France's biggest stars, including the French equivalent of Elvis Presley, Johnny Hallyday. They were preparing a segment, "Under the Roofs of Paris," that would feature the poorer folk like me who lived in maid's rooms, and asked if I would like to be on the show. My friend said I'd be perfect—the artist, foreigner, and student. I jumped at it. The following week a film crew spent the morning crammed in my room, shooting. A month or so later, the big evening arrived. Primetime: Sunday, 8 PM. I watched the show with friends, and, indeed, there it was. Four minutes of me! (You can see the video on YouTube: "Leonard Pitt in Paris.")

The next morning I walked out my door onto the street, and my fifteen minutes of fame started with a bang. A well-dressed woman entering the building exclaimed, "That *was* you on TV last night! I knew it! I told my husband, 'I know that boy. He's in our building. I see him all the time.' Very good, yes, very good!" The merchants in the neighborhood all exulted at my "*grand success à la télé.*"

People stared, whispered, and pointed at me in the street, on the bus, and in the Métro. *This is what it's like to be famous?* Two young boys spotted me on the way to the laundry and followed me all the way. As I stood inside paying for my T-shirts and underwear, they leaned against the window, cupping their hands to get a better look inside.

But the best was yet to come. About a week later, I went to the hobby store to buy more balsa wood. I entered and saw the owner at the rear. He saw me and looked into a mirror to straighten his tie. Striding over, he extended his hand, beaming. "*Bonjour!* I didn't have the pleasure of seeing you on television the other night, but I heard you were very good. Would you like to see our latest shipment of balsa? Please, step this way, sir."

*   *   *   *

When revolution hit Paris in May 1968, I made sure I was only an observer. I wasn't interested in getting my body broken by rubber truncheons and didn't want to be thrown out of France, which would have been the likely outcome had I been caught by the police. Nevertheless I had a front-row seat to the greatest social upheaval to rock France since the civil war of 1871.

Coincidentally I got a job as an extra in a feature film about—what else?—student revolt in Paris called *The Apocalypse.* (It was never distributed.) One evening, we shot a scene in the Latin Quarter using a real student demonstration as a background. Several actors and I were directed to walk down the middle of Boulevard Saint-Michel towards a phalanx of riot police advancing towards us. When we got to within about twenty feet, we turned around and walked back. About an hour after the shoot, all hell broke loose. To say the police were like animals would be disrespectful to animals. I saw a student get a tear gas grenade in the eye. The police shot straight into the crowd. The young man who was hit sat with his head in his hands as smoke poured out from the hole where his eye used to be. But that evening was only a prelude.

The students and the working class had been at odds for years, fighting the same system from different ends of society. But on Friday, May 10, the infamous night of the barricades, a soldering of social classes took place that changed everything. Hundreds of students gathered on the Left Bank in Rue Gay-Lussac and built a series of barricades across the street with torn-up trees, cobblestones, street benches, cars, and anything else they could get their hands on. The irony is that this long, wide street had been created by Haussmann in 1859, in part to prohibit the building of barricades.

The police were merciless. Officers had to beat on other police to stop them from beating the defenseless students sprawled on the pavement. Residents looking down from their apartment windows were so horrified by the brutality that some threw furniture and other large objects onto the heads of the police. Hundreds of students were arrested, and almost four hundred were injured. The dozens of cars put on the barricades were set afire and exploded, with the sound reverberating around the city.

The brutality of the police shocked the nation and played into the hands of the students. For years the French working class sneered at student demonstrators. "Children of the rich! What do they know? They don't have to put bread on the table!" But the students' bravery that night earned respect. More importantly, it gave the workers ideas: "If the students can do this, why can't we?" In a matter of days, France was paralyzed as workers around the country joined students in protest and went on strike, occupying factories and virtually shutting down the country. Anything that worked with electricity no longer functioned. People walked around Paris carrying flashlights and candles. Public transportation ground to a halt. Trains stopped. Airports operated intermittently. Theft was common as autos were stopped on the street—"Your fuel or your life!" In a matter of days the entire fabric of French society dissolved. Hitchhikers, something never seen in Paris, became commonplace. That sacred cow of French formalism, the difference between *tu* and *vous*— evaporated overnight. At the Sorbonne, occupied day and night by thousands of students and grafittied over with revolutionary slogans, teachers were addressed in the familiar *tu* form, a lapse that would have been unthinkable only a few days before.

Every afternoon I walked over to the Latin Quarter to see what was going on, and every day the same scenario played out. Students and riot police held their lines as the students lobbed bottles and bricks and the police ducked behind their shields. Large black vans parked along the Seine were filled with riot police, the dreaded CRS, who sat inside drinking spiked wine, so it was said. I made sure I was home by dark. As I walked past the vans, the police troops inside, frustrated from being cooped up all day, stomped their feet in rhythm demanding to be let loose. Darkness fell, they were let out, battle lines were dissolved, and the war began.

The government lauded the police for their restraint and blamed the uprising on outsiders, provocateurs, foreign elements who had come to France to stir up revolt. Certainly there could be no problems intrinsic to the French system. By the end of the month, it was all over. The revolution vanished. The glue holding the students and workers together dissolved as fast as it appeared. The government gave in to many demands—promises of revamping the university, improving conditions in factories, etc.—while the students and workers, in disarray, fell back to their isolated positions.

By the middle of June, Paris was quiet again, licking its wounds from the cataclysm. The events of May wreaked havoc on the country. The most immediate effect was a sharp rise in prices. One indication was a packet of ten Métro tickets. Ever since I had been in Paris, the cost had been three francs seventy. Overnight the price rose to six francs.

Once it was all over, the police took measures to ensure the maintenance of law and order. Cobblestone streets in the Latin Quarter were paved over with macadam to deprive students of their ammo. Police were everywhere hassling students. "Your papers!" became an oft-heard phrase on the Left Bank.

My steering clear of the violence was successful until Bastille Day. Paris hadn't seen a demonstration for weeks. I was walking down a little street behind the Panthéon with some friends heading for Place de la Contrescarpe. The street was full of people, everyone enjoying the relaxed holiday atmosphere. Suddenly at the end of the street a phalanx of riot police came around the corner with batons raised. Everyone froze. There were no demonstrations going on. With no provocation the police charged, screaming, "Death, death!" People ran in all directions trying to escape. I turned and ran into a square and over to a wall, hoping to disappear from view as the police ran by. No such luck. Two CRS saw me, ran over, and in those rare moments of great danger when life suddenly switches into slow motion, I thought to myself, *You've heard about it, you've read about it, now it's your turn.* The club struck me over the head, whack, whack, whack! I fell to the ground. Then kick, kick! I lay still, semi-conscious, and heard my assailants run off to find other prey, maybe a pregnant woman or a child who had been separated from its parents. Later that night I found my friend who had just gotten home from the hospital. He took a baton in the teeth. Two tourists standing next to him were shoved through a plate glass window.

Paris was no fun anymore. It was time to leave. Unfortunately my poverty kept me there. It was another year before I earned enough money to return to the States. In my final days Paris became so oppressive that I couldn't wait to leave. For all the reasons why the café can be a wondrous place, it can also be a terrible place of loneliness inhabited by solitary souls caught in an endless state of limbo—waiting for that phone call, the next job to come through, that next inspiration. Now I was one of them. The café became a holding cell where endless boredom was punctuated by cigarettes and coffee.

*   *   *   *

After a day of selling *The New York Times* at Notre Dame, I'd often stop at the café opposite Place Saint-Michel, Le Départ Saint-Michel. Monsieur Lefebvre was a regular at the café. Every afternoon he came in expecting to sit at the same table. Monsieur Lefebvre loved routine. On days when his table was taken, his discomfort was obvious. Rather than simply going to another table (there were plenty), he would stand there, irritated, his mouth pinching as he impatiently tapped his folded newspaper in his hand. Only after surveying the whole café would he sit somewhere else. His request to the waiter never varied: a cup of espresso with a small slice of lemon rind.

Once seated he carefully placed his hat on the seat next to him and patiently waited for his coffee to arrive before opening his newspaper. Having doffed his hat, Monsieur Lefebvre now had to make sure that his hair was in place. There was a certain poignancy to this man's insecure gesture of patting down his hair, trying to assure himself that he was well coiffed, above all when everything else in his life seemed to be so completely in his control. Monsieur Lefebvre tried to camouflage his baldness by growing the hair on the side of his head long enough to go over the top of his head. His full pate was never covered, but anything was better than nothing.

Monsieur Lefebvre was not a rich man. The dark suit on his thin frame was neat but well worn. The shoulders of his jacket had the sheen of infinite dry cleanings. The lapels were slightly curled. The bottom of his cuffs were slightly frayed. His necktie was not particularly well ironed.

When his coffee arrived, he'd squeeze the lemon rind to get a little spritz, add a cube of sugar, and only then would he open his newspaper. There was a swiftness to Monsieur Lefebvre's movements as he accomplished the small tasks of this daily ritual, an economy that comes from performing the same moves day after day. His hat was off in a single sweep arcing in the air as it headed for the chair next to him. He picked up the lemon, spritzed, it and put it back on the saucer with the flair of an orchestra conductor signaling a beat to the string section. Sitting erect in his chair, he turned the pages of his newspaper quickly and cleanly, folding the paper in half and then folding it again to the quarter page. But there was no joy here. This was not a Jean-Pierre who knew the thrill of speed tobogganing through everyday movements. Monsieur Lefebvre went through these motions with the cool detachment of a brain surgeon. Clearly, efficiency was the god in his life.

I enjoyed watching Monsieur Lefebvre because he was so much of who he was. Every millimeter of his person had been carefully carved out and filled with intention. He had the air of a man who was content in the knowledge that there were no more mysteries to be discovered in his person. Someone said, "Know thyself," and he did.

I wondered what Monsieur Lefebvre did for a living. Sometimes the waiter would chat with Monsieur Lefebvre. I admit, I'd bend my ear and try to catch a few words that might rise above the din to tell me something about this man. One day I heard him say *"Les rêves sont une insulte à la raison"* (dreams are an insult to reason). Was this not the quintessential French statement? In France, during the Revolution, Reason was elevated to the level of a deity, literally. In 1793 a mass celebration was held in Paris in honor of Reason with a large statue of the Goddess of Reason.

I don't remember how, but one day I learned that Monsieur Lefebvre worked at the national mint just down the street on the Quai de Conti. I never learned what he did there. Maybe he was in charge of seeing that each roll got the proper number of coins. Better yet, he seemed like the kind of person who would oversee the folding of the ends of the rolls, and very neat folds they would be.

One day his table was taken and he sat down, of all places, next to me. I'd watched him from a distance for so long that now to have him this close was a shock. I felt as if a movie star had just sat down next to me. I wanted to turn and look at him up close but didn't dare. I did peek at him out of the corner of my eye and even turned slightly towards him in my chair. That's how I learned his name, from an envelope he pulled out with some papers.

I thought of saying something to him, something typical like the French would say on a cold day. "Not very hot today, eh?" Then of all things, he turned to me and asked me the time. I was so startled I took a moment to catch myself. I looked at my watch. "Three thirty," I said. "*Merci bien*," he said, and he went back to his paper. I sat there shocked. I don't know why, but it surprised me that he asked me the time, and above all that he asked it so casually. What did I expect, a drum roll? Should the waiter have made an announcement? "Ladies and gentlemen! Monsieur Lefebvre will now ask Mr. Pitt the time!" All he did was ask me the time, and it surprised me.

I had been out all day and was looking forward to getting home. The walk from the Latin Quarter to my room is a great Paris walk. One can do many walks in Paris thousands of times and never grow tired of them: like turning the earth and smelling the rich aroma of the soil that flairs the nostrils with pleasure. From the Place Saint-Michel, walk along the Seine past the bookstalls until you reach the Pont des Arts, the pedestrian bridge across the river (built in 1809). Halfway across the bridge, stop and look back towards the Île de la Cité. In front of you is the Pont Neuf (the "New Bridge," circa 1600). Rising up behind the buildings facing you are the twin towers of Notre Dame, assuming its tranquil position of dominance on the island.

Continue across the bridge and cross the street into the courtyard of the Louvre, known as the Cour Carrée to the famous Pei pyramid. Continue to the Rue de Rivoli and up the Avenue de l'Opéra to number 16. Home.

*   *   *   *

Getting together with friends in Paris was always a dicey affair since no one had a telephone. Some days loneliness was like being seasick—minutes pass as slowly as hours. On those days I'd go to La Coupole hoping desperately to run into someone I knew. If no one was there, I'd find solace in my cup of coffee and pray that someone would show up. Dropping in on people was always risky since I never knew if they were home. If I did venture out to a friend's place, I'd pray on the way that they would be there. I'd exit the station and walk towards their place wound up with anticipation. I get to the door. No one is home, my heart sinks. Someone answers, *Thank you, God!*

*   *   *   *

Paulette walked into my room and threw her bag on the chair. "What's wrong with these men!" she said angrily. "They think having children depletes the brain. How can they be so blind?" She had applied for a job as curator at the Jeu de Paume museum and received a reply with a mumbo-jumbo excuse about why she wasn't suited. "If I were a man I'd have that job in two seconds." I took her in my arms and tried to humor her.

"C'mon," I said, kissing her on the cheek, her neck, her nose. "They're just a bunch of stuffed bureaucrats. Forget it." She slipped out of her heels and hugged me. "Let's think of happier things," I said as I unbuttoned her blouse. Her perfume, L'Air du Temps, did everything perfume was supposed to do. We fell into bed. She stopped for a second and looked at me. "Slow down, relax," she said. "Why don't you be more like those monkeys you always talk about? They're so loose and relaxed." I took a deep sigh. We lay still for a while. A stomach gurgled. Was it mine or hers? Our bodies stirred under the covers.

We lay in bed half asleep. I opened my eyes and saw her clothes lying on the chair. What a beautiful mundane moment—her bra hanging over the back of the chair, her skirt and sweater lying rumpled on the seat, her turquoise shoes fallen over on the floor. Why hadn't I seen this in a collection of the world's great photographs?

Paulette opened her eyes. "What time is it?" she asked. I leaned over and glanced at my watch on the floor. "It's two thirty."

"Oh no!" she said, bolting up in bed. "I must leave. I have to pick up the children in ten minutes. If I'm late, they'll worry."

She jumped out of bed, threw her clothes on, and stood in front of the mirror hurriedly putting on some makeup while wriggling her feet into her high heels. She grabbed her bag and came over to the bed making the funniest face and kissed me. "Good-bye, my little monkey."

* * * *

I closed the door to my room and sat down with a new book I'd bought that day. I was tired of looking for answers to my obscure questions, so after a dinner in the Latin Quarter I went to Shakespeare and Co. to find something interesting but not too heavy. I bought a copy of *A Treasury of Science*. This was the kind of book you'd find in a book-of-the-month club with essays on personalities and events in the history of science. Not challenging but informative and interesting. I scanned the table of contents and chose an article that traced human evolution from the prehominids to the appearance of modern man. Within the space of a half hour the whole panorama of evolution was laid out before me in a slow continuous fashion: small monkeys on all fours take to the trees. Their front limbs reach out to grasp and are no longer used only for support and locomotion. Objects can be handled, looked at, manipulated, and altered. The thumb develops in opposition to the other digits. A new interaction develops between the hand, the eyes, and the brain, setting this animal apart from all others. The animal puts more weight on its hind limbs and becomes more vertical. The skull changes shape as the brain increases in size, and the forehead grows larger. Now that the snout is no longer the primary way of investigating the world, it recedes. The animal becomes still more upright—stooped, but upright. The massive neck muscles diminish in size as the body becomes more vertical and lengthens. The forehead becomes larger as the brain increases in size. The body becomes more slender and gains more mobility. *Ecce homo!*

I finished reading and sat in a daze. I looked at my arms, my legs, at my hands. My body began to tingle. A powerful feeling welled up inside me. Profound experiences often come unexpectedly and in small packages. The more these moments are revelatory of a basic truth, the more difficult they are to describe. For that reason I hesitate writing about what happened next. Words cannot measure up, and what was vast will become small. Suffice it to say that I felt a deep physical connection to a past I had never known. I awakened to an awareness of my origins. I sat in my chair, awestruck.

I grabbed my jacket and ran to the elevator. Downstairs I passed the cafés, the shops, the people, and I felt like I was seeing everything for the first time. I stopped at the corner and watched the crowds pass by. A walking body. My God, what a miracle. I saw a man lift a cup of coffee. How many countless small dramas had to take place for that simple action to be possible? Electric streetlights, automobiles, buildings—what a extraordinary achievements. Everything I saw spoke of a deep and continuous connection with the past. Why hadn't I seen this before?

Suddenly I had an urge to see monkeys: chimpanzees and gorillas. The next morning, after a quick breakfast, I hopped the Métro for the Zoo. I stood at the cage with the big gorillas and watched them mope around. One gorilla sat in a corner a few feet away and looked dolefully into space. He glanced over at me. I was taken a back. The intelligence in his eyes was frightening. Who said these great animals have no feelings about being locked up? Who can look at those eyes and say they're indifferent? I detested the other people for laughing and making fun of them, for falling into the chasm between the words *human* and *animal*.

*   *   *   *

Simson asked to meet at the café Les Deux Magots on Boulevard Saint-Germain. This was the expensive café for the chic clique, the tanned winter crowd. The price of a coffee there was twice as expensive as anywhere else in Paris and was strictly off-limits for me. I glanced at the menu and groaned. Those prices! I had to admit, though, the interior—old-world ritz—was handsome and not overstated. The toilets were exceptionally clean even though they were the old squat variety (since then, they've remodeled to a more-modern restroom). The first time I saw one of those squat toilets at a café in the provinces, I was thrown. I didn't know what to do, and I walked out.

Unlike most Paris cafés, Les Deux Magots had a woman on duty with the thankless task of tending the toilets. All day long she sat at her little table down there, equipped with her arsenal of toilet tools—sponge, cloth, and glass cleaner—dispensing telephone tokens and collecting one-franc pieces from the grateful patrons.

The waiter brought our coffee, and we settled in. Simson pulled out a pack of Gauloises and lit up. "You know," he said, "if a Martian had landed on earth in the mid-1500s and visited both China and Europe, he would have had the distinct impression that the Chinese were far superior to the Europeans. They were way ahead of us in their science, medicine, and technology."

Once again Simson was talking about things I knew nothing about. In fact I knew so little that I didn't even know what questions to ask. All I could do was sit there, listen, and try to interject something halfway intelligent along the way.

"Take acupuncture, for example."

I'd heard about acupuncture. In the early 1960s, it wasn't yet officially accepted in France, but if you knew where to go, you could get treated.

"The Mafia at the AMA think it's voodoo. That's because Chinese medicine is based on energy. It's a different way of understanding the body. Once you look at things in terms of energy, everything changes. You see different relationships. The Chinese know the organs of the body, but they look beyond the mechanical functioning of the organ to its state of energy. Just imagine," he said, "someone's got a kidney problem, and they put a needle in their ear. It flies in the face of all classical Western thinking. We can't get a handle on acupuncture because we're so materialistic. We see the body in terms of individual parts, discrete entities. If we've got a kidney problem, we treat the kidney. What else? Energy scares the hell out of us. People are afraid to think about a non-material universe because they think it'll deliver us into the hands of the occultists with their ghosts, spirits, and hobgoblins. We can't measure energy or weigh it. It's too elusive. It's not like we don't believe in energy. Look at electricity. We don't know how it works, except that it works.

"For years I had terrible back trouble," he continued. "That's a tough one for Western doctors. Look at Kennedy. He had back trouble, and all they could do was give him a rocking chair. I had a half dozen acupuncture treatments, and my back is fine."

"Why did they give Kennedy a rocking chair?"

"Because of how it positions your spine. It keeps the pelvis and the spine in the right relationship and takes the pressure off the lower back. A good rocker with a slung back puts a curve in your lower back that you don't get in a regular chair. The rocking is soothing too, like a massage. But the rocker was only a band-aid for Kennedy. They didn't know what to do, so they gave him a rocking chair. Someone should write a book on the history of the chair some day." (By the way, someone did: Galen Cranz, *The Chair: Rethinking Culture, Body, and Design*, 2000.) "It's amazing to think that for thousands of years humans never sat in chairs. Most people on the planet still don't sit in chairs. Someone once told me that the Japanese call our way of sitting in chairs half sitting because we're not all the way on the ground. Who the hell ever invented the chair anyway?"

"Chairs, I never thought of that!" I said.

"It's the old European fear of the body," Simpson said. "*European* meaning *Christianity*. The ground is the devil, right? I wonder if the Greeks sat in chairs?" (They did.) "The American Indians didn't, we know that. Can you imagine what the European colonialists thought when they went to Africa and found everyone sitting on the ground? Savages just inches away from the devil. The chair ties into Christianity and the fear of the body."

"And what about the Martian? I asked. "Do you think he would have been sitting on a chair?"

"The Martian, right!" he laughed, "I forgot about him. My point is that on his first trip to Earth, he would have found China way ahead of us. The Chinese had the wheelbarrow hundreds of years before us. They also invented the mechanical clock, the compass, printing, earthquake detectors, and paper money. All way before us. In medicine they were way ahead too. We had knowledge of how to heal, we had competent herbalists, but we had nothing as sophisticated as Chinese medicine. While we were boring holes into people skulls to drain off blood thinking it would alleviate a headache, the Chinese were performing brain surgery on people while they were awake, and without any pain. And with only a local anesthetic with a few needles placed on the forehead. That's subtle. But a couple of hundred years later, everything changed. By the late eighteenth or early nineteenth century, our Martian would have found Europe way out in front of China, much more scientifically and technologically advanced."

"The Scientific Revolution. Right. That's what was happening in Europe."

"Right. But the $64 question is why did Europe have a Scientific Revolution while China did not?"

"Why do you think?" I asked.

"It's an enigma. I think it's because the Chinese think in terms of systems. That's their genius, understanding systems. Our genius is in breaking things down, isolating them, taking them apart. We love discreet parts. It's our genius, but it's also our limitation. We're great at taking things apart but not so good at putting them back together again. So we lose sight of the big picture. If anything kills us, it'll be because we've focused on some little chunk of reality that we've isolated from the big picture. We'll exaggerate it out of proportion, and it'll turn on us and do us in. And we'll have no idea of what really happened."

"In all my years in school I never heard a word about Chinese science." I said. "I wouldn't have known it existed."

"Of course. They want us to think that science was invented by the West. Gutenberg invents the printing press; Harvey discovers the circulation of the blood. Boyle practically invents modern chemistry, Eli Whitney the cotton gin, the Wright brothers the airplane, Edison the lightbulb, Ford the automobile, and on and on. One long, steady march of progress."

I stared at my cup of coffee trying to take it all in.

Simson leaned back in his chair and sipped on his drink. "It's all politics."

"Really?"

"Sure. China is communist, remember?"

We sat in silence. Simson lit another Gauloises while I sipped on my cold coffee and watched the crowd. I hated the people there. It was their money. What they spent in a day I could live on for a month. A man of great girth sat at the table across from us reading *Le Monde*. He was well-dressed in a suit and tie with his expensive coat hanging on the chair opposite him. He had large hands with short stubby fingers and wore a pinky ring. I admit, I loved hating this guy. I didn't know him, but it made no difference; I still hated him. He had thick black hair combed straight back and a full black mustache. He had a nervous tic of smoothing down his mustache by reaching up with his lower lip. Engrossed in his newspaper, his lip seemed to have a life of its own, massaging his moustache. I hated this little indulgence and his feeling of self-contentment.

Simson looked at his watch. "You know, it's time for my Tai Chi class. Why don't you come along and watch? You might find it interesting."

In the 1960s, Tai Chi was only known to a small circle of devotees in Paris. We walked to a studio tucked away in the rear of a courtyard near Place Saint-Michel. How different from Decroux's studio. No bright fluorescent lights here; only a couple of dim naked lightbulbs hanging overhead. Not a mirror anywhere. The teacher, Mr. Ko, was small in stature and was dressed in loose pants and a large T-shirt. Simson introduced me. We shook hands, and I was taken aback. His hand was so soft it felt as if I held nothing. He said that instead of watching, I must take part in the class. I looked at Simson. "Go ahead. It won't kill you."

Everyone took a spot on the floor and stood in silence, their arms held out in front. Mr. Ko made small adjustments to each person's posture. I stood in my perfect zero. He tapped me on the shoulder. "Relax the spine." Looking at my feet in a first position, he said, "Feet parallel, bend knees." What my mind understood, my body did not grasp yet. Everything he told me went against all of my training. He then demonstrated a series of movements—slow, fluid, arms floating, the body stepping and turning, the knees bent. I did my best to keep up. At the end of the lesson I thanked him and asked, "The knees, why are the knees always bent?" Smiling faintly, he replied, "Bent knee, good for energy."

*   *   *   *

I wore a cape in Paris. This seemed quintessentially French to me even though the only people I ever saw wearing them were gendarmes and guardians of the peace. The cape was beautiful not only for its style, but also for its movement as it swung in the air as I walked. I loved the movement of my hands and arms as I grasped and manipulated it when sitting down, putting it on, taking it off. It had its own little dance. I can see in retrospect that it gave me a little panache, as the French say, or, as we say, a bit of style, dash. One day I was walking down Boulevard Saint-Michel wearing my cape. I passed two young girls, Janine and Martine. They exclaimed something at the sight. I guess the cape made an impression. We chatted, or rather, we bubbled. A few days later I was in bed with Janine. It was the '60s. She was Corsican, hot blooded, intelligent, and caring. The shape of her face and her countenance were as delicate and classical as an ancient Greek statue.

Her father left Corsica for a job as a croupier in a Paris gambling casino. In Corsica he was a farmer. In Paris, now dispossessed, he kept a small plot of land outside the city and went there on weekends to work the soil. I went one Sunday with Janine and was taken by the drama and poetry of this man who clearly loved the earth so deeply but was forced into this well-paid but demeaning job. One day Janine invited me to lunch at the family apartment in Paris. We were having the soup. Her father, without taking his eyes off the bowl in front of him, said, "Janine, your friend Leonard, he's Jewish, *n'est-ce pas*?" "*Oui, papa.*"

"In two words," he said, "Hitler was right."

Actually it was three words—well, four in French, but I wasn't going to correct him. So much for the poetry of the man tied to the earth.

Chapter 14

LIFE AFTER PARIS

I RETURNED TO AMERICA IN LATE 1969 but didn't stay long. The thrill of being home wore off quickly, and I grew restless. In January 1970, I travelled to Denmark to work in a theatre company with friends from Decroux's. Theo's prophecy had come true. Denmark in the winter is a daunting experience. Living in the small town of Holstebro, where darkness fell at 3 PM, was depressing in the extreme. I only lasted until early summer. The days got longer, and the air became fragrant with the scent of lilacs. But I yearned for America. In June of 1970, I flew back to the States and landed in Berkeley, California.

Having lived in Europe so long, I missed the tumultuous 1960s completely. All the reference points that defined the lives of my own generation were nowhere on my map: the Civil Rights Movement, the Vietnam War protest, the hippie revolution, the music, the drugs. I was a stranger in a strange land.

I rented an artist's loft in downtown Berkeley on Shattuck Avenue, and meager as those quarters were (my bathroom was still down the hall, and my kitchen was an electric frying pan and a sink), I felt like a king simply because I had a large space to move around in. The hippie phenomenon had peaked by then and Haight-Ashbury was a ghost town, yet there was still an unmistakable electricity in the air that summer of 1970.

A generation of young people were out to redefine the world with an unstoppable optimism and enthusiasm. And they were willing to try anything. I began teaching right away. I put up handbills on phone poles advertising classes, and the next day the phone began to ring. I didn't know it, but I had fallen into a goldmine. Young people searching were willing to take classes in anything. One could have advertised a class in how to tie your shoe laces and filled it.

The joys of teaching are many. Having a person in front of me who does not know how to move is a challenge worth waking up for in the morning. Some people move their arms as if they were not connected to their torsos. Some people move their upper body as if they didn't know there was a lower body nearby. Some people move as if they didn't know the ground was anywhere in the vicinity.

Unraveling the conundrums of why people cannot perform what seem like simple movements focuses the mind and forces one into more acute states of observation, where *feeling* what you see becomes as important as *seeing* what you see. Next, one must know how to parcel out the information so the student can progress. Giving too much information too soon is confusing. Start with issues low in the body. As those straighten out, move higher in the body. Watching a student make progress is gratifying. Transformation takes place before your eyes. Just as important is what I learn from guiding them along. It's a cliché, but it's true. I only teach because I learn.

*   *   *   *

The questions about the ballet and the up and down of things followed me to Berkeley. The contradiction between classic Western dance—the ballet—and what came to be known as grounded movement continued to fascinate me. But now in California I was faced with an even greater contradiction: me and everything around me.

While my generation couldn't throw off tradition fast enough, I was the walking embodiment of tradition. The ramrod spine and sucked-in gut I had acquired with Decroux's work spoke of a rigid French formalism that was passé.

A single experience brought me face-to-face with "Leonard the walking, talking anachronism." Not long after arriving in Berkeley, I began working on a solo performance of abstract mime in the pure Decroux tradition that I called *Three Pieces*. With no one to collaborate with, I worked alone every day in my studio for seven months hammering out these pieces.

I designed a poster, tacked copies of it onto phone poles in town, and rented a small theatre. I still used the word *mime* then, a word I long ago abandoned. Little did I know that this word was loaded with associations different from my own. To my surprise, I had a full house on opening night. I should have known I was in trouble by the number of baby strollers in the audience. People thought they were in for a good time—fun, laughter, joy. But I was serious. I was practicing art with a capital *A*. I wasn't into coddling. I handed out no programs, so no one knew what they were watching, what the pieces were called, or even who I was. With only general stage lighting and no light changes or sound track, all the audience saw was a lithe body in a loincloth moving in a stylized fashion. All they heard was my breathing. It wasn't my intention to be inaccessible, nor was it my intention to be accessible. I was only doing what I was doing.

The first hint that I was on a collision course with the audience came after the first piece. From the darkness of the stage, I heard the squeak of baby strollers as about a quarter of the audience left the theatre. After the second piece, another quarter left. At that point I turned to the audience and, breaking my silence, said, "Good thing there's only one more piece, or else there would be no more audience left."

As I continued teaching, I searched for a path that could lead me beyond Decroux's work, but I kept running into walls. Everything changed in January 1973.

*   *   *   *

A friend invited me to a concert of Balinese dance and music on the UC Berkeley campus. I had no idea what to expect. As the curtain went up I leaned over and whispered, "If this is boring, let's leave in the middle." When it was over I was in a daze. I had never seen anything like this before. The Balinese dancers looked more like giant insects than humans. Decked out in their colorful costumes, the percussive rhythms of the gamelan music drove their bodies through space like a juggernaut with alternating rhythms of staccato and flow. Their dance movement was similar to Decroux's with its vibrant rhythms of impulse and punctuation and dynamic movements of isolation, but this dance was wrapped in an aesthetic that was foreign to me.

The power of this performance stayed with me. I began reading about Bali and listening to Balinese music, and I became fascinated with a culture where art was as much a part of daily life as fast-food restaurants were in America. Several months later, I closed my school and flew there.

My original idea was to simply observe the culture, to see how the Balinese do something as ordinary as drink a cup of coffee, open a door, walk down the street. But on a stopover in Bangkok, I met an American returning from Bali who told me that it was possible to study mask dance there. I found a place to stay in a village he recommended, Peliatan, and inquired about classes. For the next three and a half months I studied mask dance—called *topeng* in Balinese—seven days a week with one of the great masters, I Nyoman Kakul.

Kakul lived in the village of Batuan, about a thirty-minute beemo ride from Peliatan. A beemo is a small three-wheeled scooter with a shell on the back and two rows of seats facing each other. With this vehicle the Balinese have proven that the scientific law stating that no two physical bodies can occupy the same place at the same time is erroneous. Any crowded beemo demonstrates this. Classes began at 9 AM.

When I was late for a lesson I'd run down the path and arrive breathless. It didn't take long to see that this didn't matter at all for Kakul. There were no clocks anywhere in his house, he didn't wear a watch, and the concept of 9 o'clock was foreign to him. For the Balinese, at least then, the day was divided not by hours and minutes but by chores and the sun.

Lessons were held outdoors in the garden. I started by learning the classic character of the Prime Minister—the man who wanted to be king but never made it. And he's mad. This is a solo dance with a full mask.

Kakul taught me the dance in its entirety without breaking anything down. He would demonstrate a series of movements while singing the dance rhythm, or he'd stand behind me and manipulate my body like a marionette, turning my head with both hands, his foot hitting my foot to advance it a step.

After a couple of months, Kakul asked me to perform with him in a village temple celebration. Years later, I still feel the excitement. The day before the performance we went to the village to rehearse with the gamelan. And here was another insight into Balinese culture: One section of the dance was particularly difficult, so when I finished, I backed up to do it again as the gamelan played on. The musicians stopped playing, as if on cue, and looked at each other, puzzled. Kakul motioned for me to begin again. I started, and when I finished that section, I backed up to repeat it again. Now the musicians dropped their mallets and broke out in riotous laughter. Irritated, Kakul told me to start over and to dance all the way through without stopping. I immediately understood. Isolating one part of the dance from the rest was inconceivable to the Balinese. Everything is one big soup. Differentiation, reductionism, taking things apart as we do in the West was not part of the culture.

The performance came. Suited up in my traditional Balinese costume of velvet pants, sequined vest, large collar, and headpiece, I pulled it off. Dancing with a full gamelan orchestra is like dancing inside an erupting volcano.

*   *   *   *

My American friend Tom was studying gamelan in the nearby village of Teges. His music teacher asked if we would do a performance together for the village with the village gamelan accompanying us. This was a great honor. We agreed.

We were to do a comic performance with half masks, and like all Balinese dance, it would be held outdoors under the palm trees. Half masks meant we'd be speaking, a first for me. A curtain strung up on bamboo poles in a clearing defined our stage area. The gamelan orchestra was seated on the ground in front. There was no electricity, so kerosene lamps were strung up to illuminate the site. Tom and I had an array of masks we had collected laid out on a small table behind the curtain for the performance. There was a buzz in the crowd as people came from all around to see the two white Americans perform.

We agreed on a theme to get us started, and the moment the gamelan erupted, we took off. It didn't take more than a few seconds before it hit me that no one in the audience could understand a word I was saying. My wit, my humor meant nothing. Instead I had to focus on the musicality and rhythm of my voice in order to connect with the audience. I had to exaggerate my gestures and body movement. I bellowed, squealed, nasaled, and gruffed my way through our masks as we took on different characters. This was my introduction to using my voice in performance.

*   *   *   *

The next day I sat at the drink stand next to my lodging and sipped on a coffee. It was early morning in Bali. A young woman walked by, and I was struck by how she moved. She didn't walk but glided. There was a relaxation to her walk unlike anything we would see in America or the West for that matter. There was no past or future in her walk. She was not walking towards anything or away from anything. She was simply where she was at that moment while she walked.

*   *   *   *

One afternoon I went to meet Tom at his place. I was late, and I walked briskly through the village. Men sitting on a large, open platform saw me and laughed. I understood right away. No one in Bali moved that fast unless there was an emergency. I looked unusual, bizarre, hence, comical.

*   *   *   *

I sat on a riverbank listening to the croaking frogs create their own gamelan rhythms. Two women with baskets on their heads stopped on the bridge above, and one of them called down to me. "Hallo! What time is it?" Conscientious me, I looked at my watch and replied, "It's three fifteen!" They looked at each other and laughed. "Oh, it's three fifteen. Good! Well, we'd better get going! It's three fifteen, ha, ha!" The hour had no meaning to them, and they were simply playing with me.

*   *   *   *

While living in Paris I felt as though I had created a course in comparative movement studies as I pondered questions about dance and the human body. My experience in Bali heightened this feeling. Immersing myself in the culture, observing how the dance both issued from and reflected daily life was food for thought to last for years. Returning to California threw everything I knew into disarray. It was now imperative to reevaluate everything.

*   *   *   *

Back in my studio I began working with the masks I brought back from Bali and ran into the limitations of Decroux's movement. Balinese masks are full of character, idiosyncrasy, psychological quirks and foibles. All anathema to the master's art with a capital *A*. But I didn't care. I forged on.

Bali was a fork in the road that set me in my own direction. I didn't know where it would lead, and it was up to me to find out. With no idea of how to proceed, masks became the center of my work. Students who had worked with me in the Decroux aesthetic were confused as I told them what didn't work. "Put your weight in the middle. Drop your heel. Bend your knees." My guides were the masks. All I had to do was listen and see where they wanted me to go.

*   *   *   *

I began an intense reevaluation of Decroux's work. Much I discarded, and much I kept. I let go of his movement studies, the Figures, all the counterweights, the zero position as a base. But that groundedness—that was a door into a big world. As soon as one posits the notion of a grounded body, one confronts questions of how the different parts of the body connect to each other in movement.

When the body is connected, all the different parts of the body support each other. They speak to each other energetically. They are in a proper relation to each other. We all experience this as children. We've been educated into disconnection.

An example: Someone carries a heavy bucket. Their arm will extend out at the side as a counterweight. How beautiful. All the parts of the body do something different to accomplish the same end. No one thinks about this; it just happens, like hands going out in front when you fall. One's physical intelligence is complete here. Fine. The point of training is to refine this intelligence in order to increase one's expression onstage.

No one would guess that Decroux had an influence on break dancing. The isolation moves, the trademark of break dancing, began with Decroux, moved to Marcel Marceau, were picked up by Robert Shields, and were seen across America when he and Lorene Yarnell had their popular weekly TV show in the 1970s with acts all performed à la robot. This ignited the talent and imagination of Michael Jackson, and the rest is history.

And the voice. In Decroux's classes we all moved in silence as he sang the rhythm and intensity of the movement to guide us. When I began teaching, I did this too. This changed one day when a student had trouble with a movement with a very sharp rhythm. So I asked her to sing the movement to emphasize the rhythm, and she got it right away. Of course. Using the correct voice meant her breath was engaged correctly, and that was the basis for the movement. Since then I have done much work with breath and voice.

Understanding the difference between a vowel and a consonant in voice production is capital. Vowels deliver the emotion; consonants do not. Vowels are an extension of the breath and are closer to emotion. Consonants are percussive sounds and further the action. Vowels can be sculpted, stretched, bent and shaped to enhance meaning.

Listen to Édith Piaf. Listen to the immense feeling in her voice. Listen to her vowels. Her voice is drenched in tears, and we hear this best through her vowels. Listen to Pavarotti, to his vowels. What do you hear? What is the psychological quality of his vowels?

*   *   *   *

In the 1980s, during a visit to Berkeley, my parents came to watch me teach a class. Afterwards my mother said, "Lenny, I want to see Berkeley like you know it. If we weren't here, what would you do now?"

"Simple, I'd go to the café."

"OK, let's go," she said.

We went to my favorite café, and she ordered a salad. The dish was put in front of her. She took one look and exclaimed, "Lenny, would you tell me what I'm eating here?" Everyone in the café looked over at us. The salad had red leaf lettuce, something she had never seen before. All she knew was iceberg lettuce. I explained this, and she ate with skepticism. Once finished, she looked around the café and, in a voice everyone could hear, said, "Lenny, it's three o'clock in the afternoon. What are all these people doing sitting here? Why aren't they working?"

*   *   *   *

The Blake Street Hawkeyes was a gritty theatre company in Berkeley only a block from my studio. Bob Ernst, David Schein, John O'Keefe, and George Coates made some of the most interesting and lively theatre to be seen at the time. Whoopi Goldberg was a member of the company for a while just before she left for Hollywood. O'Keefe should be a declared national treasure. His one-man show, *Shimmer*, an autobiographical piece he created after the Hawkeyes broke up, is gold.

In 1977, George Coates asked me if I wanted to work with him on building a show. I didn't know what he had in mind, but I said yes. We began meeting in the Hawkeyes' studio improvising with objects as he created situations for me to maneuver through. George was very good at getting me to do things I would never have done on my own. From this work came a solo show, *2019 Blake*, the show that put both of us on the map. The piece had no narrative and was a series of actions and images that were interesting look at. The key here was the transitions. If the transitions from one image to the next are smooth and seamless, then the energy from one image feeds into the next, and an accumulation builds. If the transitions are weak, then each new image must begin from scratch. We were creating a theatre built on the art of the transition.

The review by local art critic Thomas Albright was over-the-top. This show hit a chord with the public. The theatre was jammed every night with overflow crowds hoping for cancellations so they could get in. We did a second run in San Francisco and a third in 1978 as part of a midnight series in a church basement. The last show of the series had a waiting list of over one hundred people. I did a second show at 1:30 AM on closing night to a full house. You know you did something right when a stranger stops you on the street a full twenty years later and says, "Didn't you do that show . . ."

C HAPTER 15

SEEING THE PATTERNS

SPENDING YEARS IMMERSED IN questions about the human body, trying to understand why the ballet went up and how this related to the natural condition of the body to be grounded, in time, I began seeing connections between things that on the surface did not seem connected at all. It's all about patterns. See the patterns, and another layer of meaning comes to the surface. In a strange way, I felt like history was whispering in my ear.

Pattern 1: Surveying the Landscape

Look at the 1950s: Elvis Presley, the Hula-Hoop, Chubby Checker and the twist. What do they have in common? The lower body, the pelvis. Suddenly millions of children in America were practicing one of the most primitive movements of mankind, a rhythmic swinging of the hips. There's something worth noticing there. Elvis hit like a tidal wave. When he first appeared on *The Ed Sullivan Show* in 1956, shaking and rattling his hips, he was dubbed "Elvis the Pelvis." Horrified censors lopped off his offending lower regions and showed only his upper body. The attempt at amputation didn't work. The fans wanted both. And they got them.

And here is the historical arc connecting Louis XIV to Elvis Presley. The upwardly oriented hyperextended dance body formalized by Louis XIV became a cultural icon, an idealized body that millions emulated and aspired to for centuries. The unspoken message of the posture was clear: man conquers nature, man disdains nature, etc.

Elvis was the antidote. He provided a new body that started us on our journey back down to the ground. His bent knees and fluid hips presented another way of relating to the earth. Just as Louis's upwardness was supported by other aspects of the culture of the time, other things in America during Elvis's time supported this move back down to the ground.

The Hula-Hoop spun into the spotlight in 1958. Two American businessmen imported the hoop from Australia, where they saw it used in a gym class, and established the Wham-O corporation in California. Little did they know what forces they were playing into. Manufacturing twenty thousand hoops a day could not meet the demand. Neighborhood entrepreneurs cashed in on the craze by making hoops in their garage. All it took was some PVC tubing, something to cut the tubing to length, corks, and a staple gun. I worked at my parent's toy store then, and I remember the fever around this simple toy. And it was a fever.

Chubby Checker burst onto the scene in 1960 with the twist. *Life* magazine called the dance an "epidemic," a "hip-swinging mania." They likened the twist to the dancing madness of the Middle Ages in which people danced wildly until they dropped. Other fads reinforced this focus on the lower body. In 1959, *Life* magazine reported something strange happening on college campuses known as "hunkerin'," which was slang for squatting on the ground. Photos show young boys and girls awkwardly squatting on chairs, rooftops, piano tops, and at the counter of the local A&W Root Beer stand.

This trend of getting down continued in 1962 when a popular West Indies import known as the limbo dance arrived in America. While friends clapped their hands to Caribbean rhythms played on the stereo, the dancer had to bend backwards as far as possible and pass under a bar held lower and lower to the ground.

Was it only a coincidence that surfing appeared on the California coast during this same period? Balance on a surfboard is maintained by holding the body low. The center of gravity is in the hips. The pelvis and legs must open up to the spontaneity of the ocean.

Is there a pattern emerging here? The message being subliminally transmitted throughout the youth culture was "Get down; connect with the earth!" Fall to it, squat to it, shimmy, shake, rock and roll to it! America's center of gravity was dropping fast, from the head to the pelvis. Something profound was happening, and no one saw it coming.

In the 1950s, America was a tranquil nation. The nightmare of World War II was over. The United States was the greatest industrial power in the world. Production was up; inflation was not an issue. Plastics, chemical fertilizers, and ballpoint pens confirmed our belief in the future and the ultimate good of science to improve our lives. Automatic transmissions had been introduced, and Dynaflow was a way of life. In music, the soothing tones of The Four Freshmen reflected the same coolness of the new modern jazz. On TV, *Ozzie and Harriet* and *Father Knows Best* told us that everything was all right. Everything seemed sooo smooth. But beneath the surface, things were percolating.

As parents encouraged their children to spin those Hula-Hoops or chuckled with glee as they watched them dance the twist, they had no idea that they were creating little social rebels. These children were developing a low center of gravity in their body, lower than that of their parents—out of the head and into the pelvis. Sociologically this was a keg of dynamite with a short fuse. Of course these children would develop a view of the world different from their parents. They were being wired differently. And part of that worldview was a different relationship to the earth. The lower center of gravity would promote a feeling of being more connected to the ground. It is no mystery that the kids shaking their hips in the '50s would become hippies in the '60s and '70s, and that along with protesting the war in Vietnam they would make the environment one of their central issues.

On a deeper level, the events taking place in America from the late 1950s into the 1970s can be viewed as an attempt, albeit unconscious, to strike a more balanced relationship with the natural world—humans as stewards of the earth rather than exploiters of the earth. The man subduing nature with an axe was replaced by the man carrying the watering can.

*　*　*　*

Another expression of this America out of balance in the early 1950s was the Cold War mentality that gripped the country and through a kind of skewed chemistry created a monstrous, disembodied head spewing out fear and hatred from its cancerous mouth. The government was convinced that commies, like maggots, were crawling around in our very bowels ready to devour us, or worse yet, turn us into mindless, godless robots.

While Senator Joseph McCarthy and his House Un-American Activities Committee destroyed hundreds of lives (a tragedy lost on a little boy like myself), Hollywood contributed to the nation's indoctrination with TV shows like *I Led Three Lives*, the story of Herbert Philbrick, the U.S. double agent who every week exposed a communist cell plotting the downfall of American democracy from within our very midst. The schools contributed to my fright with duck-and-cover exercises that taught me how to protect myself from an atomic blast by scrambling under my school desk and covering my head with my arms. Walking home from school every day, I looked up to the sky to see if I could spot the Russian bombers that everyone said were sure to come.

Pattern 2: Connecting the Dots

This cultural pattern in the late 1950s and early 1960s revealed a significant shift in the public mind. America was plunging into a physicality it had never known and did not want to know. In this pattern we see deep longings, repressed needs, and unrecognized fears. But there was a precedent for this social phenomenon. Fifty years earlier there had been an attempt to rediscover the ground with Isadora Duncan, Loie Fuller, the Art Nouveau movement, French fashion designer Paul Poiret, Sigmund Freud, ragtime music, and the women's suffrage movement. Connect the dots.

In the late nineteenth century, Victorian morality had banished physicality and sensuality from the social scene. Women wore corsets and bustles designed to inhibit movement, akin to Chinese foot-binding. Paris, the capital of the fashion world, was manufacturing fifty million corsets a year. The tight lacing and artificially induced small waist deformed women's internal organs, causing long-lasting physical disorders. Some women went to the extreme of having their lower ribs removed in order to achieve the desired hourglass figure. The body had become an artifact.

One bustle made of steel was recommended by doctors because it created "less heating on the spine." Men's fashions presented a similar picture of the body repressed, with stovepipe jackets and starched shirts and collars. Sexuality suffered under the label of "sinful." Masturbation was believed to cause warts and anemia. Physical pleasure itself was suspect, and marriage manuals cautioned against more than one orgasm a week.

And into this world came Isadora Duncan. It is difficult today to comprehend the liberating power she represented to her audiences. Dancing barefoot to the music of Beethoven, Brahms, and Chopin, wearing only a light chiffon-like costume inspired by ancient Greece, she brought more than a new dance to the public. She offered a new vision of a new body in a new world. Artists and poets wept with joy. In Berlin, students unhitched the horses from her carriage and pulled her home through the streets while singing her praises to the sky. Art historian Élie Faure wrote, "Yes, we wept when we saw her . . . we rediscovered the primitive purity which, every two or three thousand years, reappears from the depth of the abyss of a worn-out conscience to restore a wholly animality to us . . ." English critic W. R. Titterton wrote:

> *I remember when I first saw her, Duncan came on and struck me like a thunderclap. Will you believe me? I shuddered with awe. Once in a century, in ten centuries, comes a new idea . . . In that idea was focused all that I and others had been dreaming.*

Isadora hated the ballet and never hesitated to offer her opinion on the subject. "The ballet filled me with horror," she wrote. "This method of dancing produces artificial and mechanical movement not worthy of the soul . . . I thank God that cruel destiny did not inflict upon me the career of a ballet dancer." While the ballet sought to defy gravity and propel the body into the air, Duncan cultivated an ever-stronger connection to the earth. She wrote, "all movement on earth is governed by the law of gravitation, by attraction and repulsion, resistance and yielding; it is that which makes the rhythms of the dance."

In the late 1920s and early 1930s, Isadora's earlier inspirations lived on in a generation of young choreographers who gave the world the modern dance movement. Known originally as "barefoot dancing," these choreographers were women in contrast to the men who had guided dance through its history for the previous two hundred years.

Whereas ballet sought to conceal nature in the body, the new dance struggled to reveal the nature within us. Ruth Saint Denis, Mary Wigman, Martha Graham, and Doris Humphrey looked to nature as their model. Graham devised her principles of contraction and release based on the cyclical action of breathing; from the rhythm of inhaling and exhaling, she created a whole new choreography. Humphrey talked of "fall" and "recovery." The body moves in relation to gravity, coming into and falling out of balance.

Women's fashions too reflected the desire for greater physical freedom. In 1906, French fashion designer Paul Poiret made history by banishing the corset from the woman's wardrobe. "I do not impose my will upon fashion," he said. "I am merely the first to perceive women's innermost desires and to fulfill them." Was it coincidence that Freud appeared at around the same time with his concept of libido and his reintroduction of sexuality into the public consciousness? Freud's recognition that humans were motivated by the sexual drive was a powerful affirmation of the body. Only a few years earlier the word *leg* was too hot for polite conversation, and instead the word *limb* was substituted. Now sex itself was a subject of frank conversation. Like grass growing up through the concrete, physicality was pushing its way back into our lives.

The Art Nouveau movement also reflected this invasion of nature into the home. Characterized by design motifs drawn from the organic world, lily pads, tendrils, stalks, and vines swirled around windows, staircases, and building facades as if consuming the frozen man-made artifacts like overgrowth in a steamy tropical jungle. The soft, languid lines of Art Nouveau give the impression of nature bursting through concrete, glass, and iron.

The person recognized as the embodiment of the spirit of the Art Nouveau movement in Europe was the American dancer Loie Fuller. Born in Chicago in 1862, Fuller landed in Paris in 1892 and became famous for her "skirt dances," in which she manipulated yards of long silk that she swirled and billowed in the air with undulating forms that captured the full shock of nature's beauty. Captivated audiences were reminded of something ancient they had forgotten: Wake up! To appreciate, one must seize the moment here and now!

Artists such as Mallarmé and Rodin were among Fuller's most ardent admirers and sat reverently as she performed the Serpent, the Lily, or the Fire Dance. Fuller became such an icon that the entrance to the Art Nouveau pavilion at the Paris World's Fair of 1900 was designed with her figure flowing over and around it.

A similar invasion of physicality was taking place in America. In 1896, an African-American dancer named Strap Heel appeared in New York City at Tony Pastor's Fourteenth Street variety house. Heel was accompanied on the piano by Ben Harney, and the music Harney played was ragtime. New Yorkers had never heard the syncopated rhythms of this early jazz music and were never the same afterwards.

Within a few years, ragtime compositions were being sold by the hundreds of thousands. At first its popularity was limited to the big cities. People living in smaller, isolated communities shied away from the music because its upbeat rhythms were so associated with the lowlife. Then in 1911, Irving Berlin came out with "Alexander's Ragtime Band." Berlin's composition changed the character of American popular music and gave ragtime the seal of approval it needed to make it acceptable to mainstream white America. Ragtime spread across America like a prairie fire.

While Charles Darwin's theory of evolution—and its implication that humans were connected to the animal kingdom—was a subject of hot debate, the issue had been settled by at least one generation on the dance floor. Millions of young Americans danced enthusiastically imitating ducks, monkeys, snakes, and turkeys, encouraging a spontaneity and sheer fun of moving that challenged the stiffness and formality of conventional dance-floor etiquette. The more measured rhythms of a disappearing era—the polka, galop, and the waltz—were shoved into the background as ballrooms in every city and town hopped to the faster rhythms of the fox-trot, the turkey trot, the bunny hug, the monkey slide, the grizzly bear, the snake, the lame duck, and the chicken scratch.

The new American music and the unrestrained body it created had to fight for its freedom. In Boston, Mayor Fitzgerald (JFK's grandfather) banned all ragtime dancing in the city. The *California Christian Advocate* collected petitions against the "dancing menace" and typified the backlash: "Dancing has rarely ever been free from low animalism. It usually appeals abnormally to the lower and baser passions of mankind . . . to the physical and sensuous basis of human nature. Art to be art should refine nature . . . Strictly speaking no civilized nation authorizes or enjoins dancing." But the younger generation was defenseless against the ragtime rhythms. They spoke of twitching muscles, a tingling feeling of electricity in the body, and the irresistible need to dance.

Ragtime music was like a Trojan horse for the black population in America. Its influence on white America undermined some of the most cherished values of the very system that had oppressed them for so long. History would repeat itself years later with rock and roll.

And there was the *Rubáiyát of Omar Khayyám*. Translated by Edward FitzGerald between 1859–1880, the Rubáiyát began appearing in American bookstores in the 1890s, carrying with it a potent message of renewal. In its numerous quatrains the Rubáiyát spoke of pleasure of the senses, enjoyment in the present, and the value of living without a personal God looking over one's shoulder:

> *Come, fill the Cup, and in the Fire of Spring*
> *The Winter Garment of Repentance fling:*
> *The Bird of Time has but a little way.*

Or:

> *"Here with a Loaf of Bread beneath the Bough,*
> *A Flask of Wine, a Book of Verse—and Thou*

Beside me singing in the Wilderness—
And Wilderness is Paradise enow."

The stark world of scripture stressing the mortification of the flesh, the burden of original sin, and the glories of a life in the hereafter paled in comparison. Over a period of almost two decades, the Rubáiyát fell into the hands of millions of young people, becoming the equivalent of an early hippie manifesto encouraging a whole generation to get out of their "heads" and to "be here now!" Favored quatrains appeared on everything from stationery to note pads and wall hangings. This affirmation of being in the present could only deepen the experience of being in the body as well.

Ragtime, the Rubáiyát, Sigmund Freud, Art Nouveau, Isadora, Loie Fuller, Paul Poiret. Is there a pattern here? Each in its own way reintroduces nature to a culture cut off from its body, a nation starved of its physical vitality.

This tsunami that swept across America around the end of the nineteenth and early twentieth centuries—at times coaxing and cajoling, at other times pulling us along kicking and screaming into another way of being—eventually receded, and a coolness came over the land. Welcome to the fifties—Victorianism revisited. Then Elvis & Co. arrived.

For centuries humans have been negotiating and renegotiating their relationship to the natural world. It is our natural birthright to be connected to the earth. Our uninformed education trains us to think and act otherwise.

D. H. Lawrence expressed our dilemma well in *Lady Chatterley's Lover*, when he wrote,

If civilization is any good, it has to help us to forget our bodies, and then time passes happily without our knowing it.

CHAPTER 16

CHASING THAT THOUGHT

ONE DAY IT OCCURRED TO ME THAT if I wanted to understand the origins of Western body movement, I might do well to understand the origins of Western thought. Here was a subject I knew nothing about or ever had any interest in but which now became intensely interesting because of my questions. I didn't know where to begin. Greece, Plato, Socrates? With a little reading I found that the beginning of Greek philosophy was actually earlier, with the pre-Socratic philosophers.

The next day I was in my favorite used bookstores stocking up. I never went to libraries to research. For some reason I wanted to own the books I read and knew would mean so much to me. It was like creating family.

I only became interested in dance history when I was faced with a question that I could not answer. Similarly, the history of philosophy became intensely interesting because of my question. For almost two years I never left home without a book on the pre-Socratic philosophers. The thrill of seeing Western thought unfold was so great that even when driving my car, I'd arrive at a red light and whip out a book to read for twenty or thirty seconds while waiting for the light to change.

Several interesting things from this study stood out. Firstly, Greek philosophy did not begin in Greece, but rather in Turkey along the coast of the Aegean Sea. This was Greek-colonized Asia Minor, the edge of the Greek world.

There in the town of Miletus lived Thales, born 624 B.C., the first of a handful of men who asked a simple yet profound question: What is the "stuff" of the universe? This query brought into question the omnipotence of the Greek gods. Here was a revolution in thought. Everything to follow was important, crucial, but could not be as groundbreaking.

Thales's conclusion? The basic stuff of the universe was water. For the first time the world was conceived in terms of a material substance; matter was differentiated from spirit. Thales's thinking did not vacate the world of gods and spirits and place humans in the middle of a purely material universe. His was not an either-or world. While water was the primary substance, all things were still endowed with a soul. Gods and divinities were everywhere. Nothing was inanimate. Everything was alive. But the first cleavage between matter and spirit, a split western culture has wrestled with ever since, was established. Not to be missed here is the first move towards reductionism, a way of examining the world that became the strength of Western science and the bane of our existence. A dance stressing the body separating from the earth is a natural outgrowth from this line of thought.

Following Thales were Anaximander and his student Anaximenes, also from Miletus. Anaximander posited a universe made up of an indefinite, boundless substance he called *apeiron* out of which all things arose and to which they returned. Anaximenes said that air, not water, was the primary matter of the universe and that through a process of rarefaction and condensation, all things were created. Again, the content of their thought is not as important as the fact that they asked the same question and began tracing a line of inquiry that carries down to this day. Here in its most nascent stage was the beginning of reduction-ism—a gradual dismantling of the universe. Was this not the birth of the mechanistic worldview?

I would like to know how Thales came to ask his question. How did he gain distance on his world to even conceive that another way of seeing was possible? How many of his contemporaries would have understood his question?

I carried out this study alone, around my teaching and perform-ing, without having anyone to discuss the subject with. Someone made a suggestion. Since I lived within walking distance of one of the world's great universities, why not audit classes on the subject? I consulted a class schedule and found nothing on the pre-Socratics, but I did see a class on Plato. The teacher was happy to have me audit, but within minutes my eyes could not stay open. In no time, I was falling asleep. Nothing had changed since grade school.

*   *   *   *

The seventeenth century continued to fascinate me. That's when the Sci-entific Revolution coalesced, creating our modern world and bringing with it a new conception of the human body. I wanted to know more. To overcome the isolation of working alone, in 1989 I arranged to meet once a week at the French Hotel Café with Iain Boal to discuss this period. Iain was not only a friend but also a scholar and historian. A graduate of Cam-bridge in England, he had taught at Harvard and was now at Stanford. He knew everything I wanted to know on the subject.

During one of those meetings, Iain gave me an article on the history of seventeenth century medicine. A footnote in this article changed my life—another before-and-after moment. It was short: "Valentine Great-rakes, a seventeenth-century Irish healer." Nothing more. *Healer*? Not *quack* or *charlatan*, *healer*. Did this man really heal?

The next day I ran into a friend, Ralph Wilcoxen, on the street. Ralph was steeped in historical research. I don't know why, but I mentioned the footnote, and he suggested—preposterously, I thought—that maybe this man Greatrakes had written a book. I scoffed. "Nah, he's only a footnote." Naive me.

"If he wrote anything," Ralph said, "it'll be in the BLC." I was clueless. "That's the British Library Catalogue," he explained, "It lists every book written in the English language since the time of Adam and Eve." Did I have to go to London to see this? "No, they have one in the library on campus." I recoiled inside. *A university library? Not my world*, I thought.

Ralph noticed my hesitation and offered to take me there. So the next day, we entered the reference room and headed for a wall with over two hundred red-bound volumes of the BLC. I went straight for the *G*'s. There he was—Greatrakes, Valentine. I was stunned. Under his name were five listings: three books and two news articles. One of the books, *A Brief Account*, was by Greatrakes himself. He had written a book! The date was 1666, and he wrote this to vindicate himself against a book attacking him, *Wonders No Miracles*, written by a man of the Church, David Lloyd.

All three books existed on microfiche and could have easily been viewed in the library right there, but luckily I didn't know this, and Ralph didn't mention it. Otherwise I would have been deprived of a great adventure. Ralph did tell me that in another room in the library we could find hundreds more volumes listing where original copies of these same books could be found in American libraries. The third book listed was *The Miraculous Conformist* by Henry Stubbe. He had witnessed Greatrakes heal, and wrote a book supporting him. An original copy was in the rare book collection at Stanford. Being that Iain taught there, I called him that night, and a few days later we drove down together. While he went to lecture, I went to the rare book room. I filled out the proper form, took my assigned seat, and a few minutes later a woman handed me a pair of white gloves and a small leather-bound book. I obtained a photocopy of the slender volume, and on the ride home I read aloud to Iain.

The book was dedicated to Robert Boyle and described numerous cures Stubbe had witnessed. Iain never heard of Greatrakes, but Boyle's name surprised him. He was a major figure in the creation of modern science.

The more we examined the material, the more interesting this became. We couldn't let go of it. For the next eight years we traveled to Ireland, England, and Scotland every year to carry out research, unearthing the life of this forgotten man. Anyone wanting the full story can see my book *A Small Moment of Great Illumination: Searching for Valentine Greatrakes, the Master Healer*, published in 2006.

Someone once said, "When the universe speaks, you'd better listen." The amount of Greatrakes energy focusing on me was so strange that it seemed like the universe was conspiring upon me.

An example: When I learned that a copy of Greatrakes's book was at the National Library of Medicine in Bethesda, Maryland, I travelled there to see it. Holding this book in my hands was like doing time travel. All the aroma of the time was right there in my hands. An engraving of Greatrakes leapt off the page and took hold. I decided then and there that I wanted an original copy of this book for myself. What were the chances of finding one? The book was published in London a few months before the Great Fire of 1666. How many copies were lost? How many survived? And if I did find one, could I afford it? But I did find one, and in the most unsuspecting of places: in San Francisco. And there is more. (See *A Small Moment of Great Illumination*.)

*   *   *   *

In my discussions with Iain about the rise of modern science, I was interested in how this new science conditioned our understanding and experience of the human body. In those discussions I learned something I had not known—the repressed sexuality that lay at the foundation of this new emerging science. It is not addressed in the majority of works on this history. With one exception: Brian Easlea. His books, *Witch-hunting, Magic & the New Philosophy*, and *Science and Sexual Oppression* provide an insightful analysis. This was critical for my understanding of how the new science made sense with the creation of the ballet.

Sex and the Origins of Modern Science

At its origins in the seventeenth century, modern science was conceived as a masculine philosophy, and the object of the new science's study, the natural world, was understood as feminine. This is not a personal interpretation but rather is how it was understood at the time by the philosophers and scientists who formulated the new science.

According to philosopher Joseph Glanvill, the purpose of the new science was to discover ways of "captivating nature and making her subserve to our purposes" in order to achieve the "Empire of Man over Nature." Glanville was not alone in attributing gender to the new science along with a hierarchy with humans (men) at the top dominating a feminine nature.

The seventeenth century diarist John Evelyn wrote about Robert Boyle and noted that whenever "stubborn matter" came under Boyle's "inquisition," he always managed to "extort a confession of all that lay in her most intimate recesses."

Thomas Sprat, secretary of the Royal Society, tells us that after a "courtship of nature . . . she will yield to the forward and the bold." Then "the beautiful bosom of nature will be exposed to our view . . . we shall enter into its garden and taste of its fruit and satisfy ourselves with its plenty." Is there a repressed sexuality lurking here?

Henry Oldenburg, member of the Royal Society and long-time correspondent to Boyle, wrote, "the true sons of learning penetrate from Nature's antechamber to her inner closet." Francis Bacon wrote, "We have no right to expect nature to come to us." Rather, "Nature must be taken by the forelock. Delay and subtle argument permit one only to clutch at nature, never to lay hold of her and capture her . . . I come to you in truth and lead you to nature with all her children to bind her to your service and make her your slave."

Thomas Browne, writing in 1643, deplored intercourse as "the foolishest act a wise man commits in all his life." He regretted that humans cannot procreate like trees rather than "in this trivial and vulgar way of union."

And on and on.

In a most artful manner John Milton in *Paradise Lost*, 1667, deplores the very existence of women:

> *Oh, why did God, Creator wise,*
> *that peopled highest heaven With spirits masculine,*
> *create at last this novelty on Earth, this fair defect of nature,*
> *and not fill the World at once With men as angels, without feminine;*
> *Or find some other way to generate Mankind?*

There is no mistaking the fear, disdain, and contempt these men felt towards women, nature, and the body. They are viewed with antagonism and alienation and are to be controlled. If nothing more, the male-dominated ballet, upward bound and away from the earth, was an artful representation of this alienation. Add the Church with its hierarchy of values, and this context grows.

None of what is recounted here denies the beauty of the ballet. That point must be made. The fact that it is so captivating only points to the complexity of the issue and tells us what we already know: that life is not simple.

A Brief History of the Hatred of Women

Studying the rise of modern science, one cannot avoid running into the European witch hunts. John Milton's hateful representation of the feminine is benign compared to this grotesque expression of sexual antagonism. Vast and complicated, it is a difficult history to pin down because it played out so differently from country to country. Without getting lost in the details, several things stand out that helped me understand our cultural treatment of the body.

Number one: Contrary to popular thought, the witch hunts did not occur during the Middle Ages, but rather during the Renaissance and early Enlightenment. This means that while some of the world's great art was being created, art viewed as a rebirth of European civilization, defenseless women were being burned at the stake just down the road.

Number two: For many years, witches, both male and female, were protected by the Church. The stereotype of the witch came into being around the end of the fifteenth century, and as witch hunts grew, the focus fell largely on women. My question is: Why at this time?

Number three: At its peak, this madness lasted over a hundred years, from roughly 1550–1650. Outside a small group of scholars, this history is virtually unknown. Why does this history go untreated in any study of European history in school?

A closer look:

The Dark Ages were not so dark after all. For centuries the Church not only protected witches from persecution but even denied their existence. The Council of Paderborn (established in 785) outlawed the belief in witches and stated that anyone who believes in them is "blinded by the devil and infected with pagan errors" and is committing a crime punishable by death. In the ninth century, King Charlemagne declared the death penalty for anyone who burned a supposed witch. Burning witches, he said, was a pagan custom. The Canon Episcopi, a document prohibiting the persecution of witches, was made part of Church Canon Law in 906. Women who believed they could ride across the night sky, it said, were "seduced by illusions." In 1080, Pope Gregory VII wrote to the King of

Denmark asking him to beware of blaming unfortunate women for sickness, frosts, and other untimely events.

Then a dramatic shift took place in the late fifteenth century. Suddenly, the supposed witches of the day were found by the Church to be different from those mentioned in the Canon. They were more dangerous and had to be stopped. It's as if the Church had something stuck in its craw. *Gotta get the women, and we'll do whatever it takes!* The Canon, they now said, wasn't binding because it had never been approved by the Church Council.

But before the Church could carry out its pogrom on defenseless women, it had to turn witchcraft from a secular crime into a crime against God, religion, and the Church. Witchcraft had to be reinterpreted as a crime against Christianity, hence heresy. This would make it a prosecutable offense. Without this, the Church had no jurisdiction.

The missing link here was the Devil's pact. This invention bound the witch to the Devil, making her his servant in their work of destroying Christianity. Crimes previously prosecuted as crimes against a person could now be prosecuted as crimes against God. The Church had successfully converted a delusion into a reality. The classic stereotype of the witch came into existence as a harridan woman in league with the Devil to destroy the Church.

In earlier times, anyone who believed in witches was an infidel. Now anyone who denied their existence was a heretic. The question that attracted my attention was why did this change take place when it did? What brought it on?

A landmark work in this history was the *Malleus Maleficarum*, written in 1486 by two Dominican monks, Heinrich Kramer and Jacob Sprenger. Here is an elaborate handbook of misogyny with instructions on how to identify witches, instructions on how to prosecute them, and, worst of all, the different degrees of torture to be administered. Thumbscrews were "gentle torture." This was followed by "ordinary" torture and then by "extraordinary" torture.

There has been controversy around the actual influence of this book. Nevertheless Pope Innocent VIII issued a papal bull supporting the monks in their work, and between 1487 and 1520, the book went through thirteen printings and found its way onto the bench of many magistrates around Europe.

One chapter spells out the authors' intent and is entitled, "Why it is that Women are chiefly addicted to Evil Superstitions?" They write:

> *Women are more credulous. They have slippery tongues. They are feebler both in mind and body. Women are intellectually like children. They have weak memories. It is a natural vice in them not to be disciplined, but to follow their own impulses. All witchcraft comes from carnal lust, which in women is insatiable. Midwives surpass all others in wickedness.*

In France, a most feared witchfinder was Jean Bodin (1529–1596). According to Bodin, no punishment was too severe for a witch. He wrote:

> *Whatever punishment one can order against witches by roasting and cooking them over a slow fire is not as bad as the eternal agonies which are prepared for them in hell, for the fire here cannot last more than an hour or so until the witches have died.*

Bodin was also a highly respected judge, lawyer, and political theorist. Astoundingly, there is a high school in western France today in his name: Lycée Jean Bodin. On the school's website he is described as a "distinguished humanist."

The unfortunates who fell under the eye of the inquisitor were submitted to the most perverted reasoning. Any woman who defended herself by pointing to her virtuous life found no compassion. A virtuous life was the perfect cover for evil.

If women had the power to raise storms, change men into beasts, and inflict illness from a distance, then why could they not effect their release or kill their enemies? Answer: because God does not will it. If witches are so powerful, why are they not rich? Answer: so as not to make themselves too conspicuous. If a woman, upon learning that she is about to be accused, begins building up a defense, this is a sure sign of guilt. Why does God allow witches to operate? Answer: in order to give people the opportunity to prove they are just. He also allows witchcraft to prove that people have free will to choose between Good and Evil.

Any woman who had entered into a pact with the Devil was touched by him on her body, leaving a mark. The witchfinder's job was to find this mark. It could be a mole or a birthmark and was believed to be insensitive to pain. To determine if a given spot was the devil's mark, the witchfinder would pierce it with a bodkin, a tool resembling an ice pick. The accused woman was shaved of all body hair, then stripped naked and tied down to a horizontal plank on the town square while the inquisitor searched her body for amulets or charms she might have been hiding on her person. Every orifice was searched: nose, mouth, ears, under the eyelids, the genitals.

Inquisitors demonstrated a particular fascination with the Devil's penis, and numerous confessions extracted under torture provide descriptions that did much to feed their belief in the enormous sexual appetite of the Devil as well as the witch. Pierre de Lancre, a famous Jesuit scholar and trial judge in Bordeaux, reported that the Devil's penis was "generally sinuous, pointed, and snake-like, made sometimes of half iron, half flesh, sometimes wholly of horn and was commonly forked like a serpent's tongue. He customarily performed both coitus and pederasty at once, while sometimes a third prong reached to his lover's mouth."

There were people who stood up to denounce the inquisitors. In 1584, English member of Parliament Reginald Scot spoke out against "This outrageous and barbarous cruelty, cankered and spiteful malice, extreme and intolerable tyranny [that] is practiced against these old women."

In 1631, German Jesuit priest Friedrich von Spee was asked why his hair turned prematurely gray. He said,

> *Through grief over the many witches whom I have prepared for death. Not one was guilty. Often I have thought that the only reason why we are not all wizards is due to the fact that we have not all been tortured. And if an inquisitor could reach the Pope, he would make him confess that he was a wizard.*

It is astonishing that this history is still largely unknown and that the institution behind these aberrations still exists. If there were no Church, would God still exist?

The question again is why did this take place when it did, during the Renaissance and early Enlightenment?

I see a relationship between this history of institutional misogyny and the rise of the masculine philosophy, the new modern science as described above. The persecution of women during the witch craze was a sort of cultural lever, depress one (the feminine) to give rise to the other (the masculine).

Whereas the witchfinders found sadistic pleasure in inflicting pain and suffering on women, the misogyny of the founders of modern science, while more benign, operated at the level of metaphor, and in metaphor these early scientists lived out the attitudes and behavior of the witchfinders.

The Church Apology

In 2000, a historic ceremony was held in Saint Peter's Church in Rome that went practically unnoticed by the world. Pope John Paul II stood before Michelangelo's *Pietà* and asked forgiveness for the Church's sins past and present. The apology consisted of seven categories of sins. Category number 6 is pertinent here. It is entitled "Confession of sins against the dignity of women and the unity of the human race." The exact words read:

> *Let us pray for all those who have suffered offences against*
> *their human dignity and whose rights have been trampled; let*
> *us pray for women, who are all too often humiliated and emar-*
> *ginated, and let us acknowledge the forms of acquiescence in*
> *these sins of which Christians too have been guilty.*

Cardinal Joseph Ratzinger was then in charge of administering Church law. In former times this branch of the Vatican was known as the Inquisition. In 1965, no longer burning heretics at the stake, it took on the more benign name of the Congregation for the Doctrine of the Faith. And at the ceremony in front of the *Pietà* the good Cardinal read these words:

> *Let us pray that each one of us, meek and humble of heart, will*
> *recognize that even men of the Church, in the name of faith*
> *and morals, have sometimes used methods not in keeping with*
> *the Gospel in the solemn duty of defending the truth.*

How nice. Steal a loaf of bread and go to jail. Decimate a people, apologize, and everything is OK.

It should be noted that during the many Church scandals in the 1990s about priests sexually abusing young boys, Brian Ross of ABC News approached Cardinal Ratzinger in Rome as he walked to his limousine and asked a pointed question on the subject. The Cardinal, irritated by the questioning, slapped the reporter on the hand like a schoolmaster reprimanding an impertinent student. And it was a solid, angry slap. It was stunning to think that the Cardinal thought he had the right to do this and that common rules of comportment did not apply to him. And for those who do not know, this good Cardinal became Pope Benedict XVI.

CHAPTER 17

ECO-RAP

IN 1986, I WAS APPROACHED BY a friend with the idea of opening a theatre in San Francisco. This theatre became Life On The Water. My partners were Joe Lambert, Bill Talen, and Ellen Sebastian Chang.

Our idea was to present original theatrical work created by contemporary artists. Apparently we came along at the right time. Our first fundraiser in San Francisco raised over $5,000, and audiences were poised to attend the shows we produced. We opened the theatre with Spalding Gray performing his monologue *Terrors of Pleasure*.

Ellen, Bill, and I were theatre makers, and now with our own theatre we had a place to produce our own work. I created three one-man shows: *Not For Real*, created with and directed by the brilliant Rinde Eckert; *Spleenix*, created with and directed by the equally brilliant Ellen Sebastian Chang; and *Ned*, a scripted piece about an out-of-sorts gangster written by His High Talentness, David Barth, and directed by Ellen.

We operated Life On The Water for seven years and then decided to close so we could pursue our own work. Producing others took up too much of our lives. We paid the bills and said good-bye. It was a phenomenal seven years.

*   *   *   *

In 1991, while I was both operating Life On The Water and navigating the seventeenth-century for Valentine Greatrakes, two ideas of a different nature collided in my mind: ecology and rap music. The ecology part of the equation came up because Bill Talen, my partner at Life On The Water (known today as Reverend Billy), was producing a festival of theatrical productions based on environmental themes. Rap came up because that summer, I was directing a show for the Pickle Family Circus in San Francisco with a group of young rappers in the cast. That's when it hit me like lightening: Eco-Rap! The hyphen made all the difference: Educate inner-city rappers about dangerous environmental issues. Have them write raps about it. Hold a contest. Stage a free outdoor concert with the winners. The idea was inspiring, but what did I know about ecology or rap? Nothing. I also knew that having a good idea is easy; carrying it out is the hard part. I wasn't going to let this one get away.

With all my naiveté in place, I approached a number of environmental organizations asking each for a donation of $3,000 to get off the ground. This was preposterous, of course. I was an unknown with no organizational history in any of these areas. But one person did see the light and gave all the support he could, short of money; this was Carl Anthony, director of Urban Habitat, one of the oldest environmental justice organizations in the country. He gave advice and steered me in the right direction. With no monies donated, I had no choice but to dip into my own pocket the first year to make it happen.

I found two collaborators, and together we built the idea of the contest. With a professional ecologist as our guide, we mounted a bus with our young rappers and went on what we called a toxic tour of their neighborhood. We did four tours that first year with almost one hundred kids in all. A couple of weeks later, they performed their raps at Life On The Water before judges from the field. Prizes were awarded to the best and the top winners got to perform at an Eco-Rap concert we staged in San Francisco's Justin Herman Plaza right on the bay.

Many of the kids who entered the contest cared little for the environment but were drawn by the exposure and the prizes, e.g., free studio time, CDs, etc. "Ecology? That's a white man's problem!" one rapper said. But once confronted with the pollution in their own backyards, they became concerned very fast. And this awareness went right into their music. The results were stunning.

It turns out that Eco-Rap came along at the right time. The large environmental organizations had been under fire for being too focused on the natural world—whales, porpoises, dolphins, and redwood trees—and not giving enough attention to environmental issues affecting communities of color in the inner city. The cry for environmental justice was everywhere. Eco-Rap filled the void by bringing an awareness of these issues to a generation of disenfranchised youth and providing them with the opportunity to voice their feelings.

The concert brought the media. News stories about Eco-Rap appeared in many newspapers and on CNN, VH1, and NPR radio—local and national—as well as on local affiliates of the big TV networks. Schools recognized the value of our work and began asking us to do programs for their students.

One of the contestants that first year, A. K. Black, emerged from the crowd with an impressive brilliance. His artistry, intelligence, and heart, plus his deep concern for his community, drew us together. With some funding we received, we were able to make A. K. a partner in Eco-Rap. As Eco-Rap developed educational programs, A. K. and I, self-dubbed the salt-and-pepper act, travelled to schools around the Bay Area, turning young kids onto an aspect of life in their neighborhoods that they knew nothing about.

As word of Eco-Rap travelled, we received invitations from around the country, to events as far afield as a national conference in Colorado sponsored by the U.S. Bureau of Land Management. From national we went international. In 1995 we sent ten Bay Area rappers to Stuttgart, Germany to perform at an International rap festival. At the last minute one of the rappers dropped out of the tour. I replaced him with a fifteen-year-old girl from a high school in Bayview-Hunters Point.

Ama Deonbi was a bored ninth grader whose talent could not be contained within the four walls of high school. She was forty units behind and continually cut class to hang out with friends on the streets. She missed the toxic tour with her class because she cut that day. But when she heard her classmates rapping in school the next week, she called me to get the phone number of the toxic tour guide. The following week she performed her rap in class. A. K. and I were left speechless.

Rap performed a cappella harkens back to an era of ancient bardic poetry. Ama exemplified this. She gathered all the information and boiled it down into a poetic form that she delivered with a compelling, albeit untrained, presence. In other words, she was a natural. So when a spot opened up on the German tour, there was no question who I would send. Ama's trip to Germany was a turning point in her life. "Leonard, I had to travel seven thousand miles to cross the color line," she told me afterwards. She was the only girl on the trip, and everyone treated her with respect, she said with pride. This meant the world.

On the return trip, Eco-Rap brought thirteen young rappers from Germany to the Bay Area, all members of different ethnic minorities living in Germany who performed rap as a form of social criticism.

Eco-Rap booked them gigs around the Bay Area, and wherever they went, I sent Ama. My motto that summer was Ama Everywhere. At an

Eco-Rap event at a school in El Sobrante, there was Ama on stage telling the students, "Hey, kids, you gotta stay in school. It's cool to be smart!"

For five years I gave up all theatrical pursuits and devoted myself entirely to Eco-Rap. The success of our first year, plus our high profile in the media, eventually brought funding but never enough to take the pressure off. The burden of producing large events without enough staff took its toll. In the end I became sick. My body was racked with pain. I went to the hospital with three books and my laptop certain they would put me in a bed. "It's all psychological, Leonard," said the doctor. "Take a rest." It took a year to ease out of Eco-Rap.

The lesson learned here was about the kids. And that's what I want to tell the world. The generation of youth we worked with in Eco-Rap have been written off by our society. If it takes a village to raise a child, these kids live alone in a clearing outside of town. It's a miracle they aren't running around pulling out their hair, yelling and screaming.

The poverty and lack of social services aside, the daily violence in their community is enough to make these kids feel like they're living in a war-torn third-world country. One young girl in a program we did in an Oakland high school was machine-gunned in her bed one Saturday night while she slept.

As we all know, America is not a homogeneous whole from sea to shining sea but rather is a patchwork made up of a shrinking middle class bookended on one end by a small number of super-rich, the one-percenters, and on the other end by America the Third World, with all of its attendant pressures.

By any measure these kids have every right to be angry and cynical. But again and again I found young people who were positive and enthusiastic and who cared for their future as well as the future of their children. To a fault they were all endowed with a beautiful what I call spontaneous intelligence: facing a perilous situation, all they wanted to do was to make things better. By any measure of good citizenship, they rate the highest.

And that brings me to Ama. She taught me something I knew in my bones but had never experienced firsthand. Take a child who is troubled, who can't fit in. Take any interest they have, be it music, boxing, fly-fishing, sports, whatever. Immerse them in that interest fully. That's the hook, and with that they will find the way to their whole person. Therein lies the vehicle for their growth.

Chapter 18

WRITING PARIS

ONE DAY IN 1996, I WAS IN MOE'S Books in Berkeley hunting for anything to do with Valentine Greatrakes when I came across a book entitled *Marville Paris*. I didn't know what this was, but Paris! Leafing through the book, my life took a dramatic turn—another before-and-after moment. With more than seven hundred photos, this small volume showed me a Paris I had never seen before and challenged me on the spot.

Marville was Charles Marville, the man hired by Baron Haussmann to photograph the Paris he was tearing down and rebuilding. While I recognized the locations in the legends, I could not recognize any of the places in the photos. This was my first hint of the grand transformation Paris had undergone in the nineteenth century. It was shocking to think that I could have lived there for so long and been so ignorant of this history. I always thought that my street, the Avenue de l'Opéra, was ancient. Coming from Detroit, I would wax poetic over the centuries-old stones I lived within. Only now did I realize that the entire Avenue and all the buildings on it were barely ninety years old when I settled there in 1963.

I made copies of these photos and a few months later went back to Paris to find the same places where Marville stood to take his photos so I could see the difference. This was not easy. In most cases nothing was left. Even when buildings were still standing, there was nothing recognizable at street level because the facades have been redone modern. One must look up, to the rooftops, to the patterns of windows and balconies for clues.

To stand on a Paris street corner with a photo of that spot taken over 150 years before and to see the difference is a stunning, almost sensual experience. The scale of the work, the sweat of the labor, the achievement of carrying out this transformation in what amounted to a *shazam!* becomes very real. Moving from one corner to the next with these photos, the old city becomes palpable. On several occasions I tried to share my excitement with a passing Parisian or a shopkeeper, showing them the Marville photo to compare with the same street today. I never got more than an uninterested Gallic shrug, and I gave that up in short time. But my own amazement never ceased.

I began shooting photos of these spots to document the differences and then made visits to the archives to see more original photos of old Paris shot by Marville, and others.

On subsequent trips to Paris, I took friends on walks to show them my discoveries. I was hooked. I began studying the history of this transformation, reading everything I could on the subject. Someone once said, "If you want to learn about something, write a book about it." And that's what I did. For the next five years I went back to Paris twice a year, in the spring and the fall, for a month or two each time to research and photograph. Staying with friends made these trips possible. I'd spend weeks sitting in the archives sifting through hundreds of photos, selecting the good ones, and then go back to the same spot to rephotograph.

Photographing Paris is as difficult as photographing animals in nature. You have to know the landscape and be patient. You have to know the light.

Photographing an east-west street is different from photographing a north-south street. The light and shadow are different. And the quality of the light changes during the year. In the warmer months, Paris light is soft, pastel. In colder months it is harsher, metallic. And the trees. Trees obscure buildings. That is why March was so important. I had to get there when the trees had just begun to bud but were not yet hiding the buildings.

My first book, *Walks Through Lost Paris*, is organized around four walks with hundreds of photos showing the before and after of each stop along the way. Experiencing the city's transformation in this way creates a feeling of connection between the different locations. One can feel the body of the city. It becomes a feeling experience as much as a seeing experience. I also provide the history to animate these places.

I wrote this book under my own steam with no support of any kind. Never having been in academia, the world of grants is foreign to me. Once I finished creating the book, no publisher in America was interested. This was the era of freedom fries, and American publishers were frightened off.

With nothing to lose I travelled to Paris with my maquette, the model I made of my book. Several friends at home advised me to get real. An American who doesn't even live in Paris and is not a historian is going to tell the French about their history? Others thought the book was too specialized and would have a hard time finding an audience.

With no idea of how to proceed, I flew to Paris. Then something most fortunate happened. It was around 2001; I was in Paris and lamented to a friend, Francoise Reynaud, photo curator at the Carnavalet Museum, about the loneliness of my pursuit. Working on my own with no affiliation of any kind, I'd never had anyone to talk to, discuss.

She suggested I call Alexandre Gady, a Paris historian who teaches at the Sorbonne and has written a number of books on the city. I was terrified to make the call. A published author, a university professor? I dithered for days then screwed up my courage and almost had to grab my left hand to force myself to dial the number, all the while looking away because I could not bear to watch myself making the call. My French was fine, but the thought of speaking French around something like this, and to a real historian, was intimidating.

I dialed. He answered.

"Hello. Who's this? What? You're American? You're writing a book on what? Paris? Uh-huh, right, OK. You want to what? Meet? Uh, well, I'm very busy. OK, but just briefly. Meet me at the café downstairs."

I hung up and was out of breath. We got together, and the short meeting turned into two hours, and it was me who had to finally leave. Alexandre went through my manuscript and got it immediately. He kept saying, "Why didn't anyone think of this before?" One can imagine my elation. We became fast friends.

He insisted that I meet Francois Besse of Editions Parigramme. Besse specialized in books on Paris with lots of high-quality photos and was sure to like it, Alexandre said. I made another one of those nervous phone calls and went to the appointment full of trepidation. For me to be sitting in the office of a French publisher was a little like sitting in Notre Dame. My brain was being pulled and stretched in the most beautiful ways.

Besse puffed away on a cigarette as he went over my maquette. The one thing he said repeatedly as he turned the pages was, "Hmmm, very coherent, very coherent."

A couple of weeks later, a letter arrived with his offer to buy the book. *Promenades Dans le Paris Disparu* came out in November 2002. I wrote the book in English, and they translated. How impressive it was to read myself in French. I sounded halfway intelligent.

But the best was yet to come. Parigramme flew me to Paris for the book launch and sent me on the three-week media blitz of my dreams. Monday through Friday from 9 AM to 5 PM I was accompanied by the loveliest Parisian press attaché to radio and TV interviews and to book signings all over Paris. And this was at the height of the French-bashing fever in America. The animosity coming from the U.S. side had no equivalent on the French side. The book signings were arranged so I would take those who assembled at the bookstore on a short walk through the neighborhood. Me showing Parisians their own history? Many shook my hand afterwards and made it a point to mention their appreciation for what the Americans did for France in World War II.

One of these promotional events stands out. In the exclusive neighborhood of Place de la Madeleine is one of the rarest restaurants in Paris, Caviar Kaspia. This is a step back into the nineteenth century with a menu built around caviar with all the fixings. Once a month the restaurant holds a private lunch where guests pay to dine with an author. And one month the invited author was me! This was the experience of a lifetime.

Entering this restaurant that reeked of old-world elegance, I was greeted by a gentleman dressed in a sparkling tuxedo with a hearty handshake as if I were a regular. How did he know it was me? My mind flashed back to the last time I had anything to do with a man in a tuxedo in Paris, when I was kicked out of the Café de la Paix in 1963. What a difference thirty-eight years can make.

A second gentlemen in a tuxedo greeted me with a similarly brilliant smile and escorted me upstairs down a long corridor to a private salon where a table for twelve was set and sat me down like the grand pasha I was for the afternoon.

Minutes later the guests began arriving. Most of them were elderly women wearing furs. Lots of handshakes and smiles. We chatted away during the meal, with me trying to ooze as much charm as I could muster as the dishes came one after the other and the wine was poured. I've never acquired a taste for wine—strange, I know—but I gladly took it that day, red wine, white wine, all of it. And with the caviar it wasn't bad, I must say. By the end of the meal I was pleasantly soused. After we parted, with more hearty handshakes all around, I lay down on the couch for a short nap.

The book sold out in six weeks and became a bestseller. Imagine the thrill of seeing my book on display at the Louvre or in the Musée d'Orsay, or to walk down the street and see it in bookstore windows.

Having spent five years on this book, I thought I'd never do another one. With no support of any kind, it was just too hard. Plus, not knowing how to carry out research, how to collect and organize information, my improvised research method was to flounder and grope. My note-taking is a mess. I take notes and lose them. When I do find them, I can't read what I wrote. Worse yet are the notes I should have made. I read something that doesn't strike me as important. Then I read something later and realize that what I read earlier is now vitally important, but I can't remember where I read it.

But the pull of those old Paris photos was strong, and on a later visit to Paris, I was back in the archives poking around again. One day at the library for the history of Paris—Bibliothèque Historique de la Ville de Paris—I met a young American woman researching a project. She didn't know my book, and I had the distinct pleasure of walking over to the shelf in the very room we were sitting in and pulling it off the shelf to put it in her hands. When she learned I had no funding, she encouraged me to try for a grant. She was in Paris on a grant. "You're doing something original," she said. "You'd be a breeze." She gave me the information of her granting organization, and when I read their guidelines, I thought I looked pretty good. Apparently not good enough. Grant denied. By then I was hooked on a second book. Could I really do it? If the first one took five years, with that experience, I thought a second one shouldn't take more than three years. It took seven years.

CHAPTER 19

PARIS AND THE FUTURE, UH-OH!

THE NEWS OUT OF PARIS TODAY IS not good. Mayor Anne Hidalgo wants to transform her capital into a showcase for futuristic architecture. Dubbed "Reinventing Paris," her vast program includes twenty-three sites around the city, some going back to the seventeenth century, that have been sold or leased to developers and architects with the directive from her man in charge of urbanism, Jean-Louis Missika, to "produce urbanism and architecture of the future . . . We want to be surprised. The order of the day is, let your imagination go."

Trying to redefine Paris with futuristic architecture is a dead end. The trouble with the future is that it gets old so fast. Show us anything that was futuristic in its time and that was not old and dated before the paint dried.

But this pales in comparison to the most troubling aspect of Mayor Hidalgo's plan. She wants to build skyscrapers in Paris. The world stands agape at such news. Skyscrapers in Paris? Have the French gone mad? Isn't that why they built La Défense? Correct on both points.

One might have thought that the French had learned their lesson after the unveiling of the fifty-nine-story Maine-Montparnasse tower in 1972.

That dark silhouetted behemoth lords over Paris like the Darth Vader of architecture and has become the most hated building in the city. The public's reaction was so virulent that height limits on building were put in place in 1977 to prevent the insult from happening again. But forgetting is so easy. In 2008, in a landmark vote, the Paris City Council overturned these limits. Mayor Bertrand Delanöe began the city council meeting with a statement that made clear the why behind this shift:

> *Paris is engaged in a competition with other world capitols. We must welcome enterprises that stand at the forefront of innovation, encourage them, offer the best conditions for them to locate in Paris so they can grow and flourish.*
>
> *In order to attract these entrepreneurs . . . Paris must construct very tall buildings that equal the architectural achievements of the more dynamic cities in the world that symbolize their economic success.*

The mayor's remarks are another shade of an old insecurity that has been plaguing the French for over fifty years—the feeling that Paris has been left standing in the dust of a modernism that has passed it by.

One can understand the dilemma. There was a time when the supremacy of French culture was absolute. Their empire was vast and secure. Achievements at home confirmed their feeling of pride about their place in the world. They invented modern art, still photography, and the moving picture. The French language was *the* spoken language in the courts of Europe, the language of love and diplomacy. Their cuisine dictated taste around the world. Paris fashion had no rival. In a short seventeen years (from 1853 to 1870), Napoleon III and Baron Haussmann had transformed Paris into one of the most modern cities in the world with an unequalled vitality and dynamism. German philosopher Walter Benjamin called Paris the "capital of the nineteenth century," and he was right.

Then by the 1950s, everything changed. The French empire was in dissolution, the art world had moved to New York, and by the 1970s, Milan rivaled Paris in the fashion world. By the 1980s Paris was struggling to escape the infection of Franglais. Official bodies in Paris tried to exclude the word *computer* from public discourse for the more appropriate word *ordinateur*. *Le shopping, le marketing,* and *le parking* were all part of the same disease.

The feeling that the ground had slipped out from under the French was inescapable. Dazed and disoriented, they've been playing catch-up ever since. Unfortunately many of their attempts to regain lost prestige are through architecture and city planning. Like an insecure adolescent standing on weak legs taking a wild swing at someone, they strike out with bold yet clumsy gestures. They might connect, but the results are awkward, and worse yet, everyone can see.

Mayor Hidalgo was vice mayor under Delanöe and became well versed in his school of aggressive urbanism. The curious thing is how she and Delanöe could be so wrong on this aspect of Paris and then be so right on other issues. Their understanding of the harm the automobile has done to the city is correct. Mayor Delanöe, to his credit, widened sidewalks in many neighborhoods, eliminated parking, added bike lanes, and reduced the number of traffic lanes. His Vélib' project, placing thousands of bicycles around Paris for practically free use, has been most successful. Mayor Hidalgo has announced plans to eliminate the Right Bank expressway and return this stretch along the Seine back to pedestrians, finally ending President Pompidou's nightmarish dream of "adapting Paris to the automobile." She has named Sunday, September 27, 2015, a day of no cars in Paris. Anything that takes the city out of the grip of the automobile is a great good.

But old insecurities die hard. A surprising number of Parisians like the idea of skyscrapers. In 2012, the newspaper *Le Monde* voiced their support in an editorial titled "Let The Skyscrapers Grow in Paris":

> *Why can't we understand that to fight for human scale urbanism in Paris, to argue for preservation risks embalming the city, sterilizing it, sapping it of its vitality and turning it into a ville-musée, charming but frozen . . . Skyscrapers are not only a sign of architectural intelligence, but in the competition between world capitals they show that Paris can still demonstrate daring, a desire for architectural innovation, and an ability to reinvent its own urban landscape.*

Paris approaches skyscrapers from the wrong end of the equation. The earliest skyscrapers built in America in the late 1890s and early 1900s were an outgrowth of a dynamic economy exploding with growth. Paris wrongly expects that the symbolic value of their skyscrapers will draw entrepreneurs and world corporations to stimulate their lagging economy. Build and they will come. Skyscrapers might work in other cities, but this doesn't mean they will work in Paris. If that were true, then the suit that looks great on me would look just as great on you. Skyscrapers are outmoded symbols of power and modernity and can never create an environment with the appeal of central Paris. Contrary to the mayor's belief that skyscrapers will give the city more appeal, the city will be disfigured. This is true as gravity.

Part of the downside of skyscrapers are the smaller buildings that inevitably follow in their wake. Take a walk around the backside of Maine-Montparnasse Tower to view its spawn. Disheartening. With Google Images view Rue du Commandant René Mouchotte and see.

Paris is a fragile beauty. No city has captivated the imagination or inspired like Paris. It is a beauty different from any other city in the world.

And the skyline is integral to that beauty. Like a subtle membrane containing the city in its most delicate aspects, this skyline defines the city. Destroy this, and you destroy Paris. The city will go on standing, and people will come, of course, but the city will be diminished.

That is why the Paris skyline must be declared an inviolable part of the beauty of the city and be protected. UNESCO has established a list of World Heritage Sites, places in the world that are recognized for their historical and cultural value. The most basic criteria is that these sites be of "outstanding universal value." The banks of the Seine are on that list. And would anybody argue that the skyline of Paris is not integral to the beauty of the city?

Hundreds of songs have been written about Paris. And if Paris is given a gender, it is always a woman. And like the unique quality of a woman with a great and singular beauty, the beauty of Paris is unique. Paris is not New York, London, Hong Kong, or Dubai. You cannot deposit skyscrapers and expect the city to retain the ineffable quality that makes Paris Paris.

The pursuit of glory through the symbol of tall buildings is futile. Symbols fade. And to trade the ineffable beauty of Paris for the transitory gain gotten from a few tall buildings is a bad deal. Paris, Parisians, and the world lose.

The Lessons Not Learned

The bigger question is how well modernity fits into Paris at all. With few exceptions it is not an easy fit. One successful example is the Arab World Institute on the Left Bank designed by Jean Nouvel and completed in 1987. The intricate facade of light-sensitive panels that open and close with the light is innovative and attractive and softens the harder, rational grid design of the building, which has proven to be a fine addition to the cityscape.

I. M. Pei's Pyramid at the Louvre works, in part. There is one problem, however. No doubt the Louvre needed a new entrance. But there is nothing to say that anything had to rise above the ground. An alternative design would have been a simpler entrance with little height in order to let the courtyard and the wings surrounding it live on their own. Did anyone ever stand in the courtyard before the pyramid and go, "Hmmm . . . it needs something"? The distance between ego and architecture is often not very far, and this is an example. The Louvre directors could have had a conversation with Maya Lin, designer of the Vietnam War Memorial in Washington D.C. That said, of all the possible design choices, the pyramid is the best. The geometric shape will last forever and, contrary to much modern architecture, will not get old.

But there is an overwhelming array of modern in Paris that sticks out for its banality and inability to endure over time. In Google Images search for Les Olympiades, Tour Zamansky, or Orgues de Flandre. The most egregious example of this misguided modernism is the remake of the old central food market, Les Halles, that opened in 1979. If Paris has a heartache, this is it. Les Halles had been on the same spot for eight hundred years. Émile Zola famously called it the belly of Paris. Many would say it was the soul of the city.

When the market was closed and moved to the suburbs in the late 1960s, no one argued. But what to do with the nineteenth-century iron and glass pavilions, each the size of a city block, that housed the market? The public argued for keeping them, fill them with shops, restaurants, cinemas, theatres, offices, and apartments. No one minded walking into the future, but let's keep a connection to our past.

As soon as the pavilions were emptied, the public was quick to re-adapt them. One was converted into a popular skating rink. One pavilion was a perfect setting for large-scale theatre productions. I saw an Italian theatre production of *Orlando Furioso* there. A series of art galleries had been set up in the vaulted brick cellars underneath the pavilions that drew great crowds.

Despite all protest, the city announced plans to demolish the pavilions. One person, American financier Orrin Hein, actually tried to buy them all and bring them back to America. In a meeting with Paris Prefect Marcel Diebolt he was told, "Take them. They're yours! All you have to do is pay the transport." Surely, the American was joking, he thought. But when Hein returned with checkbook in hand, the Prefect began backtracking. The idea was impossible, he said—too much breakage. "*Trop de casse*" were his exact words. In truth the French, not unlike the jealous husband who shoots his wife dead because he doesn't want to see her go off with another, preferred destroying the pavilions, described by architect Ludwig Mies van der Rohe as a "symbol of the golden age of French technology," rather than see them go to America.

Through the media, Hein, this "Superman" as he was called, managed to exert enough pressure on the government to get one pavilion saved. It stands today in the suburb of Nogent-sur-Marne. Sections of another pavilion are in a park in Yokohama, Japan.

The city's plan for the site was revealed in an exhibition held at city hall in 1968. In a film we see stunned Parisians standing in eerie silence looking on with an expression of disbelief reminiscent of Germans citizens who were made to visit the concentration camps after World War II.

The public gazed upon steel and glass skyscrapers housing world-class banks, offices, luxury apartments, shops, etc. This new Les Halles was to be a financial capital, not only for France but for all of Europe, making Paris a vital link in the chain of financial centers around the world along with New York, London, and Hong Kong. Paris was sure to regain its place on the world stage.

This bold departure in Paris urbanism was explained by author Marcel Cornu in his book *The Conquest of Paris* (*La Conquête de Paris*), published in 1972. In 1954 the French military suffered defeat at Dien Bien Phu in Vietnam. This was devastating not only for the loss, but also because it signaled the eclipse of the French Empire. For over a century the French had operated on the belief that their cultural superiority gave them the moral responsibility, indeed the right to civilize the indigenous peoples of the world. The extent of their empire justified this belief. At Dien Bien Phu they were defeated by inferiors. The loss of face was unimaginable. The French desperately needed something to re-establish preeminence, and this giant site, like a blank canvas, held the answer.

The demolition crew set to work in August 1971, the sacred month of *les vacances*, the French vacation when most Parisians have left the city. Protest would be minimal. Photos of the pavilions lying in a heap of twisted metal are as sad as photos of great elephants struck down by big-game hunters.

With this ancient site eviscerated, Paris was in a daze waiting for the skyscrapers to go up. But remember, President Pompidou died in 1974. The new President, Valéry Giscard d'Estaing, was more preservation minded and halted any idea of skyscrapers and declared that nothing built at Les Halles would rise above the buildings around it. Six stories was the limit! Good news for the city skyline, but not good enough for a changing Paris.

Many breathed a sigh of relief at the near miss with no idea of what to expect. They found out in 1979. At the unveiling of the new Les Halles, Parisians discovered a vast complex descending four-stories underground consisting of a Métro hub, a *videotheque*, a multi-screen movie complex, and a shopping mall made of long concrete halls filled with trendy boutiques with all the flair of an upscale San Quentin. There was no feeling of being in Paris. One could be anywhere in the world. Above ground was enough glass and steel to please the most ardent modernist along with a misconceived garden unfriendly to humans.

This alienating architecture brought alienated youth from the suburbs along with a rise in drug dealing and crime. Parisians stayed away. Tourists were warned to watch their belongings.

In a city as historically rich as Paris, questions of city planning must be approached with the sensitivity of a brain surgeon picking up the scalpel. This was not the case here. Oops! The scalpel slipped. We performed a lobotomy!

After living with this pustule for thirty years, the decision was taken to tear it all down and start over. Demolition began in 2010. At this writing, the new Les Halles is in the final stages of completion.

It is worth noting that London was faced with a similar problem of a market grown too large for the city center. But while they moved the market out of the center, they kept the old structure in place, filling it with shops and restaurants. Today Covent Garden is a wonderful destination point that has enriched London. The remaking of Les Halles was a disaster of urban planning that impoverished Paris.

*   *   *   *

There is a mini-Manhattan in central Paris that hardly anyone knows about, and the French are in no hurry to show it off. This is the Front de Seine in the fifteenth arrondissement, a complex of twenty buildings going as high as thirty-two stories built in the 1970s all within view of the Eiffel Tower.

By the 1990s, the quarter had become an eyesore with none of the hoped-for allure. The city began looking for a fix, something to rejuvenate the neighborhood, and they found it: a shopping center—Beaugrenelle. Completed in October 2013, a visit would confuse one into thinking one had taken the wrong bus and ended up in a Detroit suburb.

Each of these vast projects has shown Paris to be a living organism. The graft of the foreign body of an inappropriate modernity has been rejected by the host. Paris is the neurotic dog chewing on a sore in a futile attempt for an unattainable satisfaction.

In 1971, André Fermigier wrote in *Le Nouvel Observateur*:

Paris of the second half of the twentieth century is a miserable failure . . . [it] resembles more and more an underdeveloped country bristling with capitalist symbols and poor counterfeits of an architecture that has meaning in New York, but which here is the architecture of lies.

Today three projects begun while Hidalgo was vice mayor under Delanoë threaten the Paris skyline. The forty-two-story Tour Triangle designed by Swiss architects Herzog and de Meuron for the fifteenth arrondissement is the most contentious. While Mayor Hidalgo assures the public that the city will be gaining "one more work of art," a majority of people living in the fifteenth are against it. The project won a city council vote in June 2015, but an appeal has been lodged.

Second is the new courthouse (Palace of Justice) designed by Renzo Piano (famous for his Pompidou Center) that is going up in the seventeenth arrondissement. For centuries the Paris courts have been located on Île de la Cité. Indeed, Marie Antoinette was tried and sent to the guillotine from there. The new courthouse, at 160 meters tall, is going up despite opposition from a cadre of lawyers who prefer the ancient location in the heart of the city.

A third project are two skyscrapers, thirty-eight and twenty-seven stories each, called the Duo as they stand in tandem, conceived by Jean Nouvel for the thirteenth arrondissement not far from the new National Library. As with all of this tower-building, nothing includes housing. Everything is for offices, hotels, restaurants, etc. The building permit for the Duo was granted in September 2015. There is none of the grace or refinement in these buildings of Nouvel's Institute of the Arab World. These shiny towers, both tilting off-center away from each other, are excellent representations of the architecture of speed. They will make sense as one speeds by in a car. To the pedestrian they will lack everything once the initial luster has faded.

The irony in all of this building is that hundreds of thousands of square meters of office space stand empty in Paris awaiting new tenants who want to move to the city.

Given this scenario, the question we must ask today is what will Paris look like a hundred years from now? There is little doubt—Central Paris, the Paris of the postcards, will sit at the bottom of a bucket surrounded by very tall buildings. The tourist driving into the city will pass signs along the way with arrows pointing towards *Centre Historique*. And those who know this history will look around central Paris and remark how everything in their beloved city looks the same but, oh, how different it all feels.

*　　*　　*　　*

The threat to Paris today is not only from very tall buildings. Smaller projects bode poorly too.

The Samaritaine department store in central Paris, occupying five buildings between the Seine and the Rue de Rivoli, was bought in 2001 by the luxury group LVMH (Louis Vuitton, Moet-Hennessy), owned by the richest man in France, Bernard Arnault.

When La Samaritaine was closed in 2005, it was announced that the giant site would be reconfigured into a premiere tourist destination with a luxury hotel, designer shops and offices, and all the provisions needed to cater to wealthy tourists. Affordable housing and a childcare center were thrown in to appease critics.

One aspect of the plan is particularly troubling. The new Samaritaine wants a strong "architectural gesture" on Rue de Rivoli to signal the rebirth of the site. The Japanese design group Sanaa was brought in to create this "gesture." Their plan calls for a facade six stories high made of undulating glass extending the entire length of the block. Not only is the design objectionable to preservation-minded Parisians, but worse, four buildings on the Rue de Rivoli would need to be torn down—three from 1852, one from 1740. To see images of the proposed facade, Google "Samaritaine redo Sanaa."

Protest to stop the "shower curtain," as it was dubbed, lead to lawsuits. While legalities proceeded, the work continued, and to the horror of many, the four buildings were torn down. A gaping hole greeted Parisians walking down the Rue de Rivoli.

In a reversal, the building permit for this project was annulled in May 2014. Too late for the lost buildings. The design, it was judged, violated the comprehensive Paris urban plan that states that new construction "must integrate into the existing urban fabric." Architecture of rupture is not permitted. Supporters of the Sanaa project argued that there is no rupture. The glass wall will reflect the Haussmann buildings across the street, thus providing coherence and continuity. The annulment went to appeal, and in January 2015 it won. Paris will have its shower curtain.

The new Samaritaine is destined to become a site of future regret in Paris, as with Maine-Montparnasse and Les Halles. One day we'll hear of some alteration to take place, color added to the six stories of glass with the excuse that times have changed, etc.

There is an irony in this loss of a signature part of the La Samaritaine. In 1927, the founder of La Samaritaine, Ernest Cognacq, purchased a classic mansion on Rue Saint-Paul in the Marais, the Hôtel de Vieuville. This stunning residence, built in the late sixteenth century, had architectural details that included Renaissance dormers, an extraordinary wrought iron staircase, and hand-painted wooden beams, making it an architectural treasure. Mr. Cognacq and his wife Louise Jay were noted art collectors and had amassed a great collection of eighteenth-century art. Indeed there is the Cognacq-Jay museum today in the Marais. One might have expected that Cognacq bought the Hôtel de Vieuville to begin his museum. Instead this erudite and cultured gentleman tore down the Hôtel de Vieuville to build a warehouse for his department store. If there is anything right about the Sanaa project, it is this poetic justice meted out to Mr. Cognacq, posthumous may it be.

*   *   *   *

This picture of future Paris would not be complete without an acknowledgment of three forces that have been gnawing away at our favorite city for years. Gentrification, globalization, and massive tourism.

Globalization is the insidious intruder that enters through the front door with a smile and takes over the whole house. What is Paris with fifty-four McDonald's? That's a low number given the decades they've been in Paris. Starbucks has been in Paris for a much shorter time and already has thirty-nine cafés, and the number grows. I would not care to see the Starbucks five-year plan for Paris. And let's not forget the KFC, Domino's Pizza, and all the rest.

There was a time when every inch of Paris offered a new experience for the visitor. Today, less so. Globalization is the great leveler. Everywhere begins to look like everywhere else. The French should try being French. It worked for a long time.

But protectionism has reared its beautiful head. A Starbucks was to open on Place du Tertre, the tourist mecca at the heart of old Montmartre, and was fought by locals who won. Similarly, when news got around that a McDonald's was trying to open in the lively Rue Montorgueil neighborhood, locals resisted and won too. This is all good, but it does little for the city as a whole.

Secondly, massive tourism, a staple of Paris life, has taken an ugly turn of late. The Pont des Arts, the nineteenth-century footbridge across the Seine, was visited by some lovestruck couple in 2008 who had the idea to seal their romantic bond with a padlock affixed to the bridge's grillwork signed with their names and the date. The idea caught on. By 2015 there were hundreds of thousands of padlocks weighing tens of thousands of pounds, not only on this bridge but others in Paris as well. Whole sections of grillwork on the Pont des Arts have collapsed under the weight of the locks. The city, not wanting to spoil the romantic image of Paris, was slow to respond. Several collapsed sections were replaced with plexiglass panels that were graffitied over. Other sections were covered with panels of plywood, which were also graffitied.

In June 2015, it was announced that all locks will be removed and that the grillwork will be replaced by glass panels. This is a loss to the beauty of the bridge. No doubt the panels will be graffitied over too. To see this, Google "love locks Paris."

Lastly, gentrification, a world-wide phenomenon, has taken its toll over the years and is the bulldozer with no *off* switch, reducing the economic diversity of the city and making it more and more a city for the wealthy. The Marais quarter, one of the priciest quarters in Paris today, was built up in the seventeenth century with mansions for the nobility, but then turned slum after the wealthy moved out in the 1700s and a flood of poor refugees from Eastern Europe began arriving around 1900. The plan in the 1950s was to tear down and rebuild *à la moderne*. Enthusiastic residents who could see the beauty behind the grime stepped in, and with their encouragement, Cultural Minister André Malraux created his now-famous Malraux Law of 1962, prohibiting all demolition and providing incentives to owners to bring their buildings back to their original glory.

A neighborhood that Paris had turned its back on began to sparkle. Rents went up, and the local artists, artisans, and crafts people and the larger working-class population who had given the quarter its character were forced to leave. This once-shunned neighborhood became one more stomping ground reserved for the wealthy.

More recently, the quarter of Saint-Germain-des-Prés suffered a similar fate. Once home to artists, intellectuals, musicians, and writers, Cartier jewelers opened up on a prime corner across the street from an

Armani store. A block away is Louis Vuitton, who recently opened a second store around the corner. Two within a block of each other. So much for bohemia.

More recently yet, Rue des Rosiers, the main street in the Jewish quarter, began showing signs of gentrification some years ago as local stores closed and chic boutiques opened in their place. Then in 2007 the street was pedestrianized. This was the deathblow. Some places are improved when they are made walking streets. That could never be the case here. Despite protest from locals, this street, once the salt of the earth, is one more haunt for tourists who, with no idea of what they are missing, think they're experiencing the real Paris.

Paris will always be ready for the Rick Steves photo op. The tourists will continue to flock. But globalization, gentrification, massive tourism, and a too-often-inappropriate modernism continue to transform the city. Anyone who has watched Paris evolve for decades cannot help but notice how the city has changed. Has a tipping point been reached? Someone once said, "We'll always have Paris." Hmmm . . .

Note: The terrible events of November 13, 2015, change everything. I was in Paris less than two weeks before. The recurring thought in my mind during my two-week stay was that *Paris is a distressed city. We live in a broken world and Paris expresses this more than other places I know.* The attack on Charlie Hebdo was a grim introduction into this reality. So what happened does not surprise me, but the scale shocks. There is no way to know how this will play out over time, how it will affect the life of the city, the economy, tourism, urban development. All we can do is hope and pray that our favorite city will marvel again in all its beauty.

CHAPTER 20

THE KEY TO A BRILLIANT PARIS FUTURE

A REMARKABLE ARTISTIC EVENT TOOK place in Paris in October 2013, and unfortunately it was completely missed by city administrators. The populace didn't miss it though, and they stood in line for up to five or six hours to observe this phenomenon. I speak of an abandoned ten-story apartment building in the thirteenth arrondissement called Tour Paris 13 that was given over to a hundred street artists who came from around the world to cover every surface of the building, inside and out, with their art. Here was a grand display of extraordinary art of the twenty-first century—I repeat, extraordinary art of the twenty-first century. The man with the vision behind this project was Mehdi Ben Cheikh, director of Itinerrance Gallery. To pull off this stroke of genius he needed the cooperation of the arrondissement mayor, who had the presence of mind to recognize the brilliance of the idea.

The mystery is why the idea was not picked up by the larger city administration to become something greater. One Paris observer wrote, "The Tour 13 is an immense gift to Parisians." An understatement. After the artists finished applying their art, the building was open to the public for a brief thirty days, and then, incomprehensibly, it was torn down.

While the French pursue a course of action that has failed in the past—skyscrapers—they missed this grand opportunity before their eyes. Paris Tour 13 represented *the* kernel for a resplendent future Paris. And as the kernel is unrecognizable from the flower it produces, the many possibilities lying dormant in Paris Tour 13 were present and waiting to burst upon the world to surprise us with it many unexpected manifestations.

A bland apartment building from the 1950s was transformed into an exciting urban scene with a palpable buzz all around. This is exactly what people crave in their experience of a city. Imagine that a café had been installed on the premises. And another café had opened across the street. And next door, a bistro. Add to this a building nearby for artists where they could live and work at affordable rent.

Creativity engenders creativity. Artists from other disciplines would be drawn by the excitement. A culture will bubble up in ways we cannot predict today. The mind boggles at the possibilities and at how the French could miss such an opportunity.

Art lies deep in the heart and soul of Paris. History has proven this time and again. What other city has drawn so many artists to its heart as Paris? Picasso did not leave Barcelona for London. Marc Chagall did not leave Russia for Rome. And the artists who came to Paris to adorn Paris Tour 13 came at their own expense with no remuneration other than a place to sleep. That is the power that Paris holds.

Paris shimmers best when it reveals this artistic side of its nature.

Skyscrapers may work in other cities—New York, London, Dubai—but they cannot work in Paris. This is not a question of taste. It is a matter of fact. Skyscrapers are contrary to the nature of Paris. They cannot and will not enrich the city. Paris will be diminished, and these new towers will stand as monuments to alienation.

Change is inevitable. Agreed. But building skyscrapers is trying to compete with other capitals on other capitals' terms. This is wrong. Compete, Paris, yes, but on your own terms. Remain faithful to your Self. And that Self is the arts.

In its heart and soul, Paris is a city of art. There lies its strength. Art has always spurred growth in this city. Instead of building towers of glass and steel that are dead before they are finished, give Paris another Paris Tour 13, and let it grow. Paris Tour 13 showed us the future, not only in the great talent on display, but also in the readiness of the Paris public to respond with such enthusiasm.

There lies the future of Paris.

The power of art to generate and regenerate is well known. Give Paris another Paris Tour 13. The public will respond. Paris will become richer, and the world will applaud.

History has shown that real creativity does not need tall buildings or sumptuous quarters to flourish. France's contributions to world culture came out of hovels and makeshift studios. And out of these humble quarters grew whole industries. One of the most creative places in the world today, Silicon Valley, was born in a garage and has no tall buildings.

What Makes Paris Beautiful?

The beauty of Paris demonstrates a simple truth: the new gets old, the old gets better. Has anyone flown into Paris on a stopover to La Défense? There is nothing wrong with new. Rather, the problem is "new" as defined by modern architecture in any of its variants, be it postmodern, deconstructivism, brutalism, etc. There is no patina there.

Had I lived through Haussmann's remake of Paris and saw Art Nouveau appear, I would not have complained. And a few years later, Art Deco. No complaint. But after World War II, modern swept in and wiped out whole swaths of cities, putting in an aesthetic with no staying power.

What we need is a new new. A new that endures.

Paris sets the gold standard. We walk the same Paris streets over and over again and never grow tired of them. Each time is like turning the soil of a rich, fecund earth that gives off a heavenly aroma. Even though we never enter most of the buildings we walk by, we are immensely satisfied in their presence. They make us feel good. We never ask ourselves, "Geez, couldn't they have done better?" No, this is as good as it gets. Has anyone ever analyzed what this pleasure consists of and what makes it so difficult to recreate today?

These buildings and streets invigorate and stimulate our senses. Go to Rue Cassini on Google maps to see four post-Haussmann buildings at numbers 1, 3, 5, and 7. Built between 1903 and 1906 they are sure to please. How did architects get it so right for so many hundreds of years? And how could they have suddenly gotten it so wrong?

Any school of architecture should teach a course on Paris. What they got right, they got supremely right. What they got wrong, they got supremely wrong. And discerning the difference is instructive. Even determining what "right" is is instructive.

That a refined French sensibility could have developed over centuries to create streets and urban settings that inspire, stimulate, and make us feel good, and then to have evaporated so quickly to give way to so many dead streetscapes leads to a disturbing conclusion: the French have suffered a complete aesthetic collapse. A fog of amnesia has descended, clouding perception and thought.

Victor Hugo wrote about the greatness of Paris, "This city does not belong to a people but to peoples . . . the human race has a right to Paris." And the French would agree. That is why I hold Paris to a higher standard. If they want to be seen as the most beautiful city in the world, then they should act like it.

If Paris really wanted to demonstrate innovation, wanted to show it could reinvent itself in the twenty-first century, it would inspire its young architects and urban planners to build a new aesthetic, a new modern that can endure over time, a sustainable modern that goes beyond the short shelf life of today's modern to create a feeling of place as satisfying as present-day historic Paris. This aesthetic does not exist. It must be created. Therein lies the challenge. Create. Don't imitate. Paris follows in the footsteps of a tired, worn-out modernism that has proven over and over again to have no staying power. Give us a new new. An enduring new.

Paris sets the standard. I do not speak from nostalgia but from a desire to elevate the human experience to a level we have known but have forgotten. There is no need to repeat what has been done before. Innovate. Analyze, compare, observe, ask questions.

For those who argue that a city must be of its time, I ask, whose time? And defined by who? And what of the result? Maine-Montparnasse, Front de Seine, Porte Maillot, the Tour Zamansky, and Orgues de Flandre were all of their time.

*   *   *   *

Some people suffer from a visual impairment that is similar to being color-blind or tone-deaf that I call *architectural dysphasia*. These people look at a building and see nothing through their feelings. While the average person will experience beauty, awe, boredom, or even dread, the aphasic sees only shape, structure, materials, volume, light, utility, cost, and budget. They do not read the expression of a building, and because of this, they do not know how the building makes them feel.

Ask them how they like a building, and there is the pause of reflection. They go into "thinking mode" rather than "feeling mode." Feeling needs no time. It is immediate. Thinking is all about time. It mediates feeling and takes us away from ourselves. Responding with feeling reassures us in who we are. Responding with thinking confuses. The aphasic person experiences a building by proxy, telling us what the building reminds them of or what it looks like. This doesn't tell us what the building means to them.

A street in Paris that illustrates the point is Rue Vilin in the nineteenth arrondissement. Once lively and inviting, today it is clean and dead. Plaques on the buildings at the entry into Rue Vilin with the name of architects demonstrate this architectural dysphasia.

If we accept that the old buildings on the street were uninhabitable, that reconstruction was an absolute necessity, why then is new construction always absent of life? Why is a policy of urban anesthetizing so consistently inflicted upon these neighborhoods?

When Lily Tomlin worried about what the inventor of elevator music was thinking up next, now we know. He's been redesigning Paris.

Three Alternative Approaches That Work

1. LE PLESSIS-ROBINSON

Le Plessis-Robinson is small town of about twenty-six thousand people situated six miles to the southwest of Paris. Le Plessis was designed as a Garden City in the 1920s. A plan for a railroad that was never realized doomed the town to isolation. For years Le Plessis suffered high unemployment, with most of its population living in bland, Soviet-style public housing blocks.

Then in 1989, a new, young Mayor, Philippe Pemezec, decided to turn this boring, listless town into an environment that people actually felt good about. Amazingly he met resistance. People had become attached to the dreariness of their town. Towards the revitalization of Plessis, he wanted to employ design ideas that were, um . . . traditional. Mention this word in architectural circles today, and scorn rains down in the silent disapprobation of peers. But the world is not perfect. View photos of Le Plessis via Google Images and determine for yourself: success or failure?

Do you feel drawn in or pushed away? Urban planners from around the world have traveled to Plessis to see the innovative approach that has revitalized the town. No one from the Paris city administration has made the trip.

I was taken on a two-hour tour of the town by the vice-mayor and was mightily impressed. Compare this to the newest large development in Paris, Paris Rive Gauche. View Avenue de France with Google Maps. Everything is clean, efficient, and soulless. Given that nothing is perfect, which of these settings would we feel comfortable with over time: Plessis or Avenue de France? Which do we think has the greater potential for longevity?

2. POYNTON SLOWS DOWN

Poynton is a small town in central England. For years people lingered in the town center and chatted as they went about their business. Then came the traffic. Today twenty-six thousand vehicles a day pass through the town's main intersection. This killed the town center and created a chasm, cutting the town in two. This once-pleasant spot became a no-man's-land where crossing four lanes of traffic on foot was a perilous journey. Local business suffered.

There was a proposal to divert traffic to a side road around the town, but this was rejected because civic leaders knew it would only move cars faster and isolate the town. Traffic engineer Ben Hamilton-Baillie had a better solution. Based on the idea of "Shared Space" formulated by Dutch traffic engineer Hans Monderman, his idea was not to remove the roadway. Instead, leave it in place, but slow everything down.

To the consternation of town residents, Hamilton-Baillie removed all traffic lights, traffic signs, and curbs. He eliminated the sidewalks and reduced the number of traffic lanes from two to a single lane in either direction. All lines painted on the ground to define traffic lanes were removed.

Then he built two roundabouts in the middle of the large intersection to help guide vehicles on their way. Everything Baillie proposed was counterintuitive. It made no sense. People feared that without traffic lights, cars and trucks would only drive faster. With no sidewalks, people would be run over, and so on. Yet it worked, and superbly well.

Completed in late 2012, people driving into the intersection and seeing no traffic signals had the natural response to slow down and pay attention to each other. With everyone taking time and making eye contact, pedestrians found they could cross the intersection in better time and in a much more relaxed manner.

This is an excellent antidote to the worst effects of speed. Now that things have slowed down, people linger. The businesses have seen an increase in foot traffic. People from other areas have come to visit. The rediscovered animation of the center has bubbled through the rest of Poynton, bringing an old-time pleasure of being there while not compromising any elements of the modern world.

Rightfully, the measure of success for this project was how to maintain a richness of human experience instead of the old notion of efficiency and moving large, heavy metal objects along their way as fast as possible. If someone could only bring the same sensibility to the field of architecture and create buildings with people in mind, places that made us feel good about being there rather than paying homage to ideas. (For more on this, see the YouTube video "Poynton Regenerated.")

3. FOURTH STREET—BERKELEY, CALIFORNIA

Fourth Street is only a stone's throw from a railroad line that runs along the San Francisco bay, and for much of the twentieth century the street was ideally situated for small industry that was dependent on the railroad. As industry dried up and the buildings emptied, Fourth Street became a ghost town. The firm of Abrams, Millikan and Kent bought one of the empty buildings in the 1980s and redesigned it to become a design center for the homeowner. Then they opened a restaurant next door. This combination of enterprises brought the public, and over a period of fifteen years, the firm developed the street building by building, lot by lot, into a premiere location with shops and restaurants that became so popular that it displaced the center of gravity of the city from the famous Gourmet Ghetto to this new location. Fourth Street's popularity made it a regional shopping center, drawing people from miles around.

The key to this street's success is simple. Denny Abrams, lead designer of the street, made it clear. He and his partners abide by an unspoken code of excellence driven by the desire to provide a premiere experience for the user. In other words, people count. Every element of their design was conceived for the effect it would have on those walking on the street. A more conventional developer would have torn down the old buildings and constructed a strip mall with a layout that serves the convenience of cars—a parking lot on the street with the buildings behind that.

Fourth Street is a real street. The parking lot is behind the buildings. Revolution. Strolling, lingering, and sociability are part of the shopping experience. At a strip mall, you park your car, shop, and go back to your car.

The result is that Fourth Street, like the prized Galerie Vivienne in Paris, has the rare quality of being a public space with a strong feeling of intimacy. And there lies its success.

CHAPTER 21

THE ORIGINS OF
THE AESTHETIC OF
MODERN ARCHITECTURE

AS MENTIONED ABOVE, WHEN I TRIED to understand why the ballet developed an aesthetic that took the body off the ground and into the air, I came to recognize forces beyond the dance itself that played a crucial role in influencing the dance's development, e.g., the formalized language of the body in the French court where the ballet was born, as well as Church attitudes towards the body, space, and nature. I call these Priming Forces. These are never obvious but are very present and operative in the choices we make.

Similarly, I tried to understand why the particular aesthetic of modern architecture arose when it did in the early twentieth century. Flat rooftops, flat surfaces, and the complete absence of embellishment became signature of the new architecture. Why not earlier?

Many reasons have been cited: an adoration of the machine, the availability of new building materials, the desire to create a built environment free of pomposity and overdonemanship, the need to build in quantity and in haste after the devastation of two world wars. Then too, a number of architects saw the new modernism as a solution to housing for the working class. Now they could build simple, clean housing with lots of air, light, and green space. This is all true.

But none of this can explain the success of the modern aesthetic in architecture and its longevity. Why didn't it fade away like Art Nouveau or Art Moderne? They both lasted little more than twenty years. But the modern aesthetic has lived on, and through many iterations. The success of modern in the 1950s was fueled in part, I believe, by a desire to put the trauma of World War II behind us. Radically changing the built environment helped put distance between us and the war.

But there is something else, something more subtle, a priming force that has not been recognized because on the surface it is so unrelated: this is the introduction of extremely high accelerated motion (EHAM—the acronym is mine), otherwise known as moving fast, or in a word, speed.

The recent invention of EHAM, speed, moving ever faster across the earth and through the air, has brought about a shift in human consciousness that I put on a level of the invention of the wheel or the domestication of animals. It has changed how we think, perceive, relate, and create. It has gone unnoticed because its many effects are so pervasive and on the surface appear so unrelated. Because it is everywhere no one sees it. Ask a fish what it thinks of the water, and it'll say, "Water? What water?" Another reason why this has gone unnoticed is because of the many benefits EHAM has brought, such as great wealth, power, and convenience.

Some explanation is in order.

For millennia, humans lived at walking speed. And much of the world still does. People could move faster with carts, carriages, horses, and eventually the bicycle, but our human sensibility was dominated by the pace and tempo of the walk.

At walking speed, the visual detail of our surroundings is part of our experience. We are moving slow enough to take it all in, and this enhances our connection to the world. In the simplest sense this connection is sensual. We see the full variety of three-dimensional form in nature and in the built environment, and we respond to it. We might like it or not like it. We love it or hate it. We see form that touches us with wonder or deflates our spirit. We are in the physical world.

The invention of the train in the nineteenth century introduced humans to a rate of speed until then unknown. But this was still an infrequent experience for most people. The pace of the walk continued to dominate.

Then came the invention of the automobile. And because it took over so quickly, became a repeated experience with greater frequency, it integrated into people's lives more rapidly than the train, thus making speed more a part of daily life. And then came the airplane. Unthinkable speed. Even though air travel was rare for most people, our consciousness became permeated with the notion of bodies moving ever faster. Speed began to occupy a new place in our consciousness. To the forward thinkers of the time, they knew that the future was all about speed.

And as speed became increasingly dominant in our lives, a funny thing happened. Our perception changed. We saw the world differently, even when not moving.

How does moving at high rates of speed affect how we see? The details of our surroundings blur and eventually disappear from view. We're simply going too fast to see them anymore. As we see less detail in our environment, three-dimensionality fades from our perception. Things flatten, and the great diversity of form is lost. Everything takes on a sameness.

As solid mass and three-dimensional form receded from view, light and volume became foremost in our perception and thus became dominant design principals of the new architecture. What we take in, we put back out. It is no accident then that the new architecture was made up of flat rooftops, straight lines, and sleek surfaces devoid of embellishment. This is the architecture of speed. We internalized this experience and put it back in the world of our built environment. Had we remained a walking culture, our built environment would be vastly different today.

The most forward thinkers in architecture in the early twentieth century felt the shift taking place. They knew intuitively that the future was all about speed and reflected this in their work long before it entered the mind of the average person. They internalized this experience of speed and put it into their work without understanding the forces at play or what drove the phenomenon.

The adoration of the machine expounded on by Le Corbusier—"A house is a machine for living"—was in perfect synch with this new perception. The simplification of form that became dominant in our way of seeing was a perfect match for the machine that also eliminates anything extraneous. The one validated the other. It was natural that the notion of form follows function underlying machine design would become a precept of modern architecture.

The machine validated everything we had learned to see and not to see. The absence of embellishment, sacrosanct in the new aesthetic, confirmed what we were already seeing in the larger world. New building techniques and construction materials came along to give body to this new way of seeing.

*   *   *   *

Modern architecture made its public debut in 1932 with the landmark show at New York's Museum of Modern Art entitled "The International Style." Curated by Philip Johnson, the show featured the work of forty of the strongest architects of the time, including three who would become icons: Le Corbusier, Ludwig Mies van der Rohe, Frank Lloyd Wright, and Walter Gropius.

Johnson promoted the new aesthetic with an evangelical zeal. The book he wrote with Henry-Russell Hitchcock, appropriately entitled *The International Style*, articulated the principles of the new architecture and became the equivalent of a bible for the working architect. As described by Johnson, it was "severe," and if you "stepped out of it, you stepped out of it at your peril. We thought we had saved the world. It was almost a moral movement."

There was something disturbingly über alles in the attitudes underlying this rising modernism that sought to impose a uniform style of architecture around the world that discounted all local history, tradition, culture, topology, and climate conditions.

Le Corbusier was clear: "Reforms are extended simultaneously to all cities, to all rural areas, across the seas. Oslo, Moscow, Berlin, Paris, Algiers, Port Said, Rio or Buenos Aires, the solution is the same, since it answers the same needs."

This is the architecture of speed. Everything is seen in a blur and is reduced to a deadly sameness. Any design element referring to the past was rejected. Here was the Esperanto of architecture, a universalism that works as an idea but fails in the real world.

Take this view and transpose it into the political realm, and, hmm . . . it bears a strong resemblance to what we call totalitarianism. And at the time modern architecture was getting its bearings, there were two totalitarian systems in the world: the German Nazi Party and the Soviet Union. It may be no surprise that both Johnson and Le Corbusier were Fascist sympathizers.

In 1939, Johnson witnessed the invasion of Poland as a news correspondent for the newspaper *Social Justice*, published by right-wing Roman Catholic priest Father Coughlin. Johnson wrote, "The German green uniforms made the place look gay and happy. There were not many Jews to be seen. We saw Warsaw burn and Modlin being bombed. It was a stirring spectacle." Le Corbusier thought nothing of working for the collaborationist Vichy government in France during World War II, even though they turned down his services.

The appeal of the International Style eventually evaporated. Philip Johnson observed this himself. In extended interviews in the late 1970s and early '80s, he admits to the shortcomings of what he so confidently brought into the world. "What you see so boringly around you in New York is all a result of our work in 1930. Everything looked like a box, every church looked like a box, a library didn't look like a library. Ride down Fifth Avenue today," he said, and "you get bored before you start looking."

Ah, the wisdom of age.

It is worth noting that Le Corbusier described himself as "an entity free of the burdens of carnality." Anyone who diminishes their connection to their physical nature, their physical desires, etc., has only one way to go, and that's into the mind, into the realm of ideas. In teaching the physical arts for over fifty years with thousands of students standing before me, I've seen this phenomenon over and over again.

And when the dissociated mind encounters the messiness of the real world, unpleasant things can happen. Short of resolving this lack of integration, the only way out of the conflict for this confused, mediated half-person is to impose absolute order. Doubt is replaced by certainty, and ambiguity makes way to reassuring clarity. This adds up to a brand of cerebral behavior that can be very appealing. If the person has an innate charisma, which their affliction does not preclude in any way, the chances of their success are enhanced.

Sigfried Giedion's work *Space, Time and Architecture*, first published in 1941, articulated the rationale and principles of the new architecture and became a handbook for any student of architecture or urbanism. The book was pivotal in modernism's introduction into the public sphere.

Some architects eventually found modernism's break with the past an idea that had worn thin. Enter postmodernism, written about extensively by Robert Venturi. He tried to right the imbalance, and he left his mark, but it has not endured. The past is still held in disdain. Architect Thom Mayne made this clear when he spoke about his new skyscraper, Le Phare (destined for Paris's La Défense), that will be the tallest building in the Paris region.

Mayne said, "There's a whole group of people that want to build new buildings that look like old buildings. It's ridiculous, right? It would be like . . . cherishing a horse and buggy." For Mayne, working in Paris represents "an opportunity to use all of the devices available to us that in fact give meaning to the centuries of history of this two-thousand-year-old city. History becomes the most interesting when it's compared to the present." Gobbledygook.

His studio, Morphosis, is in Los Angeles. Few cities in the world have been so shaped by the car as LA. Speed is in the DNA of the city. In some neighborhoods a person walking down the street is viewed as suspect. I wonder if Mayne might see things differently if he had an office in Florence, one of the world's great walking cities. The reader is invited to view his buildings: Cooper Union in New York City, or Diamond Ranch High School in Pomona, California.

The rejection of the past and the internalizing of speed is clear in the contemporary design of columns. No modern column will ever have a base at the bottom or a capital at the top. Modern columns are dogmatically bare at both ends. Anything other than a clean top or bottom risks being labeled as pastiche, kitsch, retro, old-fashioned, or, worse yet, traditional. An example in Paris is at the corner of Rue Rambuteau and Rue Beaubourg, part of a development from the 1980s.

But there is something deeper in the classical design of columns that has been lost: an understanding of the importance of beginnings and endings and the purpose they serve as transitions in design.

The bottom of a column is a beginning. The top is an ending. These are transitions of importance. And if they were marked for centuries it was because this representation of the life cycle, this beginning and resolve, provided a feeling of satisfaction and fulfillment. Columns in classical Japanese architecture resolve differently than the classical Western column, but they do resolve. This demonstrates the universality of the resolution.

The unmarked column leaves us wanting. Those who do not recognize this have been co-opted by speed. This recognition of the importance of beginnings and endings and the need to mark them as transitions is so basic that it goes beyond architectural design.

When I was in Bali I noticed how actors, upon exiting the stage, would circle around first and then leave. They are marking the transition. French comic Jacques Tati showed the same care in his film *Jour de fête*. In one scene, he runs down a country road chasing after his runaway bicycle and changes directions abruptly to run up a hill to head off his bicycle on the other side. At the abrupt change of direction, he does a large arm gesture to mark the transition, the end of one length and the beginning of the next. Without this, the moment of change would have been flat. He knew this. It is so simple and so universal that it escapes our attention. A covered entry over a door into a house is more satisfying than a door without one. Putting aside the utility of the covered entry, the fulfillment it provides in marking the transition is vital.

There is an art to marking beginnings and endings. Architects have known this for centuries.

The out-of-body nature of modern architectural design with its propensity to live in ideas to the exclusion of the physical world is evident in the writings of one of the earliest modern architects, Austrian Adolf Loos. His book *Ornament and Crime*, written in 1910, likened embellishment to a state of degeneracy bordering on the criminal mind. Only primitive societies, he wrote, embraced embellishment and the decorative.

Loos demonstrates the unsustainability of reasoning disconnected from the real world of mass and three dimensions. Embellishment was doomed, he wrote, because it would go out of style. Buildings without embellishment were closer to pure form and therefore stood above time. Because they were closer to the universal, they would never go out of fashion. Instead the reverse is true.

No one visits Hagia Sophia in Turkey and wonders, "What were they thinking?" No one walks around Saint Mark's Square in Venice and scoffs. If buildings with embellishment have endured it is because their richness of form resonates deeply in the human psyche. It is the barrenness of modern that suffers from short shelf life.

There are exceptions. Eliel Saarinen's work at Cranbrook, a private school in the Detroit suburb of Bloomfield Hills, is quiet and handsome and has lost none of its allure through time. In Paris, the Palais de Chaillot holds its place well. But these exceptions do not make the rule.

Embellishment has worked through the centuries because it resonates deep within us and reflects out own physicality. We exist in three dimensions. We have curves, bumps, and lumps. We have detail. We have flaws. We are new, worn, old, beautiful, perfect, imperfect. We are in the physical world. And we see all of this reflected in embellishment. That's why for millennia, every age has developed its own aesthetic of embellishment. It reflects our human physical experience. It's only when we have left the body, left the physical and taken refuge in the mind, that we banish embellishment of all kind. That is the architecture of speed.

Modern architecture's rejection of mass, three dimensions, and detail is equal to the classical dance's striving to overcome gravity. Both forms of expression represent a distancing from the physical world and in this, a rejection of nature.

The irony is that both are so fiercely physical, almost in spite of themselves. Rather than expressing the inherent nature of their physicality, they are more the expression of ideas and concepts detached from the natural world.

The Architect's Dream

It is worth repeating that as speed became more assimilated into the public mind's eye, mass, detail, and three-dimensionality disappeared from view while light and volume became dominant. In the extreme, structure itself becomes irksome. The relationship of glass to structure in buildings is indicative of this shift. As modern design gained favor, walls of concrete, stone, wood, or brick gave way to greater surfaces of glass, giving dominance to light. Structure was less present. Given the choice, architects would have eliminated it completely.

Sanaa exemplifies this. The museum they designed in Lens, France, as a partner to the Louvre is a show of light and volume. Three-dimensional structure is practically invisible. Here is the equivalent of the Classical Ballet in architecture. As the dancer tries to escape the physical world, so does the architect. Sitting in the front row at a ballet performance, the sound of the dancer's footsteps across the stage are irksome, like someone flushing a toilet in the next room. For the architect of evanescence, structure and the physical world of weight and the three dimensions represent the same intrusion into their world of light and space.

The dream for many architects would be to create a structure made of light only—to be able to manipulate light so it could be shaped, sculpted, and ultimately take on a tensile strength to support weight. There would be no glass windows even. In their place would be projected bands of light that would control the inflow and outflow of air, the creation and retention of heat.

Grasping a non-material door handle of a non-material door, one's hand takes the shape of the handle but feels nothing because there is nothing there except manipulated, bundled light. The advantages of such non-objects are many. They can't wear out or break down. They can't get dirty and transmit germs. They last forever because they are not there. They function perfectly. The only problem would be around power surges or failures. But with faith in technology, this too could be solved.

This Sanaa museum is located outside the city in a natural surrounding—it is an isolated structure and benefits from that setting. Their Samaritaine design has no such benefit. The failure of both Sanaa and the Paris city administration to understand how context plays into architecture lies at the heart of the present dispute.

Speed Ripples Out

The effects of EHAM on our culture become clearer when we begin to see the patterns. EHAM is part of the very soil of our culture, and as with any soil, many different plants and flowers will sprout. Modern architecture is only one manifestation of EHAM. There are others.

The Impressionists were the first artists to express the dismantling of the visual field brought on by EHAM. The first exhibition of this new art was held in 1874 in the studio of photographer Felix Nadar on Boulevard des Capucines in Paris. The out-of-focus of Gauguin, Manet, Renoir, et al, was an early reflection of a new technology that carried us whizzing by the landscape.

In the early years of the new century, the Italian futurist movement of Luigi Marinetti reflected the growing assimilation of EHAM. His famous futurist manifesto of 1909 was explicit: "We affirm that the world's magnificence has been enriched by a new beauty: the beauty of speed." Marinetti understood that the revolutionary nature of speed carried an implicit rejection of the past, and he called for the destruction of all libraries and museums. The only thing he clung to, perhaps out of sentimentality, was his intense hatred of women.

Cubism and its distortion of the human figure took this dismantling of our visual field further. Then the 1950s brought unimagined speed with the jet age! Automobile design reflected this shift, with tail fins imitating airplanes that grew larger as the decade progressed.

Moving at extreme speed pulls us away from the physical world. (That's worth repeating.) By the 1950s, EHAM had become so much a part of our way of life that all the elements of the physical world had disappeared from our mind's eye. We must look for the pattern. It is no accident that Abstract Expressionism in the arts, with its rejection of anything approximating recognizable form, be it human or otherwise, came about at the same time as the jet age and freeways that sped us along through cities and countryside, giving us a word reduced to a blur.

The figurative in painting became as unsavory as embellishment in architecture. The ordered, three-dimensional form that we recognize at a walking speed fades into a blur at jet speed.

Seen within this context, Jackson Pollock was not so much the lone genius revolutionizing painting as he was an artist feeling the temper of his time and responding to it with no conscious realization that he has doing so. Those Priming Forces were exercising their influence. Atonal music is one more flower from the same soil. Recognizable form in architecture or music disappears with the internalization of speed.

EHAM and the retreat of the physical had no better example than Twiggy, the bone-thin super model of the 1960s! This emaciated young girl became a cultural icon by the age of sixteen and dictated a look that is still emulated today. The shapely woman, for millennia an ideal of femininity, became old-fashioned and was banished.

The most positive representation of EHAM are the arts that responded with such creativity. Beyond this though, EHAM is foreign to the nervous system, and without compensations it is degrading of the human experience.

That is why it is so necessary to recalibrate, to slow down, to find a slower mind-pulse after the experience of speed is over. Some have an easier time than others. Our physical health can be assessed by how fast we recover our resting heart rate after a workout on a treadmill. The longer it takes, the worse shape we're in. A similar test needs to be devised to measure our rate of recovery from EHAM.

The repeated experience of the intensity of speed over time without recalibrating to a slower rate of mind-pulse is destructive to the nervous system and leads to self-defeating and destructive behavior. Many people manage to rediscover the slower rate of mind-pulse naturally. Many use yoga, Tai Chi, or meditation. Film director David Lynch, a long-time practitioner of Transcendental Meditation, has created a foundation to get a million children around the world meditating, and the results are most impressive. Go to YouTube and enter "Violence in School Ends Thanks to David Lynch."

But many become addicted to the intensity of speed. This explains something about young people and video games. The games today are not the cops-and-robbers of my youth. Today's technology creates an experience with many of the same physical sensations of actually being in the midst of the violence. Once the game is over, the intensity experienced by the young player continues resonating inside, often priming them to make wrong choices, such as acts of violence. What we take in, we put back out. That's why there is no one-on-one relationship between video games and violence. There cannot be. And the games' defenders will make this point. But this doesn't deny a direct relationship, subtle may it be.

Those who internalize the intensity of speed and cannot recalibrate to a slower rhythm suffer from an unrecognized disorder similar to PTSD. I call it RISD—Resonant Intensity Speed Disorder. But there is a difference. PTSD derives from experiences that were traumatic. RISD is just as harmful, but it derives from experiences that are fun, and misleadingly so.

Have we noticed how we've become a culture of intensity junkies? The intensity of speed has made us crave intensity in everything we do. This is one of the effects of EHAM. We see it everywhere: Extreme Pizza, Extreme Couponing, Extreme Home Makeover, Extreme Sports Channel, Extreme Weight Loss, Extreme Home Construction, Extreme Markers for Kids by Crayola. In 2015, Ringling Bros. and Barnum & Bailey promoted their new greatest-show-on-earth production, Circus Xtreme. Extreme anything is a dead end. There's nowhere to go. It can never deliver the satisfaction one seeks and leaves one empty.

For those rooted in the physical world, balance, grace, and harmony will remain essential to the fulfillment of their well-being, and they will express this in the work they create. Those who have assimilated speed with no means of recalibrating or slowing down become disjointed and unbalanced and live in a state of cerebration and less in feelings. This explains why beauty is an outmoded concept in many architecture circles. Beauty carries with it balance and integration. Speed denies this.

Victims of violence will give violence back. Those who receive love give love back. Those who have absorbed speed give it back in the subtlest of ways.

*   *   *   *

But there is more. The most destructive effect of EHAM is how it kills intimacy in human relations. Simply put, one is going too fast to care. Intimacy is all about connection and participation and demands time and attention. Speed disconnects, both psychologically and physically. The antidote: slow down, pay attention, be kind to strangers. We are strong when we stand in support of each other.

Intimacy and architecture are not two terms often put together in the same thought. The intimacy we feel in the built environment derives not from any particular architectural design, be it big or small, new or old, but rather from the feeling that a building or streetscape evokes within us. The intimacy is in our feeling of connection with the built environment. The beauty of Notre Dame is grand, majestic, timeless, yet it is a beauty that whispers to us. We connect with it because it is so deeply satisfying and provides a feeling of well-being, and therein lies the intimacy—in the feeling of well-being it gives us.

At the other end of the spectrum from Notre Dame is Rue Nationale in the thirteenth arrondissement of Paris. Before being rebuilt in the 1960s, this was a street of cheaply constructed, shabby buildings. Apartments were small with no bathrooms. Everyone on the floor shared a single toilet in the hallway. The public bath was a weekly ritual. The six-story buildings had no elevators.

Despite this poverty in amenities, the rich street life on Rue Nationale provided an emotional glue that created a strong sense of well-being to all who lived there. Everything on this bustling street spoke of intimacy. There were forty-eight cafés, twenty-six butcher shops, ten bakeries, and twenty-nine mom-and-pop grocery stores. Shopping was a daily social ritual that took hours to complete. People stopped and chatted and took time for coffee with friends. The importance of this interaction and the sense of connection to the neighborhood it created cannot be underestimated.

Then the architects and urban planners got in the way. These buildings were torn down, and high-rises with all the modern comforts were built in their place. Apartments were large with plenty of light, and each had their own bathroom. But no attention was given to the life on the street.

After the makeover, the forty-eight cafés on Rue Nationale became one café. Ten bakeries became two. Norma Evenson wrote a fine analysis of this street in her book *Paris: A Century of Change, 1878–1978*. As Evenson points out, life in the neighborhood went from an outdoor, Mediterranean setting to a Germanic setting with everything shunted indoors. In effect, the street was rendered dead. Neighborhood residents were left living with all the modern comforts but in lives of isolation.

For hundreds of years architects designed buildings that made us feel good. Be it a grand city, a small town or village, it all felt good. In Paris one can walk by buildings from the seventeenth, eighteenth, nineteenth, and early twentieth centuries, and with all the stylistic changes, it all feels OK. And OK is OK. We enter few of the buildings we pass, but it makes no difference. We are happy to be in their presence. There is a lesson here:

a building dialogues with a city through its exterior, by its facade. This is the point of intersection between the building and the city. If the facade is engaging and draws us in, the city is richer, our experience is richer.

The drive into Paris from the airport is the lesson we have not learned. We keep recreating the same bland nightmare. The architecture of alienation spills across the landscape like a B Hollywood horror movie. Jane Jacobs aptly called it The Great Blight of Dullness. An existential ho-hum fills the air and blunts the mind. Looking at this flatness, all we can do is scratch our heads and wonder, *What were they thinking?* Like a creeping malignancy, the sadness of the suburbs reaches into the city and gives us Rue Nationale, Les Olympiades, Front de Seine, Avenue de Flandre, and Rue des Amandiers. I repeat: we need a new new.

*   *   *   *

While many cities, including Paris, are making an effort to slow down, the countervailing force today is the digital world, which brings a new version of speed with its own brand of intensity that we must accommodate, and for many this comes with difficulty.

CHAPTER 22

DISSOCIATION IN ARCHITECTURE

VITRUVIUS OF ANCIENT ROME WAS the first to state the necessary conditions of good architecture: Firmness, Commodity, and Delight. "Firmness" meaning well constructed. "Commodity," that the building serve the purpose for which it was built. "Delight," the most elusive feature, meaning that the building should please.

Years later in 1907, John Ruskin, writing in *The Stones of Venice*, described the three branches of virtue required of any building. One of these is "That it look well, and please us by its presence whatever it has to do or say." Well said. Buildings do have a presence. Some buildings draw us in. Others repel. Much modern architecture would have a hard time arguing that it has lived up to the virtue of "pleasing by its presence." A number of today's iconic architects even strive for the opposite.

One example is the Aronoff Center for Design and Art, opened in 1996, designed by Peter Eisenman for the campus of the University of Cincinnati.

Widely celebrated at its opening, Charlie Rose devoted a full hour to the new building on his TV show televised from the building itself, with a panel of America's biggest names in architecture including Michael Graves, Charles Gwathmey, Richard Meier, and Bernard Tschumi.

Standing outside in front of the building, Eisenman tells Rose that he is not that good with exteriors. This is an understatement. He then tells us how he designed the interior to intentionally upset people, to give them a feeling of being "disturbed, dislocated." With the precision of a highly perceptive but unintegrated intelligence, he tells us that we have become a sedimentary culture wherein "the body has become cut off from the mind and the eye." He thinks that by disturbing us, we will be jolted into a new state of awareness that will reconnect the mind, the eye, and the body. This works fine as an idea but not as a reality. This is hair shirt architecture. The hair shirt was a medieval garment made of coarse hair and worn on the skin to irritate the body as a form of penance or punishment. Like the hair shirt, Eisenman designed his building to rub people the wrong way, and for a higher purpose. While the actual hair shirt is justified by theology, his building is justified by ideology.

But there's a difference. People wore hair shirts by choice. These buildings are inflicted on people who have no choice. People don't live architecture through ideology, no more than they choose friends or lovers by ideology. We live friends, lovers, and architecture through feeling.

At the end of the broadcast members of the audience were invited to ask questions. One woman spoke of her frustration that "80 percent of the people who pass by this building don't get it." When her sister came to visit, she had to tell her that finding the center's front door would be a challenge. The woman standing before the TV camera wanted to know, "What responsibility do you feel you have to make the general population get it?"

Charles Gwathmey came to the building's defense. "The frustration of finding the front door," he says, "makes an awareness more acute, makes the experience more threatening . . . and tends to heighten ones sensibilities . . . this is what art has always been about." If art is only to "replicate and repeat the known then . . . one never grows." How nice. And in the meantime, what are the uninitiated supposed to do? What is the prescription for rising above one's frustration? Fittingly, fourteen years later, the building was in need of a $6 million overhaul. The new gets old.

Eisenman's center reduces architecture to an exercise of the mind. For the average person, a building is a physical, sensorial experience. Personally, I wear a building like a suit of clothes. I prefer that it fit, that I feel comfortable in it.

In a public discussion some years earlier at Harvard University with architect Christopher Alexander, Eisenman cited a building that he found at first glance to be ill proportioned. Given a closer look he found that he actually liked it because, as he said, it stood as a reminder that not all is right in the world. More hair shirt architecture.

I suggest he go beyond this exercise of the mind and embody his belief. He should wear a shoe with one heel a quarter inch higher than the other or a pair of pants one size too large to remind him that not all is right in the world. Short of that, I suggest that he study Tai Chi in order to obtain a direct experience of the physical before the mind has entered the picture.

Would anyone theorize about clothing fashion, the need for it to challenge us, to open our minds, to extend us beyond our accepted boundaries? Yes. And those are the outrageous, unlivable fashions presented by unreal bone-thin models on the catwalks of Milan that make us recoil from high fashion because it is so removed from the real world of real people.

Eisenman and his colleagues are highly intelligent rational thinkers. But their hyper-intellectualism has led them into a state of self-obfuscation where they miss the simpler reality of how people actually experience architecture. An excess of thinking distorts perception and kills feeling. The Aronoff Center is an extreme representation of the architecture of speed, an architecture in the service of ideas and not people.

I feel for the students who attended this gathering at the Aronoff. They were no doubt intimidated and confused before these highly intelligent, interesting, and esteemed men and women who continue propagating this, The Great Bamboozle. Many of these students likely did not understand the ideas put forth and thought it was their fault, that they had to work harder to "get it." They were mistaken. There was nothing to get.

Eisenman believes that "Architects who did not derive their work from ideas were not only bad architects, they were not architects at all." What does this say about the architecture of Indonesia, with its spectacular use of bamboo, or the architecture of Africa, or Bhutan? He also famously said, "San Francisco has no architecture."

In our age of modernism with flat, unadorned surfaces rejecting anything that can be construed as a reference to the past—beware the pastiche!—building exteriors should be taken out of the hands of modernists and given over to stage set designers. This may sound strange, but think about it. Good stage designers have knowledge of design in history. They have an acute sense of the visual and can design with imaginations that are not boxed in by ideology, no matter how subverted. And importantly, they aim to please. Let them delight us.

The Architect in Me

In 1996 I had a chance to put all of my thoughts and beliefs about architecture and the built environment into practice in the real world. I decided to build a cottage in my garden. I had no preconceived idea for a design when I began. All I knew was that I wanted it to feel, warm, soft, and delicious. I wanted people to be inside and feel like they were being held in two large hands that protected them.

I then had to translate this feeling into real-world materials and design. The first thing I understood was that it needed a pitched roof, not a flat roof. A pitched roof gives more a feeling of being contained. Flat does not. Next, I had to abolish the straight line. But it had to be subtle so it was *felt* more than *seen*. Greek columns are not straight but are gently curved. That was an aesthetic choice, not a structural choice, and for the same reason. The curve softens and gives liveliness to the structure.

I also knew that the stucco surfaces must not be too perfect. They had to look weathered but without any sign of a human hand. I drove around Berkeley with the stucco man to show him what I did not want, what was close, etc. Avoiding smooth surfaces and perfectly straight lines helped create the softness I wanted.

You have to know what you want so you don't get what you don't want. Because if you don't know what you don't want, then you'll get what you don't want.

When it came to the roof, I knew I needed slate instead of shingle. Not only did this give a softer feeling, but slate also brings something ancient and secure, increasing the feeling of security. And instead of laying the slate perfectly aligned like a checkerboard, as they would have done, I told the slate man to push one piece up or down to make it irregular, to knock off a corner, to rough it up a little. This irregularity would soften the effect.

Inside I followed the same ideas. The exposed beams came from a hundred-year-old hotel that had been torn down. I hired a man with an adze to take off the straight lines of these perfectly milled beams.

I imagined the space as a person and wanted this person to be an interesting conversationalist. A bay window on one side and a dormer on the other broke up the space. On entering, one sees a fireplace flanked with bookcases at the other end. One of the bookcases is a faux door leading to the bathroom in the turret.

From my observation, not enough architects are sensitive to the feeling their buildings give off. It would be interesting to give architecture students a project to design a small building, maybe a one-room structure, that exudes, say, whimsy, foreboding, boredom, or grace. Is this possible?

CHAPTER 23

BACK TO SCHOOL FOR ME

ONE NIGHT, I WAS INVITED TO A friend's house to meet another Detroiter who also lived in Berkeley. "David's a great guy," Marilyn said. "You gotta meet!" Not only were we from Detroit, but we'd also grown up on the same street. We didn't know each other because he was a few years older than me, and that made all the difference in the world.

David Rosenthal had been a criminal defense lawyer for thirty years in one of the toughest communities in California, the Iron Triangle neighborhood in the small town of Richmond, about ten minutes north of Berkeley. Once a lively, prosperous city, Richmond fell into a state of social distress at the end of World War II. The shipyards closed, throwing thousands into unemployment. Then the Ford factory moved south, and deadliest of all, a shopping mall was built a few miles away, draining the city of its retail and leaving a dead downtown.

For years David had worked with families plagued by violence and instability and had seen nine- and ten-year-old children irretrievably damaged by their toxic environment made up of poverty, crime, and broken families. He knew there had to be a better way.

In 1988, a fire broke out in a Safeway warehouse in Richmond. By the time the fire was doused, eleven acres of warehouses had burned to the ground. For days a giant plume of toxic smoke wafted over the Iron Triangle, covering automobiles in soot and making the air dangerous to breathe. David led a class action lawsuit made up of ten thousand plaintiffs, and each name on the list received $5,000 from Safeway. He thought this might improve the life of the population, but it did nothing. Life in Richmond went limping on.

In 1993, a chemical plant in Richmond had a toxic release of sulfuric acid over the Iron Triangle. The air was fouled, and once again breathing became hazardous. Thousands went to the hospital. The lawsuits were numerous. The amount of money at play was huge, almost $300 million. David saw to it that a portion of this money was set aside for "community development," and it was this money that ultimately allowed him to pursue his dream: create a school. Begin with preschoolers, four year olds, and keep them in a healthy, nurturing environment for most of the waking hours of their day. At the end of the year they would move to kindergarten, with twenty more preschoolers arriving to take their place. Keep feeding the school from the bottom until it reached sixth grade.

He called it Richmond College Prep. The word *college* alone was a mini-revolution in itself. Nobody thought of college in this town. David was sure that given the chance, these disadvantaged children, largely African-American and Latino, could succeed as well as their white counterparts living in the better neighborhoods.

At our dinner David went on an on about the boring meetings he had to sit through with city and state administration. He just wanted to get it done. His accomplishment is impressive, not only for what he created, but also because he didn't have to do it. He could have retired and lived the good life, but instead he chose to get his hands dirty by tackling a festering social disease. Here was a lawyer with a heart.

When the school was finally up and running, he asked me to come out and volunteer. "Read to the kids, or help them with their arithmetic," he said. I could barely contain my lack of enthusiasm. The word *volunteer* is one of the most boring words in the English language. By the time I get to the second syllable, *vol-UN*, I'm yawning. I can't even finish the word. By the last syllable I've fallen asleep. *Vol-un-tee* . . . snore. I recognized the greatness of what he had done, the out-of-the-box thinking it took for a retired lawyer to create a preschool when he had no background in education. But *volun* . . . ? I can't even type the word.

One day, to alleviate my guilt, I thought, I'll go out just once and be done with it. Well, surprise! The school was only a couple of portables set up on an empty lot with a small wooden building across the street for an office. A visit is deceiving. To walk through the classrooms, everything looks normal. Little kids sitting on the carpeted floor playing, being read to, having a snack. But to think of where they'd be if not here, the scene becomes dramatic.

I worked with two children on my first visit, and I was stunned. It was clear that my small effort had a huge payoff. The children thrived on the one-on-one contact. If nothing else, just spending time with them told them that someone cared. I could see it in their eyes. I was hooked.

I became a regular, went out twice a week, and watched the school grow. From the original twenty children, now ten years later, the school has over four hundred students and goes to the sixth grade. We're still in portables, many more, but who cares? They do the job. The school is free, and enrollment is open to all, first come first served.

Many of my friends have become volunteers. (Whoops! I just typed that word.) There's a large playground today and even an edible garden— Grandpa Allen's Learning Garden, a bequest of my friend and fellow volunteer Allen Trachtenberg who loved the children and left them this gift in his will.

One day, I sat with nine-year old Latasharae. She read *Blueberries for Sal* and read well. Afterwards I learned that she didn't know what a blueberry was and had never seen one. The next time I visited the school, I made sure to have blueberries with me. I offered her one. She looked warily and took one.

"Go ahead. If you don't like it, you don't have to eat it." For a little girl like her, this blueberry was as big as an apple for an adult. She took a tiny bite and chewed, her face in a state of waiting. Then her eyes lit up. "This is goood! Can I have another one?" And from that day on I never went to school without blueberries. From there I graduated to dried figs imported from Turkey. The kids had never heard of figs, dried or otherwise. "Go ahead, take a taste. If you don't like it, you don't have to eat it." They loved it. And there was a geography lesson here as well. "Where do you think these figs come from? They're from a country far away, the only country in the world named after an animal. Is it the country of giraffe? Horse?" The laughs were uproarious. "It's Turkey!" Lesson learned.

One day I was working with eight-year old Jason and learned that he had never seen the ocean. Richmond is minutes from the Pacific Ocean, and he didn't know it even existed. He had never seen a bridge, a seagull, a ship, or a wave. The next Saturday I took him and his grandmother who he lived with (she was forty-nine years old) for a drive into the Richmond hills for a look at the Bay. Neither had ever been up there before.

Jason was stunned. His eyes were big with amazement. "What's that?" he said, pointing across the bay. "That's San Francisco," I said. "Oooh!" he swooned. "I want to go there!" So the next Saturday I picked them up, and off we went. I learned quickly how to maximize Jason's fun on this outing: "See that bridge over there? We're going to cross it. See that hill? We're going to the top." Giving him the anticipation increased the fun of the experience.

After driving up and down the hills of San Francisco, taking in the views, I drove to the Mission District to a Mexican restaurant for a burrito.

I wanted Jason to see a colorful, lively street unlike what he knew in Richmond. As we sat enjoying our burritos, I chatted with Jason's grandma. The conversation came around to diet. I told her how I try to be careful about what I eat, etc. I asked her what she had for breakfast. She took on a sheepish smile. "A soda and chips," she said. Imagine Jason's diet at home. He munched away on his burrito and then tapped me on the shoulder and with a big smile said, "Hey, Mr. Lenny. Today's a good day."

And a good day it was, and it gave me an idea. Most of the kids at school, like Jason, lived in one of the most beautiful spots in America with no idea of the glorious nature around them. So I created a program: Junior Explorers. On a Saturday morning, I'd meet up with several of my friends at school, and with four or five cars filled with excited kids, we'd drive off in our caravan on the outing of their little lifetimes.

We drove across all the bridges between Richmond and San Francisco, saw the bay from every angle, got to San Francisco and stopped in the Marina, went up and down the hills, and had lunch on Treasure Island to take in the views. Each child got a map, and at various spots along the way, we'd stop and look at the map and then at the view so they could see where we were on the map, where we had come from, etc. This was a hands-on geography lesson. Sitting on a vista point overlooking the Golden Gate Bridge, with San Francisco on one side and with Berkeley and Oakland on the other, I could see their brains changing shape right there as I pointed out the vastness of the Pacific Ocean and told them that if you went far enough towards the horizon, you'd hit China.

These children were assaulted by images and names of places, cities, and countries around the world but had no way to put all this information together into a coherent picture. Their picture of the world is fragmented. A geography class helps, sure. But nothing replaces the experience of being out there.

On the way home we'd phone the kids' houses to let the caregivers (you can't say *parents* because too often that's not the case) know that we were on our way back so they could pick up their children at school. One call was an insight. The mother couldn't meet us. She didn't have enough gas in the car. Could we drive her son home?

Most of the caregivers in this Richmond population have no disposable income, so trips anywhere are out of the question. The children can't even go outside and play. They can't ride their bicycles to a friend's house or just around the neighborhood. It's too dangerous. So they stay home. And often on bright, sunny days, they sit in dark rooms. Curtains or blinds are too expensive, so in their place, sheets hang on windows.

I did Junior Explorers for about two years. In the end it became too difficult at the scale I was working, so I became a one-man Junior Explorers program, taking 2 or 3 kids out on my own. The school thrives today, and in late 2014, the local newspaper told the world that our school had the highest academic achievement of any school in the city.

CHAPTER 24

A FAMILY PORTRAIT

WE WERE NOT A WEALTHY FAMILY in Detroit. We got by. Uncle Al was the most successful in the family with his wholesale toy business. In 1956, he helped my parents open a toy store just in time for the Christmas season. They named the store after my brother Murray. In a few years, Murray's Bargain Center morphed into a hardware store, a less-seasonal hence more-stable business. The store was open seven days a week, and my parents worked side-by-side most every day for decades.

My mother always wore a kitchen apron in the store with a pocket full of lollipops and gave them away freely to the kids coming in with their parents. Years later, those same kids came in with their kids and found Mrs. Murray (that's the name she took on at the store) still there. The success of the business was largely because of her personality. She loved to connect with people.

One day in the early 1970s, she went to visit her friend Becky, who owned a jewelry store. Business was brisk, so my mother got behind the counter and sold a ring. She could sell anything. Afterwards she asked

Becky how much she made on the sale. "Oh, not much. Maybe a couple of hundred dollars," she said. My mother was stunned. "A couple hundred dollars? We sell a gallon of paint and make twelve cents!"

She drove back to the store and told my father that she wanted to sell jewelry in their hardware store. "Sarah, you're crazy!" he exclaimed. Their clientele were all working-class from the Ford Motor factories in the neighborhood. A hardware store didn't seem like the ideal place to sell jewelry.

"Give me a small cabinet with a little jewelry in it. That's all I want," she said. "That's the craziest thing I ever heard of," my father retorted. So, on her own, she got a small cabinet and filled it with rings, necklaces, and pins. To discourage her, my father stacked up bags of fertilizer next to the cabinet to drive people away. My mother lit incense sticks and put them on the jewelry counter.

Guess who was right in this story? Mama knows best. The jewelry was successful beyond anyone's expectations and became a huge part of the business. One third of the store was eventually given over to display cases with inexpensive pendants to $10,000 diamond rings along with a staff of five and a full-time jewelry-repair department. It turns out that working-class folk are far more comfortable buying their diamond rings in a hardware store than a fancy jewelry store. And who would have guessed, but these working-class folk love to buy jewelry.

Years went by. My mother eventually retired from the store and in 2006, at age ninety-four, she was at home recovering from an illness when she died in her sleep. The paramedics were called. My brother Barry got there first. As they tried unsuccessfully to revive her, Barry wanted them to know that the woman lying in front of them wasn't just anybody.

"Any of you guys know Murray's?"

"Yeah, I do," one of them said.

"This is Mrs. Murray," Barry said.

"This is Mrs. Murray!" said the paramedic. "She sold me my wedding ring thirty years ago!"

Following Jewish tradition, the next day the family assembled with the rabbi to hear stories about my mother in order to write the eulogy for the funeral. And that's when I heard something I never would have believed had I not heard it right there from my brother himself.

By the early 1970s, the family hardware store was doing well and was comprised of three departments: jewelry, hardware, and auto parts. Uncle Al with the successful toy business ended up going bankrupt after expansion plans failed. Now it was my parents' turn to help him out. "Take your pick, Al. What'll it be, auto, hardware, or jewelry? We'll open you a store somewhere." Al chose auto. Excellent choice.

Murray was living in Los Angeles then with his wife Ina and was teaching special education in the Watts district. With a baby on the way, he was looking for something better. So he came back to Detroit, ostensibly for a year or two, and joined Al in the new auto parts business. They opened a little store selling discount auto parts, the first discount auto parts store anywhere. Their timing was perfect.

Al had a special talent at merchandising, or simply put, he knew how to put things on a shelf and make it all look good. This does not come natural to everyone. He and Murray put in the time did the work, and then one store became two stores, then many stores, and Al ended up doing better than he ever did in the toy business.

One day in 1992, Al went into the hospital for something relatively minor and while lying in bed died of a heart attack.

Uncle Al was like a Damon Runyon character with a wry sense of humor that could turn difficult situations into something actually fun. He made work better than work. Now that he was gone, Murray was alone, and the fun was gone. So by the mid-1990s he decided to sell. But he wanted our parents' approval. After all, they were the start of everything. So he called a meeting with them and was nervous. What if they didn't like the idea?

The meeting took place in the family den. My father, the silent one, sat on the side with his chin resting on his clasped hands as he leaned forward looking at the floor.

Murray sat facing my mother.

"So, Murray, you've got something on your mind. Tell me, my son, what is it?"

"Ma, I want to sell the business."

"You what?"

"I want to sell the business."

She looked at my father. He said nothing.

"Why, Murray? What's the matter?"

"Al's gone, Ma. It's no fun anymore. All I got is headaches. I want out."

She looked at my father. He didn't move.

"Murray, you got somebody who wants to buy?"

"Yeah, Ma, I do."

She looked at my father. He didn't budge.

"You gonna make some money?"

"Yeah, Ma. A gazillion dollars."

She looked at my father. Not a word.

She motioned for Murray to lean forward and said, "Murray, c'mere."

He leaned in, and in a whisper she said, "Sell the fuckin' thing."

I shrieked when I heard this. "What! Mama said that! I don't believe it!" "Lenny, those words came out of her mouth," Murray said, "And papa was sitting right there."

On the day of the signing that finalized the sale, Murray sat at a long mahogany table in Manhattan with an army of lawyers, his and theirs. After signing page after page, his head lawyer called the bank to relay the news. Murray, thinking the deal was done, got up to leave. His lawyer took him by the arm. "Murray," he said. "Hold on. That call only means that the money is moving."

Everyone sat in silence for ten or fifteen minutes. The phone rang. Murray's lawyer picked up. "Hello?" Pause. "Fine, thank you." He turned to my brother and leaned over. "The money has arrived," he said softly.

Murray sprang up onto the table and with a fist pump in the air exclaimed, "Touchdown!"

And out the door he went.

*   *   *   *

My parents eventually retired from the store, and Barry took over. He ran it until 2005, and then he too yearned for something beyond what had become The Grind. He wanted to sell but wanted our mother to know first. She was ninety-three then. Our father had passed away a couple of years earlier. This was a big deal, more than selling the auto stores. This would bring fifty years of family history to a close. Driving to the house, he was nervous. He sat down with Mother in the den.

"Ma, I want to sell the business."

He explained how he felt, what he wanted to do. She listened in silence. He finished and waited for her to say something. She nodded in assent. "Barry, I'll stand behind you like a post."

*   *   *   *

It was 2010. I sat facing Barry and could hardly see him through my tears. He was in his hospital chair, thin, pale. He was saying good-bye. He told me how much he loved me. "You've been a great brother," he said. "I know you know that."

When he phoned two years earlier to tell me that he had the big C, pancreatic cancer, my first thought was, *Is this possible? My little brother? How can I live without him?* When we were kids and shared the same bedroom, every night before I went to bed I would whisper into his ear as he slept, "Barry, I love you." Now this?

In the months to come he did everything modern medicine prescribes—the surgery, all the chemo, all the tests. The days went by, and he and his wife Jane looked for hope anywhere it lurked, in a number. Oh, those numbers.

Barry needed a CAT Scan. So he called a local hospital in Iowa, where he was living. "Cat Scan? No, we don't do that here," the woman said. "But I can give you the number of a vet in town." True.

In his last days, Barry was pale, gaunt; his hair had gone totally white. He looked a hundred years old, but strangely he looked good. I know—how good can you look when you're dying? But still, he looked good. By that I mean he had a presence I had never seen before. And it was a remarkable quality of presence. This was not something I concocted out of my imagination, out of fear or sadness. He had a bearing about him that I had not seen before on anyone. I know this sounds strange, but sitting in his bathrobe, it was as if he were wearing a great collar on his shoulders, as if in recognition of the good life he had lead, the gods on high had conferred upon him The Great Mantle of Life. That is what I saw, and that is the phrase that sprang to mind.

Barry and Jane had been meditators for decades. In his illness, he never missed a beat. Twice a day he closed his eyes, and for as much as an hour, he would float into his mantra. One day a couple of weeks before he died, when he could still sit at a table and eat with everyone, he let out an exclamation, an aha moment of finally getting what it was all about. "If I only had a few more years to meditate!" he said. It was clear to me that this evolution of his spirit had much to do with that presence I saw.

The day before he died we all sat with him, our chairs pulled up close so we could touch him. Me, Jane, his children Jesse and Joanna, and Jesse's wife Aviva.

With his head hung down and his eyes closed, we didn't know if he was awake, asleep, maybe meditating. Then, without moving, he blurted out, "Jesse, sing!"

Everyone startled. Jesse looked around, embarrassed. He had never sung in his life. But Barry wanted his son to sing. What song could he possibly know well enough to sing? Only one. "Row, row, row your boat, gently down the stream. Merrily, merrily, merrily, merrily, life is but a dream." He began singing, and each of us chimed in in turn to do a harmony.

After Barry died, we sat with him for about twelve hours. Friends sat with us too, remembering, telling stories. It's amazing how much laughter can bubble up at times like this. Then in the Vedantic tradition, his body was washed, wrapped in muslin, covered in brilliant flower petals, and sprinkled with oil. Prayers were said. I leaned forward to kiss him one last time, to say I love you, and to wish him a final good night.

Barry's decision was to be cremated. After a short ceremony at the funeral home, all of us wheeled his cardboard casket downstairs to the oven, touching him as we went, sending kisses. The director asked who wanted to deliver him to the flames. I couldn't do it. Jesse stepped forward. "I will," he said. His reason was simple: "Cause I want to kill the fucking cancer." And that's what he did. He killed the fucking cancer.

*   *   *   *

Murray's son-in-law, Greg, was a great guy with a winning smile and killer good looks. Everyone liked him the moment they met him. He was a great husband to my niece Erin and a loving father to his two-year-old son Asher.

Greg worked in the North Tower. That says everything. When the plane hit, he called Erin. "There's been an explosion. I'm getting out of here. Love you." He did not survive. Not a shred of him was found.

For weeks, months, Erin attended funerals and memorials for Greg's friends who were also lost that day. Depression doesn't describe the feeling.

Christmas and New Year's came and went. The next year rolled by. Christmas came again. Nothing new. Then at New Year's, Erin was in Aspen with her parents. On New Year's Day, Murray said, "Erin, get dressed. We're going to a movie." "I don't want to, Dad. Go without me." Murray insisted. "Erin, we're going to the movies, and you're coming with us. Get dressed."

Reluctantly she got off the couch, dressed, and off they went. Sitting in the movie theatre before the lights went down, she scanned the crowd and caught the eye of a guy with dark hair and fine features. In that instant, there was a buzz between them. On the way out she caught a glimpse of him again. There was that buzz again. The next day she told a girlfriend about the good-looking guy she saw at the movies. "Did you talk to him?" "How could I? I was with my parents." We later learned that he told his brother the next day about the great-looking girl he saw at the movies. "Did you talk to her?" "How could I? She was with her parents."

The following week Erin was back in New York. She went to the gym, and who got on the machine next to her? Yes. What an alignment of stars! "Didn't I see you in Aspen?" he said. "Yes." Small talk followed. She left and got on the elevator. He ran over. "Can I see you sometime?" Erin had dated before, but every time the guys learned that she was a 9/11 widow, they disappeared. Now she was up-front and told him right there. He was undeterred. His name was Jon.

My brother began hearing the name *Jon* more and more from Erin. "Erin, what's going on?" "Nothing, Dad. We're just friends." Then one day Murray was in Central Park doing his morning walk, and Asher came careening around a corner on a new bike with Jon steps behind. "Asher, where'd you get the new bike?" "Jon got it for me, Papa!" Once again Erin assured him. "Just friends, Dad."

Then came the Jewish holidays, and Murray and Ina were invited to Jon's parents' place for dinner. "Erin, what's going on? Something's going on!"

"Dad, it's nothing. We're just good friends."

A few months later, Murray got a phone call from Jon. "Murray, I'd like permission to marry your daughter."

Need I say more?

With the engagement real, Erin told Asher that he could now call Jon *daddy* because they would soon be married and he would be his real daddy. But as well as Asher and Jon got along, this little fellow would not call Jon *daddy*.

The wedding took place in Aspen, the place of their first sighting. When the ceremony was completed, Asher walked over to Jon, looked up, and said, "Daddy, would you pick me up?" Two children later, this family lives happily on.

Raising Stephen

One day in 1993, I got a phone call from Child Protective Services of Orange County in Southern California. Eight-year-old Stephen had been taken away from his mother by the State of California and was being cared for at Orangewood, a state-run children's home. They were looking for a foster home to take him in. Was I interested? I knew Stephen. His mother was my first cousin. Although I hardly knew her, I knew a lot about her. CPS looks for a foster placement within the family first. If that doesn't work, then the child will be placed with a family living somewhere near the parents.

Everyone in my family knew of Stephen's plight—the instability of his life, living in and out of homeless shelters. There were no drugs or alcohol in this picture—only incompetence. On two occasions I brought him up to Berkeley for a few days during a school break so he could see that there was more to life than the dysfunction he knew. Now this. Did I want to become a father? What should I do? I was fifty-three years old with no big attachments and had no hole in my life that needed filling. He was lovable as could be. But could I handle it?

I phoned my family. Overwhelmingly the feeling was to take him in. My mother put it succinctly: "Lenny, if there's room in the heart, there's room in the house." I knew there was room in the heart. The state came out to inspect my place, interviewed me, and I was OK'd. I flew down to Orange County for a hearing before a judge, who would make the final decision about where Stephen would live.

I told him beforehand that while we knew what we wanted, the judge might decide to place him with a family closer to his mother. I was impressed with the proceedings. Contrary to my expectation that we would be run through in all of five minutes, they took the better part of the morning going over every aspect of the case in great detail. The judge decided in our favor—Stephen would come to Berkeley. I went across the street, picked him up at the children's home, and off we flew. On the plane he tapped me on the knee and said, "Hey, Lenny, the dream came true."

Of course I had no idea what I was getting into. What I discovered was that Louis XIV had moved in. On his first day of school I made Stephen a peanut butter and jelly sandwich. After school I asked him how he liked the sandwich. "Fine," he said, "except next time, make sure you get the peanut butter up to the edge of the bread. And the jelly too. Up to the edge of the bread. I don't want to bite into the sandwich and get only bread." Louis XIV, right? My solution was as follows: I took Stephen to the cupboard, showed him the bread, the peanut butter, the jelly. I showed him how to make the sandwich, and never made another sandwich again. And since then, every sandwich has been perfect.

He was thrilled to be in Berkeley, and years later he told me that the most exciting thing for him was that now he had an address, an actual address of a real house where he lived instead of moving around all the time.

California state law dictated that he speak to his mother three times a week. I had to audit their conversations, take notes on content, etc., and every few months send this log to the state. Every three months we had to return to court in Orange County, where a judge was to review every-thing and determine if his mother was ready to take him back. She had two years to comply. If not, we could move towards adoption. Two years passed, she was not judged capable, and I adopted.

When Stephen was ten years old, my family threw a big party for him in Detroit, a party to welcome the newest Pitt into the family. We were all born Pitt. But he was a Pitt by choice! That made him special. My brother Murray played the master of ceremonies for the afternoon in perfect Georgie Jessel fashion, and speeches of welcome were made. Gifts were offered.

In Berkeley there were many difficult days as this little kid tried to sort things out. One day he looked strained, confused. I had a hunch. "Stephen," I said, "You can love your mother and not want to live with her. It's OK to feel that way." I could see the weight lift from his shoulders. Good as this was, it was little more than pouring a cup of water onto a raging fire.

I found three female therapists and made appointments with each so he could choose which one he liked best. He made his choice, and therapy got underway. This helped. Stephen is now thirty-one years old. The chal-lenge continues.

When Stephen came to live with me, I was not in a relationship. Had I been, that would have set a precedent, and it would have been OK. But I wasn't, and I knew I couldn't embark on one now. Naive as I was, I knew one thing: I had to get my wagons into a circle around this little boy. Other-wise he would feel threatened, and I'd have hell to pay. So I became a monk for thirteen years. OK, I had a couple of dalliances, but that's all.

At the end of that time, Stephen was twenty-one. And I met a woman. She had a theatre project in mind and asked me for some ideas. Through our many conversations, her qualities came forward, and things began to sparkle. Coincidentally (and this is spooky), Stephen walked into the house one afternoon just after I had met her and said, "Hey, Lenny, why don't you get a girlfriend? It's OK now. I wouldn't have liked it before, but it's OK now."

Well, I fell. And I fell big. For me, the monk, it was like walking out of a dark cell into the bright sunlight that I hadn't seen in years. But it didn't work out. A slight understatement. More accurately, I stood at ground zero of a nuclear explosion and made it out alive. Not bad. Well, I did get pneumonia twice in a row but came out OK.

CHAPTER 25

SURPRISED BY LOVE

STEPHEN WALKED INTO THE HOUSE one day and told me that his girlfriend was pregnant. I hit the roof.

"Are you crazy! How'd that happen? You studied safe sex in high school. You taught it to other kids. Pregnant! You mean you didn't use a condom?"

"It was the heat of the moment," he said.

"There's always heat of the moment," I said. "That's no excuse!"

He sat in stony silence. I railed.

"You can't do this. This is terrible! You're driving into a brick wall."

This went on for days.

Stephen had issues. He was unready for fatherhood. His girlfriend Viva was wonderful, but at twenty-two and as a grad student studying to become an opera singer, and with school debt, this was not her moment either.

"There's no happiness here," I said. "Go ahead, have the baby. But you're not going to live with me, and don't come to me for money!"

I argued for abortion or adoption. Viva saw the light and began arranging for adoption but then changed her mind. I walked around under a cloud of gloom and doom.

When Viva went into labor, I made sure I was at the birthing center with Stephen. No matter how I felt, I wasn't going to miss this. Viva wanted a natural birth and was in a shallow pool of warm water being guided into motherhood. But labor went on late into the night, and I had a lecture on Paris to give the next day, so I went home to get some sleep. Unbeknownst to me things got complicated, and she had to be rushed to the hospital for a C-section. By the time I got there, Miles was six hours old. We knew it was going to be a boy, but ten and a half pounds!

I took one look, and my heart stopped. I had never seen a newborn for real before. And my blood. In a split second my brain exploded and took on a new shape, and it was called Love. I stood gazing in awe as an onrush of feelings came over me I had never felt before. It was like living in a house all your life and one day you stumble through a hidden door into a room of wonders and marvels.

They ended up living with me, and I gave them money.

Stephen and Viva were slow at first to understand how fast I had come around. So I told them straight out: "This is the greatest gift that's ever been made to me in my whole life." To make the point more clear I reminded Stephen of something he'd said to me a couple of years earlier: "Lenny, how can I ever repay you for all you've done for me?" Now I told him, "Stephen, debt paid."

Because I never raised a child from birth, I had no idea what I missed. Now many things I never understood, and did not know that I didn't understand, suddenly made sense. Here at the tender age of seventy I was discovering things that everyone else knew. I felt like I was living life in reverse.

For example, now I understand what people mean when they say, "Oh, I'd never travel or move to such and such place. I don't want to be that far away from my grandchildren." Of course. Every day is a day of growth, change, and discovery. Who would want to miss that?

Another moment with Miles that changed my life came when he was eight weeks old. And I didn't see it coming. He was still a little blob with his eyes and head rolling in all directions. I held him in my arms, talking to him, cuddling, and cooing, when all of a sudden his head stopped and he fixed his gaze on me. I froze. Wide eyed, he looked straight at me. And he held it. This was the first look of his life, and it was on me. He kept looking at me. A thousand thoughts raced through my mind.

I swear I could see Miles's brain growing, connections being made before my eyes. He looked at me for what seemed like a long time. I knew I had to hold that look for as long as he wanted, that I had to be silent and not turn away. This was his moment, and he had to be sated. He had to be in control. I had to let him know the beauty and intimacy of simply looking. Then his head snapped and bobbed away. I was breathless.

Some loves are so deep that we are unalterably changed. That's how I felt. Each of us has a shape to our emotional life. Our personal experience combines with our genes and comes together into a signature shape of who we are. This thought had never occurred to me, but it did now because I could feel the shape of my emotional life change. Truth be told, I've become a mushy puddle of tears. I'll choke up at anything.

Miles has brought me many gifts I could never have dreamt of. Now when I'm walking down the street and see a woman with an infant, I'm the one who strikes up a conversation. "Baby time! How old? Sleep through the night?" It's fascinating, and I would be perfectly happy to sit in a circle of women and talk about babies. Crazy, but true.

It was exciting when Miles began crawling at about six months. But something else was in preparation as he learned to crawl, and I didn't see it coming. Every night when he goes to bed, his mommy and daddy bring him into my study so I can give him a kiss goodnight. But one night—he was eight months old—I went to give him a kiss, and out of nowhere, for the first time, he leaned forward and reached out to me with open arms. I melted. Learning how to crawl, he had learned more directed movement in his arms, and now he could assert his desire through them, and I was a recipient of this newly learned knowledge.

At thirteen months it occurred to me that Miles was like a being from another planet who had fallen into my lap. He knew nothing about life on earth and was hungry to learn everything. And it was up to me to show him what life here was all about.

Example: One day I walked out of the house with him in my arms and thought, *He's never smelled a flower!* So I plucked a sprig of jasmine from the fence and held it to my nose to show him how to smell. I inhaled deeply and gave out a big "Ah!" Then I put the jasmine up to his nose. He didn't know what to do, but the fragrance was so strong that he took it in and smiled. I smelled it a second time with a big "Ahhh!" and then held it to his nose. Now he leaned in, smelled, and let out a big grin. Lesson learned.

A week later we were in my garden. While I plucked a sprig of jasmine, Miles reached out and pulled off a tip of lavender next to it and surprised me by putting it up to my nose with a big smile. I took it in and let out a big "Ahhh!" Then I held the jasmine to his nose. He smelled and with an ear-to-ear smile let out a big "Ah!" He then placed his lavender tip delicately back on the bush.

People tell me that Miles is lucky to have me. I say I'm lucky to have Miles. He has taught me so much.

One thing I have learned: When a child has their focus on anything, no matter what, don't disturb them. One day Miles sat playing with the plastic top of his bottle trying to figure out how it fit over the nipple. He tried to put it on, dropped it, picked it up, tried to fit it on the bottom. He kept trying. Remarkably he did not grow frustrated. Finally he got it! Do not disturb! I gave him the pleasure of his focus and unbroken attention.

When Miles was an infant in my arms, and he would get fidgety, I realized how little it took to calm him. Sometimes no more than a turn of my body, even a shift of weight could do it. These changes, small to us, were huge for him.

Whenever he reached out to touch something almost within reach—a window, a door—I could feel this desire in him and how important it was that he complete that moment. And I made sure he had that touch. And I could feel his satisfaction in completing that tiny desire.

When he was on my lap, I made sure he had something under his feet so he could push with his legs. I could feel what that meant in his body, how good it felt to him, how that contact and pushing nurtured his physicality and connectedness.

Part of my job is to be attentive to what interests Miles and to nurture that in him. One evening I sat in front of the computer with him on my lap and searched on YouTube for some music that he would like. He was about three months old. I came to the third movement of Beethoven's *Moonlight* Sonata played by Murray Perahia, and Miles became quiet. He watched for the whole six minutes without fidgeting. We did it again the next day, and he sat just as quiet, watching all the way through. And we did this every day for about a year.

In the days that followed, he broadened his horizons to include The Chieftains, Riverdance, and of course the ultimate, Elmo! I'm too old to have known Sesame Street or Elmo, but I've made up for lost time, and with Miles on my lap, it's never boring.

Socializing a child is critical, and I take this to heart. Every day we're together, I take him to the café. The distance is not great, and I've always felt guilty for driving there in the past. But now with Miles in the stroller, I walk there, singing to him along the way in English or French. The café, coincidentally, is called the French Hotel Café. He knows everyone there—the baristas, the regulars—and he has charmed them all. Pretty girls have come up and started chatting out of the blue. I've tried to decipher his charm. Was there something I could learn? Was it the diaper? Should I try one with just a little bit showing over my jeans? Was it the drool?

The whole gamut of life is present at the café, from infants to the very old. Luckily this is not a trendy place where only the young go. It's important for Miles to see the whole spectrum of life.

Down the street, The Cheese Board is a place of food and fun. The cheeses from around the world, the shelves of breads, buns, and brioche, and the freshly baked pizza provide a mix aromas that are magic to a little one learning about the world.

Peeking behind the counter to watch the baking—the kneading, pulling, cutting, sprinkling—is endless fascination. Children love verbs. They understand them. Verbs are physical, and this is their language. The live music in the afternoon is an addition to his enjoyment.

Other things I learned: Whenever I'm in a store with Miles and he goes to reach for a box or a can on a shelf, I never say, "Don't touch that, Keep your hands off!" or some variant. Instead, I put my hand on his hand and gently say, "We have to leave it." The difference is that to say "Don't touch that" makes it adversarial, a him-and-me thing. "We have to leave it" is us working together. And no surprise, he rarely tries to take the item off the shelf.

When he was a toddler and we walked outside, I would let him explore to his heart's content. I'd take his hand and let him lead. I followed him. I wanted his mind to expand, to take flight.

His first discovery was the speed bump at the entrance to the parking lot next door to the café. He went over it dozens of times in fascination. Next was the curb, in fact any curb. He stepped up, stepped down, and over again. Doorstops, drain pipes, cracks in the sidewalk, steel grates around trees. All of this demanded close inspection.

One day, I received an unexpected compliment. A woman was sitting in her car apparently watching us. Miles and I were on our favorite block, and he went about exploring: curbs, bicycle pedals, dirt, etc. As the woman pulled away in her car, she leaned out her window and yelled, "You're giving your grandson the greatest gift of all. Patience! Free play!" And with that she gave me a vigorous thumbs-up. I looked up *free play* online, and it seems that I had been practicing an entire theory of child play.

The flower sellers down the street, Mariam and Sarah, are treasures. Imagine a twelve-month-old toddling up to a pot of flowers and leaning forward to smell.

A friend at the café made an interesting observation. "People come in here with their children and usually handle them like a piece of furniture. They put them here, there. But you give Miles time to explore. He walks around looking like a little man just taking care of business." I was pleased.

Miles will not remember any of the things we have done together in these early months and years. This is to be expected. What does count, though, is the quality of our relationship. A relationship of love and support will create a young person with self-confidence, intelligence, and an optimism about the future. A fractured, unstable relationship will create a young person living with insecurity and all the terrible compensations this brings on.

The negative side of becoming a grandfather is the fear I now live with. When Miles was about a year old, he swallowed a penny, and it got stuck in his windpipe. Stephen was alone at home with him and saw him gagging, choking, trying to get his fingers into his mouth. Luckily the penny lodged so that it did not block his breathing, and he quieted down. But clearly something was wrong. An X-ray at the hospital told the story, and the penny was taken out.

So now I get to worry that some new misfortune will befall us. And I realize now what my parents most certainly felt when, as a newly minted twenty-one-year-old, I sailed off to Europe in 1962 with practically no money, little idea of where I was going, and not knowing a word of a foreign language. And I also understand now what my mother must have felt when my first postcard arrived telling her I was OK, and how many times she must have read and reread that postcard, and what it was like for her and my father when I came home for my first visit a year and a half later. So many things.

And the regrets. Having Miles highlights the loss of those in my family who have passed away. How my parents would have loved him. And now I have so many questions I would have wanted to ask them. What was it like raising three boys? Did they childproof? What was I like? How did I eat, sleep?

Most poignantly, it brings a reconsideration of so many people in my family. I think of the love and sweetness that everyone showered me with when I was small, and now I would like to thank them.

Every day I think of all the things I want to do with Miles, the experiences I want to give him. Prime of course is taking him to Paris. How old must he be for such an experience to have meaning? May the gods grant me the years to see it happen. By the time Miles graduates high school, I'll be eighty-nine years old. May the gods . . . (For more about my relationship with Miles, see the YouTube video: "Surprised by Love: A Grandfather's Late Life Discovery.")

Stephen and Viva are no longer together. Stephen lives with me. Despite this, Miles and I remain close. He comes to stay with us on weekends, and I often go to visit him during the week.

What I Learned From Miles

If you love your little one, love holding them in your arms and have to resist eating them up because they are so edible, then get down on the floor with them. Sit on the floor, lie on the floor, stretch out, get on all fours. You'll become a magnet. They'll lean, sit, crawl, climb, and fall all over you. You'll roll around with them in your arms. And best of all you get to steal lots of kisses. The intimacy is delicious. The lessons learned about trust and love are invaluable and will last a lifetime. Once you've spent time on the floor with your little one, sitting in a chair with them in the room feels, well, almost unnatural. The separation feels strange.

One day I was babysitting. I couldn't get Miles to nap. He kept climbing out of bed. So I lay down on the living room floor. He came over, climbed on top of me, and stretched out the length of my body like I was his bed with his head on my chest, his arms and legs flopping over the sides. He lay quiet, still. After a minute or so he slid down to the floor next to me. I put my arm around him. He laid there still for a minute or two, his head inches from mine, eyes open, staring out into space. Slowly his eyes closed. He put his arms around me, and we both fell asleep. The sweetness is beyond compare. Get on the floor.

*   *   *   *

The Miles I love today is not the Miles of a month ago, six months ago, and certainly not a year ago. Every week brings something new. And now I see, as I love him today, that I'm still loving all the earlier Mileses that I loved in the past and still see in him. To love over time is to love in layers. And they are all present all the time. Now I understand how my family loved us, me and my brothers. I never understood my mother's enthusiasm whenever she saw us after a separation. But that's what it was. She was loving us in all of our layers. She was still loving the little boys she loved so many years ago, and I didn't know it. My mother gave me an emotional lifeline to the world. I forgot about it for years. Miles gave it back to me.

*   *   *   *

Given the likelihood that I will not be around forever for Miles, I wanted to tell him something important. I didn't know how to tell him. I knew I had to pick my moment. We were walking down the street on the way home from the park. He asked me to carry him. I picked him up. Because he's getting heavier, after a while, I had to change arms. As I did, he put his face close to mine. There was the moment!

I held him close. "Miles," I whispered. "We'll always be together. Always, forever. Even when we're not together, we'll be together, always forever. You know why?"

He looked at me with those big *Why?* eyes.

"Because we love each other. Love makes people close. I carry you inside me right here all the time." I put my hand to my chest. "And you'll always have me inside you right here all the time." I touched his chest. "That's how we'll be together, even when we're not together we'll be together, forever always." He gave me a hug and went, "Meouw." He was three years and three months old.

A Mind Explodes With Discovery . . . And I'm There!

I was walking across the garden with Miles in my arms. It was twilight. The sky was clear, and the moon shone bright.

I pointed up in the sky. "Miles, look at the moon."

"Oooh! What shape do you call that?" he asked.

"That's a crescent moon," I said. "It's shaped like a croissant. Like the croissant you had this morning."

"A chocolate croissant!" he said gleefully.

"Yes!"

He wiggled out of my arms and lay down on the ground.

"Look, Papa, I can see good!"

I was startled at his discovery.

I lay down on the ground next to him.

One star was faintly visible off to our left.

"Look, Miles, see the star?"

"So cool!" he said.

"It's going to get dark real fast now, and we're going to see lots more," I said.

The stars began appearing one by one.

My heart throbbed to be lying on the ground with a three-year-old who was seeing all of this for the first time.

Then suddenly Miles did something amazing. He jumped up and ran into the house. Moments later, he came running back out with a pair of old opera glasses I kept on my desk. He lay down on the ground next to me looking up into the sky. We had looked at each other a few times before from a couple of feet away in my study, but that he would make this connection to such great distance, I was impressed.

"Look at that star," he exclaimed. "That one's really high up. So cool! Papa, can I get the flashlight?"

He wanted to see the star better.

A week later, Miles wanted to go for a walk around the block after dinner. He made sure to have his favorite book with him. After dark we were in the garden, and he lay down on the grass. "Papa, let's look at the stars," he said. I lay down next to him. He crawled on top of me and curled up in my arms, looking up into the sky. I thought I was dreaming.

*   *   *   *

Stephen and I took Miles into the Berkeley hills one evening to see the sunset. He had never seen one before. From our vantage high on the hill, we saw Berkeley spread out before us and beyond that the bay, San Francisco, the Golden Gate Bridge, Mill Valley, and the ocean. Miles was very taken. The sun slowly went down behind Mount Tamalpais. As it slipped away, he wanted to know where it was going. Once it disappeared, he was all excited. "Papa, where did the sun go? Where is it, where did it go?

"The sun went to sleep," I said. "Just like us, it has to rest. It has to sleep so it can come back tomorrow and give us light and warmth."

"That's amazing!" he said.

Then he did something he had never done before. When Miles is with me, he never gets to sleep before 10 PM. He won't nap during the day. But that day he fell asleep in the car on the way home, just like the sun, and he slept through the night. He was in tune with the universe. The next morning he awoke at seven thirty. "Good morning!" he sweetly said as he sat up. Then he bounded over to the window, and looking out, he said, "Papa, can we go see the sunset?"

CHAPTER 26

THE ONE THING MISSING FROM OUR BEAUTIFUL LIFE

I WRITE FROM MY SEAT AT THE CAFÉ. The French Hotel Café in North Berkeley. I've been coming here every day, seven days a week, for about thirty years. I arrive at 7 AM and often spend hours in my corner. Cafés are ideal for writing. The combination of intense concentration and distraction is a natural rhythm, like breathing in and out. Sitting with earplugs and the brim of my cap pulled down low, I'm cocooned in my little world and work away. If I see someone approaching and don't want to be interrupted, I tip my head down half an inch so our eyes do not meet. . . happiness! Tip the brim too late . . . misery.

Not many of my friends come here. They think it's a dump. But what a glorious dump it is. The French Hotel Café has not been homogenized or pasteurized and in its imperfections is perfect. This could be an old neighborhood café in Havana—more so when the Latino baristas play their jaunty, brassy Mexican music.

Look beyond the surface and you'll find the whole world here, the entire life cycle in spectacular display. Every shade of human relations, every subtle nuance of group interaction plays out here with a cast of characters made up of the most sophisticated, intelligent, and urbane, to the quirky, eccentric, and idiosyncratic, even the most marginal types you would never see anywhere else. Put this array of humanity together and you have the cantina scene from *Star Wars*—weird, bizarre, beautiful, and in this town thoroughly unnoticed.

Every day the regulars stream in on schedule and always aim for the same tables. This is when humans discover their inner animal and settle into their spot with an instinctive feng shui that finds the one place that suits them best. No thought or reflection is needed. It's all about the feel of the place.

God forbid someone should inadvertently sit down at a regular's table. If habitués arrive to find their spots occupied, they can't help but feel miffed. Discombobulated, they slink off to sit in the hinterlands, and that can be as far as two tables away. Then a subtle game of chess plays out. Their eyes never leave their desired tables, even when not looking at them, and as soon as the interlopers make the slightest move to leave, the presumptive owners of those tables, not wanting to look too obvious but really wanting those damn tables, ready every muscle in their bodies to make the move to secure what is by all rights theirs.

There's the early morning crowd, the late morning crowd, and the afternoon crowd. Each one is its own cast of characters. Some come in looking for someone, anyone to talk to. Others only want to sit alone with their books or newspapers. Can you see someone every day for years, not know a thing about them, never say a word to them, and still have a strong opinion about them? Absolutely.

The Chair Man likes the table next to the door. "Chair Man" because he sits for hours hunched over his graph paper with a caliper, straight edge, and pencil, drawing his latest chair design. Math Man likes the fourth table up. Central Casting could not provide a better version of the harried mathematician. Clothes rumpled and the table covered with papers in turn covered with equations and numbers of all sorts, he sits slouched, hand to chin in thoughtful contemplation, pondering who knows what for hours a day.

One regular slapped another regular in the face as they sat at a table outside on a summer day. Some years later a regular stood up livid with anger, yelling at another regular. They no longer sit together. Two regulars, a man and a woman who have never spoken to each other, got into a tugging match over who got to the table first with yelling and name calling (from him). He won.

A young couple sat drinking their coffee clearly on the verge of consummating something romantic with furtive gestures seeking approval. A few days later they returned with an obvious ease and had clearly crossed a threshold. At the other end of the cycle, regulars Al and Anne have been married sixty-two years. At eighty-six, they have the vitality of people half their age. She teaches a workout class for seniors.

A man sits staring into space, his brain lodged in his cranium as if it landed there by accident, a part-time resident not really sure what it is doing there. An elderly couple sit together daily and read. In their wellness of being they spend long periods in silence and are just fine.

Alan is in his thirties and is not all there. He waves innocently at anyone as he walks by, and if they smile, he'll sit down at their table. He's not capable of a conversation beyond what a nice day it is, etc. Sometimes he sits alone with his glazed look and watches the people pass by. The baristas never bother him and offer him his favorite drink, a hot chocolate with lots of whipped cream. This block is his village, and everyone looks after him. As it should be.

Many regulars have reached that stage in life where they are so fixed in their person that they have become stylizations of themselves, like pen and ink caricatures who jumped off the page of an artist's sketchpad. And I don't mean that in an un-nice way. It is simply life.

A tall, lanky, elderly man peddles up on a bicycle that is too small for his large frame and sits on a seat set too low. Hunched over the handlebars, his knees almost rise to his chin as he pedals awkwardly along. He is bone thin wearing an old pair of pants, an old shirt and jacket, and a rumpled cap. He walks with a slight limp and has a large hairy growth the size of a grapefruit on the side of his face. He looks out of place even in Berkeley and would be a better fit in the English countryside of the 1930s bicycling into town. He's an afternoon man who sits alone with his coffee cake and black coffee and never says a word to anyone.

And there are those regulars who make a difference in the world. Barbara Cohn is an epidemiologist who carries out groundbreaking research on women's breast cancer and was featured on the network news for her important work. Ruth Morgan directs a non-profit, Community Matters, and does the crucial work of providing educational programs to help the incarcerated become better people and aid those released to readapt to society.

And now to my point:

Many people living in California are in search of the good life. No one talks about it, but everyone knows what that good life is: the Mediterranean lifestyle—the life of French Provence or Italian Tuscany. This is implicitly understood and needs no explanation. Like *An American in Paris*, no one asks why it wasn't an American in London, or Rome. It is no accident that no one talks about emulating life in Sweden or Belgium. No one waxes poetic over a dish of Swedish meatballs, pickled herring, or a potato casserole. I've never seen anyone's eyes light up as they described a Flemish beef stew or a dish of Belgian mussels. But pasta, olive oil, bouillabaisse, or a good duck confit? That's something else.

So the news from a friend that they will be vacationing in Italy or the south of France elicits basset hound eyes of longing and old-fashioned *envie*. And in our quest we fill our houses with knickknacks brought back to this country by the carload to help us evoke that much-sought-after Mediterranean lifestyle.

But beyond the "stuff" of Provence or Italy, there is something else we are looking for. It's a rhythm, an unhurried life where work gets done without the harshness of the constant rush. And it is about beauty—a desire to surround ourselves with objects that evoke warmth, graciousness, and a simple joie de vivre.

Something all of these objects have in common is a lusciousness of detail that is lacking in our modern aesthetic. Be it a wrought iron door handle, an old wire basket, a properly aged folding chair, a lamp or candleholder, there is an appreciation for detail, a delight in the decorative.

But there is still something missing from this beautiful life we strive to create. The key, the organizing principle to that Mediterranean lifestyle, is the café. Nothing symbolizes the congeniality, the rhythm or sheer joie de vivre we ache to recapture more than the café.

My years in Paris taught me how central the café is to the French way of life. Families meet at the café, important meetings are held, deals are concluded, ideas are hatched there. The full breadth of life takes place in the café. Who in Paris would think to go to a movie, the theatre, or the opera without going to the café afterwards? Americans—we go home.

The reason why we don't get it is simple. For all the social revolutions that this country has undergone, from the roaring '20s with its rejection of buttoned-down Victorianism to the Beat era of the '50s to the hippies and the sexual revolution of the 1960s and '70s, this country is still at heart an intensely puritanical culture. The keystone of that puritanism is the denial of pleasure in all forms, e.g. physical, sensual, etc. And we are fated to forever negotiate and renegotiate our relationship to that puritanism. Hand in hand with that essential puritanism is a Protestant work ethic.

And you don't have to have been raised Protestant to have that work ethic embedded in your DNA.

This creates a predicament for those of us living in warm, sunny California. While we surround ourselves with things that fill our lives with warmth and beauty, lurking inside us is a Puritan mentality used to living in a small, dark room in a cold climate. The cold draws us in and isolates us. It is no accident that opera was invented by the Italians, a warm, outdoor culture used to projecting a voice across distances, and that England, a cold, indoor culture, was the home to great literature.

So we work at recapturing our pleasure of the senses. We have mini-revolutions in the world of coffee, bread, wine, "California cuisine," and, most recently, dark chocolate. The last bastion of that cold climate mentality is our blind spot around the enjoyment of the café.

And the moral to this story? Discover your warm-climate person within! Go to the café! Take something to read. Meet a friend. Take your children to the café! Go every day; become a regular. Open your own café if you must. And then see to it that another café opens next door or across the street. And then a third within easy reach. Not enough can be said for the power of synergy. That's what we all crave. A scene! Yes, go to the café with a friend and enjoy *la vraie belle vie*!

CHAPTER 27

HOW CAN I FORGET, CHOCOLATE

ONE DAY IN DECEMBER 2003, I stopped by a friend's house with a bar of dark chocolate in my pocket that I had just bought. Coincidentally, her husband had bought a bar that day too, and it was sitting right there on the table. I suggested that we try both bars to compare. What a revelation. Each bar illuminated the other, bringing out a variety of subtlety that we never would have noticed tasting each bar by itself. It was so much fun I suggested that we try it again the next day and that we add a couple of more bars. I told a friend who wanted to join, and there we were four of us sitting around a table with six bars of dark chocolate ready for tasting. Everyone took obvious pleasure as we discovered the many beauties of this simple act. The tasting was full of surprises, but it was the variety of our responses that was so riotous. One bar that delighted one of us fell totally flat for another.

It was so much fun that we decided to meet again, the next time in my cottage. And we'd invite a few interested friends. Ipso facto, we had a club. Everyone agreed to bring a bar, but dark chocolate only. Milk chocolate need not apply. We made up rate sheets to note our scores, anywhere between 0 and 10.

Eventually there were sixteen of us, and over time, that many bars turned out to be too many. Sixteen people describing their responses to sixteen chocolates is interminable. We eventually whittled it down to six bars. We agreed to meet monthly. And we've been doing it ever since for ten years. We celebrated our tenth anniversary in December 2015.

The fun from sitting at a table tasting chocolate is a surprise that never tires. The reader is invited to visit our website at www.berkeley chocolateclub.com.

CHAPTER 28

AND IN THE END

I NEVER MARRIED. THIS IS ODD, I admit. Even I think so. I always imagined myself married with kids, lots of kids. I imagined a kid farm. I love kids. That's why Miles and I get along so well. We understand each other. One day, in the late 1950s, I was on the bus riding to high school and thought about the girl out there in the world that I would one day marry. I wondered who she was, where she was, what she was doing, what her name might be. I guess she's still out there.

I can't explain it other than to say that my intense focus on the work of creating has narrowed the field and limited my possibilities. It is not that I drive myself but that I am driven. That's my brain on fire. This focus is very good for living in the now. The liability is that I've missed opportunities because to take advantage of them would have meant taking my eyes off what was in front of me. Some of these opportunities were relationships.

If I lived my life like I drive my car, I would have gone much further. I'm fearless behind the wheel. On the road I'm aware of everything around me. I have a highly developed sense of space. I know where I'm going and how to navigate through the fast-moving objects around me to get there. I know how to strategize in movement: when to accelerate, slow down, pause, stop. I know how to be poised to move and how to begin moving. Friends have told me that I must have once been a New York cabbie. I'm a movement person. Be it my body or my car, it's movement. It's all a dance.

In contrast, in my life I can't take my eyes off the next project right in front of me long enough to strategize anything in the future. That's why I've never capitalized on the success of my performance work or my books. I accept this as who I am, and I live with it. As I have said, all the fun goes to the obsessed. I am obsessed, and I'm having fun. I know this single focus has unintentionally hurt people, and I am sorry for that.

I came close to marriage. More than once. But as someone once said, I'm always zigging when I should be zagging.

In the late 1970s, it was Angela, an uncommon beauty from Sicily. She lived in San Francisco with her boyfriend, the medical researcher. She took some classes from me. The classes ended. We met for coffee and fell in love. She returned home to Sicily, and the letters flowed. I had performances booked on the East Coast and thought, being that close, why not visit her? I found a cheap ticket and made the flight. A friend insisted that she was married to the researcher. Nah! Impossible. Once my plans were finalized, I phoned to tell her I was coming. Then I asked her, "Angela, are you married to Vito?" Silence. Then in a whisper, "Yes."

"Why didn't you tell me?"

"I was afraid you wouldn't want to see me anymore."

Turns out she was unhappily married. It was her only way out of the house as a young woman.

"Leave him," I said. "I can't," she replied. "My father will either kill me or die of a heart attack." I flew to see her anyway. Crazy, I know.

She picked me up at the airport, and we sat in the car for an eternity wrapped in each other's arms. Vito knew I was coming, and whether he knew we were involved or not I couldn't tell. We never met. After a few days, Vito went to a conference in northern Italy. She asked him if I could stay at their place. He was OK with it.

When I had to leave for Rome to get my return flight to the States, she had to meet Vito in the North, so we took the train to Rome together, spent one night in a hotel, and the next morning said good-bye. I asked her to kiss my ring so I would always carry her with me. And that was that.

*   *   *   *

Whoever said there's an afterlife, I'm going to hold them to it. I've got my next life all planned out. This one is too full to do everything. I'm going to be a musician, marry, and have a family. Is there something like transgender in the arts? Transartist? I've done many things except the one thing I was really meant to do: music. Sounds impossible, but it's true. Me, out of the closet, I'm a musician. Music is my measure of all things. It's in my bones. I feel it. I sit at my desk with an accordion at my feet, two ukuleles, two recorders on the shelf, a tin whistle, an ocarina, and a beautiful 1906 mandolin leaning against the wall. I've fiddled with them all but not enough to really play. And I love to sing. I know the obvious questions, and I have no answers. I just got distracted.

For Those Who Wonder, "Why Are We Here?"

We are here to help the universe fulfill its destiny in an endless state of becoming. This is only partially true. To say "we help" implies a separation between us and what we are helping. I put it this way though because it is an easier approach to understanding something that is not easy to understand.

In truth, we are not helping anything because there is no separation. We are the becoming. This is true for all things in creation—humans, animals, plants, everything animate and inanimate. Everything carries out this role of fulfilling in a different manner according to its own nature. We humans do that by existing in a proper relation to things. This relation is one of balance and connection to all things around us. In terms of human behavior it means to carry oneself honorably with respect for all things.

Our ability to think, consider, cogitate carries with it what we so proudly call *consciousness*. It is a so-called higher power that includes the ego, and this has confused us. Misunderstood cogitation has created dissociation, leaving us with a feeling of being cut off from things, other people, nature. It has created hatred, wars, racism, and climate change, all misconceptions of an unachieved consciousness.

This is what I know to be true. I did not read this anywhere. No one told it to me. It simply came to me as a reality of things. This is my brain on fire.

EPILOGUE

BERTHE EVENTUALLY EXTRICATED herself from Hubert, met a man, left her apartment on the Avenue de l'Opéra, and married. I hope she's doing spectacularly well.

Richard and Saskia eventually split up. While he continued to live in Paris, she went back to Amsterdam, where she became part of a group devoted to personal growth. She committed suicide in the late 1970s.

Richard continued dabbling in women and also became a very wealthy man. When his stepfather developed terminal cancer, his mother decided that life without him would be impossible, and so they made a pact to commit double suicide. Things didn't go according to plan. She died, and he survived. He not only survived but lived on for several more years. In the end, Richard found himself with a large double inheritance. He bought properties in Paris and fixed them up. When I visited him in the late 1970s, he suggested that I stay in his apartment near Boulevard Raspail. He told me to pee in the bathroom sink, it saves money, and please, don't drip on the floor. Be sure to replace any food eaten. I declined his invitation and never saw him again.

Simson still lives in Paris and has retired from the French Radio. He enjoys a life of writing, has produced two scholarly works on Egyptian religion, and goes to the café every day.

Paulette lives in central France. Theo died of cancer years ago. Decroux died in 1994. I eventually found Penelope. I ran into her by surprise in New Zealand in the 1980s while on tour with my one-man show *Not For Real*. I was in the house of my producer and found a message by the phone. "Leonard, call Penelope at 2 PM." I was stunned. She'd seen a poster advertising my show in a shop and had nearly fainted. I phoned, and we met the next day. The last time I'd seen her, she was nineteen. Now she was forty-one and just as beautiful. Husband number one had died and had left her with two children. She remarried, an economist, had two more children, and was living in New Zealand for a couple of years. We stayed in touch. Refinding someone from your youth who meant so much is a gift of the universe. Life goes on.

ACKNOWLEDGMENTS

WRITING IS A FIERCELY SOLITARY PURSUIT. But any writer is only the tip of an iceberg, and my iceberg is vast. There are those close to the tip who read this manuscript in whole or in part and lent valuable advice and encouragement, including Michael Parenti, Mary Campbell Gallagher, Tom Farber, Daniel Rancour-Laferriere, Marie Tapert, Michael Corbett, Hank Rosenfeld, Viva Millan, Sarah Fry, Max Jacobson, and Georgette Delvaux.

And there are those further down the pyramid who have buoyed me and provided inspiration at stages along the way long before I began writing anything. Their wind in my sails has been the most delicate fragrance of the most precious flower. There are so many. To begin: Laurel and Hardy, Charlie Chaplin, Buster Keaton, Red Skelton, Sid Caesar, George Karl, the other-worldly Danny Kaye. My teachers: Leonard Johnson, Étienne Decroux, I Nyoman Kakul, Ida Bagus Anom. And those who came later at the right time to help me fulfill my many pursuits: Alexandre Gady, Francoise Reynaud, Iain Boal, Michael Fried, Piero Amadeo Infante, George Coates, Ellen Sebastian Chang, Joe Lambert, Bill Talen. And above all, my family: my parents, Irving and Sarah; my brothers, Murray and Barry; all my aunts and uncles and cousins and in-laws. I have the good fortune to be of a family where we get along. Thank you all.